Other work by the same author:

Co-author of *Seeing The Unseen: A Past Life Revealed Through Hypnotic Regression*

Editor of and contributor to *The Handbook of Hypnotic Interventions: Treating DSM-IV and ICD-10 Disorders*

Change Management Excellence
Putting NLP to Work

Revised Edition

Martin Roberts PhD

Crown House Publishing Limited
www.crownhouse.co.uk

First published by

Crown House Publishing Ltd
Crown Buildings, Bancyfelin, Carmarthen, Wales, SA33 5ND, UK
www.crownhouse.co.uk

and

Crown House Publishing Company LLC
4 Berkeley Street, 1st Floor, Norwalk, CT 06850, USA
www.CHPUS.com

First edition published in hardback in 1999;
reprinted 2001 (ISBN: 1899836144).
This revised paperback edition published in 2006.

Clipart used on pages 181 and 198 is © *CorelDRAW*

British Library of Cataloguing-in-Publication Data
A catalogue entry for this book is available
from the British Library.

10-digit ISBN 1904424678
13-digit ISBN 978-190442467-3

LCCN 2004111451

Printed and bound in the UK by
Cromwell Press
Trowbridge
Wiltshire

Dedication

To my dear wife Glenys for the support she has given me on my road of personal exploration and the help and encouragement that she has given me to get me to write this book. Her editorial assistance has been invaluable particularly in the checking of the manuscript for sense, style, diction and sentence structure.

Table Of Contents

List Of Figures iii

Acknowledgments..v

Preface to the Revised Edition vii

Foreword...ix

Introduction...xiii

Part One   **Introducing NLP And Modern Developments In Change Management** 1

Chapter One   Background 3

Part Two   **Developing Excellence In Communication And Understanding How Other People Tick** 15

Overview 17

Chapter Two   The Important Role Of Rapport In Communication 19

Chapter Three   Developing Precision In The Language We Use 27

Chapter Four   Bringing It All Together......................................49

Part Three   **Developing Excellence In Change Management**.....53

Overview 55

Chapter Five   Thinking And Understanding With Greater Precision..57

Chapter Six   Understanding The Causes Of Failure 75

Chapter Seven Preparation In Advance of Choosing A Change Mechanism 103

Chapter Eight   Choosing The Problem Solution 139

Chapter Nine   Resolving Conflict And Aligning Attitudes And Beliefs 157

Part Four   **Understanding The Function Of Time In Planning Change** **189**

Overview 191

Chapter Ten   Using Time Functions In Strategic Applications......193

Part Five   **Understanding Modelling and Modelling NLP-style**..**219**

Chapter Eleven   Modelling...221

Part Six   **A Short Consideration Of Popular Packaged Solutions** **235**

Overview 237

Chapter Twelve   Packaged Solutions 239

Appendices...**253**

Appendix One   The New And Updated Meta-model 255

Appendix Two   Dr Mayon-White's Change Management Strategy ..259

Appendix Three   NLP Resources And Contact Points 263

Appendix Four   About The Author 273

Bibliography 277

Glossary Of Terms 285

Index 295

List Of Figures

1. Causes of UK Change Management Failures 80

2. Features of Badly-formed Problems 82

3. Multiple Cause Diagram for the XYZ Company 92

4. An Example of a Rich Picture in Schematic Form 95

5. An Example of a Rich Picture from XYZ Company 96

6. Defining the Well-formed Problem 100

7. Critical Success Factors of XYZ Company 119

8. Main Board Members' Preferred Change Programmes of XYZ Company at the Start of the Investigation 120

9. Business Forces Diagram for a Business in Balance 134

10. Business Forces Diagram for a Business out of Balance following a failed TQM Project 135

11. Successful Problem-solving 141

12. The Well-formed Solution 147

13. Logical Levels 171

14. Logical Levels Diagram 173

15. Overlapping Subsystems 174

16. New Capability which does not fit in with the existing Organisational Identity 175

17. An Identity Conflict 176

18. Perceptual Positions 181

19. Time-line 198

Appendix One. The New And Updated Meta-model 255

Appendix Two. Dr Mayon-White's Change Management Strategy 259

Appendix Two. The Key Features Of Dr Mayon-White's Change Management Strategy 260–261

Acknowledgments

If a book includes the term Neuro-Linguistic Programming (NLP) in the title then rightfully the first acknowledgment must be to the co-developers of this incredibly powerful and interesting branch of psychology, John Grinder and Richard Bandler. Without their contribution this book could never have been written. However, many others besides have helped me on my path of discovery about NLP and added new dimensions to my personal model of the subject by way of publications and personal contact. In the USA, the most notable of these are: Robert Dilts, Judith DeLozier, Leslie Cameron-Bandler, Steve and Connirae Andreas, Tad James, Wyatt Woodsmall and Michael Hall. In the UK, John McWhirter, Eric Robbie and Ian McDermott are among many who have contributed to my better understanding of the subject and have also provided a valuable resource for testing out many of my own ideas.

All of us have experiences in the past that can qualify under the statement "I would not be where I am today without ..." In my case this applies to the many people who encouraged and influenced me during the thirteen very formative years (1968 to 1981) that I spent in the employ of International Computers Ltd. Special mention has to go to: Geoff Cross, CEO; Peter Ellis, Group Marketing Director; Peter Simpson, Director, Group Strategy and Development; and the late Arnold Jewitt, Director, Marketing Division. My heartfelt thanks also go to a group of very special colleagues who played important roles in supporting me and my sometimes "off the wall" ideas, particularly: Tom Jones, Reg Shaw, Pam Barlow, John Hartley, Harvey Dodgson, Martin Jordan and Jan Foxton (Heather); also to my first wife, Doreen, for her encouragement and understanding during this challenging period in my life.

Later, in the late 1980s and early 1990s I had the opportunity of working within the Raytheon Corporation, and it was during this period that many of the ideas contained in this book began to take shape. Many people within the company supported me during this period, and I thank you all. However, a special thanks to John Smith, Sally Smedley, Dr Peter Partington and Yvonne Jacklin for encouraging me and allowing me space to develop what at that time must have seemed some really crazy ideas.

More recently, and during the formation phase of many ideas in this book, I have had the opportunity to work with some of the brightest innovators in the art of Change Management. How many of these ideas would have come into existence without the stimulation provided by this group is difficult to say. They also acted as a wonderful sounding board and often offered additional material that turned my ideas into something of a more direct and practical application. So a great big thanks to all those who contributed to the short-course programme at the International Ecotechnology Research Centre at Cranfield University in the period 1989 to 1993. Of particular note are Bill Mayon-White and Geoff Elliott. Sadly, two other significant members of this team and major catalysts for my exploratory work during that period are no longer with us: the late Dr Roger Crane and Jim Stuart.

Many thanks to Professor Helen Muir, head of the Applied Psychology Department, College of Aeronautics, Cranfield University, and Dr Peter Brooks of the same faculty for involving me in the development of the short-course programme entitled Human Factors in Information Technology. Although probably they would not have been aware of it at the time, this programme caused me to formally record many techniques that I had been presenting on campus but had never previously written down. I would also like to thank them for their championing of my appointment as a Visiting Research Fellow of the University during this period.

Over the years I have been privileged to work with many executive officers and senior managers who have contributed to my learning about how organisations work. I thank these brave people for having the courage to allow me to experiment with their enterprises.

Finally, I wish to express a great big thanks to all those who have helped in the production of this book.

Preface to the Revised Edition

It is now almost eight years since I embarked upon writing this book. Much to my great delight it was well received and has remained popular ever since. At the time of the first reprint in 2001, the opportunity was taken to make a few minor alterations and add a small amount of text. Most of the changes resulted from feedback that I received from my readers, and I thank them most sincerely for taking the time to contact me and to give their views.

During the 1970s and 1980s, the domain we know as NLP grew at an almost exponential rate. New ideas and concepts were added almost continuously during those two decades. In the 1990s, NLP went through what is perhaps best described as a period of consolidation with little really new being added. This was also a period when over 150 titles on the subject appeared, almost a 700% increase over everything that had been previously published. Of varying quality, collectively they served the purpose of bringing together many of the diverse ideas and concepts that NLP had introduced and made them understandable to a far wider audience. A large proportion also concentrated on the applications of NLP rather than simply the technology. So far, since the advent of the 21st century nothing much has really changed. No new NLP models and no new wonderful discoveries such as Meta-modelling, time-lines or submodalities have arisen. New books are still appearing, though less than previously, with the majority, as in the 1990s, concentrating on application.

However, we have seen a large amount of rebranding occurring in many sectors where NLP has been adopted and adapted. The first and perhaps most obvious one involves the role of the coach and mentor. Whilst nearly all schools of psychotherapy have moved away from the title of "therapist" to that of "life coach" or "mentor", NLP has been one of the first out of the blocks. Mentoring and coaching have also become the "in" words in the business community as well as in many other domains, although both were in fact already in use in the 1980s. Whilst the names may have changed the technologies have not, although they are often dressed up to look or sound quite different. However, when you lift up the bonnet of this latest, slickest sports model, you find NLP written all over the engine. So we now see NLP, chameleon-like, changing its appearance to suit the market but the technology remains largely the same.

A similar occurrence has taken place in the world of education. NLP was at one time seen as a tool to use with special needs and gifted children. Now it has found its way into all aspects of education from early learning through to university level and onward into training in business. Again you do not always find the name NLP attached to the technology but in many cases this is exactly what it is.

This absorption of NLP techniques into other fields is a very healthy thing and it does provide proof that NLP has a sound basis. Ever since those very early days NLP has been criticised for not having had a sound scientific foundation. Well, now the proof is easy to see and is all around us: bright children becoming brighter, therapists, sorry, life coaches, achieving so much more, and business folks learning new, more efficient ways to interact with their colleagues. As they used to say, "the proof of the pudding is in the eating".

I have often been asked why I did not include any information about NLP modelling in the first edition of this book, particularly as I had written several fairly controversial articles about the subject almost concurrent with its publication. My reason was simple: I did not feel that I could go along with many of the claims made for the efficacy of NLP modelling in a business setting. However, I did not have enough information to hand to substantiate what I thought was the true situation. After I had published a series of four articles on modelling in *Rapport* (Volumes 42–45) and analysed the results of the feedback I had received, I had most of the information that I needed. So I have put this together to provide an additional chapter in this revised edition in which I lay out my case surrounding the technology and efficacy of modelling, NLP-style.

Martin Roberts
St Clears, 2006

Foreword

When my wife persuaded me eventually to write this book, my first problem was in deciding which of a number of potential audiences I should be addressing. I could have written a book that introduced some of the concepts of using NLP in Change Management scenarios to business consultants and managers involved in change. Conversely, I could have produced a manual for people who already had an understanding of NLP and wished to apply and adapt their knowledge for use in bringing about change in a business environment. Having often been asked by both groups about these applications, finally I chose to attempt to do both. I fully recognised that this might be a difficult task. For to address both audiences simultaneously would not be easy, as both had their own way of using language and had invented separate sets of expressions that were uniquely their own.

This was something that was familiar territory to me, having had a catholic background in my consultancy assignments over the years. Indeed, I learned very early on in my youthful days designing computer systems that Socrates had got it exactly right when he said, "If you wish to have a good table or chair made for you that will be comfortable and give good practical service for many years, you had better learn the language of carpenters". So with this statement in mind I will attempt to avoid the use of jargon from both the business world and NLP. However, when I am forced to resort to the relevant jargon I will also attempt to provide an adequate explanation of its meaning.

It seemed unlikely that I could satisfactorily answer all the questions that might be provoked by this book. Therefore I decided to include a number of case studies taken from actual experiences to show how these techniques can be brought together and used beneficially in a business environment. I have used examples drawn from a great number of different real-life situations, and, in order not to cause embarrassment, I have not attributed these to any particular organisation(s). Likewise, to avoid similar problems with identity the main case study running through the book is named the XYZ Company. Again, the example is made up from experience gained in several different businesses over a number of years.

My second problem in writing this book stemmed from the first. How simple or complicated should I make it? Having sought advice from both business consultants and NLPers (people who have a good understanding of the subject of NLP) I came to the conclusion that it would need to be a mixture of both simple and complex ideas, demonstrated by past relevant experiences. At the end of the book I have provided an extensive bibliography for those who wish to delve deeper into specific subject areas. I have also included recommendations for further reading within the text for those who wish to expand their knowledge of a particular subject or application.

My wife urged me to lay down a record of the new material that I have personally contributed to this field. When I came to analyse what was specifically my own invention I came to realise that much of what I had developed stemmed from my association with some very bright people with whom I came into contact at Cranfield University. So this book is to some extent the result of a group effort, and I can only echo Isaac Newton's famous words when asked about his great contribution to the science of physics, "If I have seen further, then I was merely standing on the shoulders of giants". This book does contain many new ideas and concepts that have not previously been published and these, when correctly applied, do increase the success rate of Change Management projects by many magnitudes.

If I were asked now what was the most significant tip I could give to a budding Change Management consultant it would be above all else, "Keep things simple". All too often in the past I have seen managers turned off by being subjected to long diatribes about the detailed elements of a particular technology. Most managers do not have the time or the patience to understand the technology involved in NLP. What they really want to know is how your offering can make improvements to the effectiveness of their business. When a manager acquires his new company car he is very unlikely to want to know precisely how the gears in the gearbox intermesh or anything else about the "technology" involved. He is much more likely to want to know about performance, safety, what colours it comes in and how it compares with other competitive makes and models. So, to summarise: do not attempt to "sell the features" of NLP but instead "sell the benefits" that your approach can bring to their business.

Always remember the more senior the manager the less time he has available to him to learn something new. Most senior managers would consider spending more than a couple of days a year on any course as excessive, so do not attempt to get them to do an NLP practitioner training however short it can be made!

A word or two of caution at this point. While many NLP techniques have found their way into the business community, it has not been adopted per se as a complete technology by them or the principal consultancy organisations who are their major sources of advice. Most, if not all, of the large consultancies in the UK and in the USA have thoroughly evaluated NLP on a number of occasions. However, they have never adopted significant elements of the technology apart from those that have direct application to communication skills, sales and marketing. This is a close parallel to what occurred when other psychological techniques were adopted by the business world. In particular, Transactional Analysis and Behavioural Modification stand out as having only parts of their respective technologies adopted by the consultancies and business in general.

There are several reasons for this, but the prime one is locked up in an equation where the value of the knowledge obtained is measured against the time required to acquire the knowledge, and time is an extremely valuable commodity, particularly in business. Thus it has always been the easy-to-learn elements of the various psychological approaches and the associated "quick fixes" that have been adopted. Sadly this has often meant that some techniques which had immense potential for use by business were not taken up, as they were seen as either too complicated in application or took too long to learn. I have not made that mistake with this book and have invested considerable effort to de-mystify many of the more advanced NLP techniques and to place them firmly in a business setting.

The rest of this book is about the techniques that I and others have developed and found to be of positive application in the world of business. Wishing to make the content easily understandable to everyone has meant that sometimes I have not delved too deeply into the underlying technology. Instead, I have provided references to other books that can provide a deeper or more specific understanding of the particular subject. There are now more than two hundred books published that can generally be termed "NLP". If you are totally new to the subject, I would recommend that you read *The Principles of NLP* by Ian McDermott and Joseph O'Connor (1996) or *My Little Book of NLP* by Georges Philips and Tony Jennings (2000), both of which provide a very good, basic introduction.

Everything in this book has been tried and tested many hundreds of times in a variety of business settings. Not just by me but also by my associates and a few other people whom we have let into the secret of what, and how, we have brought about what some have claimed have been "impossible" changes – and, in other cases, repaired the damage done by others who applied change programmes incorrectly. To a large extent this book reveals the secrets of our approach to Change Management and the techniques we used to achieve excellence in our work. As I now reach the age when most people retire and two of the co-developers of this work have gone to seek their Maker, I believe this is a fitting time to reveal to a larger audience the secrets of our success.

I trust this book will stimulate you into making your own discoveries and perhaps enable you to go on to invent some applications of your own. When you do, and if I have played a part in providing the stimulation, I will have achieved my objective.

Introduction

Structured into five parts, each part of this book addresses different aspects of the overall subject area. The first part looks at the history of NLP, what the term stands for and how the subject has developed over the last twenty or so years. It provides a background covering the development of NLP from other therapies and its gradual spread from the therapeutic arena to other areas such as business applications. Finally, it looks at how some of the current business and personal development gurus have been influenced by this technology.

In the first part also, attention is given to the development of Change Management techniques over the last thirty or so years. Of particular concern is the high level of failures associated with many of these modern packaged solutions such as Total Quality Management, Business Process Re-engineering and Information Technology in general.

The second part looks at communication skills. This is perhaps how NLP is currently best known in the world of business. Clearly if you are a manager or a consultant and you cannot communicate effectively you are not going to be very good at your job. For those with experience in the field this can be an opportunity to revise or hone your skills. Those coming from an NLP background have an opportunity to gain an insight into how to apply, in a business setting, the technology you have already learned.

The third part deals specifically with the subject of Change Management. It covers the research undertaken by the Ecotech Group at Cranfield University into the causes of Change Management failures and the methods developed to avoid repetition of the same mistakes. It deals in particular with three models devised or adapted from many fields including NLP, which provide a means for improving success with all Change Management projects. Additional models are also included to assist with resolving conflict within organisations and aligning attitudes and beliefs.

The fourth part looks at the function of time and the different ways we can view and use our perception of time. Again two new models are included which can make significant improvements in Business Strategy Development, Planning and New Product Innovation.

The fifth part of the book looks at popular packaged solutions which have arisen from developments in the field of modern management science over the last two decades. As a very large proportion of Change Management failures have been either directly attributed to or closely associated with these types of solution, the main focus is on avoiding the major pitfalls.

Finally, at the back of the book are a number of appendices which are included as an adjunct to the main text.

Part One

Introducing NLP
And
Modern Developments
In
Change Management

Chapter One

Background

The Holy Bible starts with the phrase, "In the beginning was God ..." and it is difficult to beat that for an opening phrase so I won't attempt it! Instead, I will borrow the concept and start by saying that in the beginning of NLP there were two highly innovative Californians, Richard Bandler and John Grinder, and it is these two who are credited with being the originators, or co-developers, of the subject. However, before delving too far back into the pedigree of NLP, it is perhaps apposite to deal with the term NLP itself, as newcomers to the subject sometimes seem to be confused by the name. One of the most popular misconceptions is that it has something to do with a new form of computer programming rather than what it really is: a technology for understanding how the mind works.

By far and away the best description I have seen of NLP is in a book by Steve Andreas, Charles Faulkner and other members of the NLP Comprehensive Training Team, which goes as follows:

What is NLP?

NLP is the study of human excellence.
NLP is the ability to be your best more often.
NLP is the powerful and practical approach to personal change.
NLP is the new technology of achievement.
NLP is the acronym for Neuro-Linguistic Programming. This high-tech-sounding name is purely descriptive, like cross-trainer shoes, a golden retriever, or a classic convertible coupe. Neuro refers to our nervous system, the mental pathways of our five senses by which we see, hear, feel, taste and smell. Linguistic refers to our ability to use language and how specific words or phrases mirror our mental worlds. Linguistic also refers to our "silent language" of

> *postures, gestures, and habits that reveal our thinking styles, beliefs, and more. Programming is borrowed from computer science, to suggest that our thoughts, feelings, and actions are simply habitual programs that can be changed by upgrading our "mental software."*
>
> *Andreas, Faulkner, et al (1994)*

I trust this has cleared up any confusion that the term NLP may have caused. I should like to add one small but vital observation. In my experience it is almost impossible to gain a useable understanding of NLP from just reading about it. You simply have to experience it for yourself in order to be able to use it effectively. The best way to achieve an experiential understanding is to practise what you learn. Therefore, in order to assist in this regard, most of the "technology" in the following text contain examples which can be explored further.

So back to the origins of NLP. The geographic roots of NLP can be found at the University of California, Santa Cruz, in the early 1970s. At that time Richard Bandler was an undergraduate mathematics student. Initially he spent much of his time studying computer science. Richard did not come from an affluent background and had a part-time job as a storeman and gofer with a local publisher to help pay his way through university. The publisher was Science and Behavior Books whose area of excellence was books on psychology and psychotherapy. Being an extremely inquisitive character it did not take Richard long before he had become intrigued by the work of some of the therapists/authors with whom he came into contact.

During this period the owner of the publishing company, Robert Spitzer MD, gave Richard the task of transcribing over forty hours of film showing the father of modern Gestalt Therapy, Fritz Perls MD, working with his students and clients. Dr Spitzer had made a commitment with Dr Perls in the late 1960s to publish the films with an additional commentary to be provided by Dr Perls once all the filming was completed. The commentary and films were intended to form a complete introductory training for students studying Gestalt Therapy. However, with the film work only partially complete, Fritz Perls died in early 1970. Dr Spitzer set

Richard the transcription task as he felt the outcome once published could form a fitting epitaph to Dr Perls.

The outcome of Richard's work was threefold. The first was a book called *Eye Witness to Therapy* (1973) with much credit being given by Dr Spitzer to Richard. The second was a switch by Richard from the mathematics course at the university to psychology. But perhaps the third was the most important, because Richard started "doing" Gestalt Therapy with his fellow students. He achieved this by simply mimicking everything that Dr Perls had been doing on the videotapes. He even went so far as to grow a beard, chain-smoke, and speak English with a pronounced German accent. It was around this time that Richard came into contact with Dr John Grinder who was at that time an associate professor of linguistics at Santa Cruz.

Dr Grinder's background is an interesting one, although slightly enigmatic. It is known that John had served with the US Army Special Forces in Europe during the 1960s and subsequently with US intelligence services. He has said that it was there that he acquired his ability to rapidly assimilate languages, accents and dialects as well as taking on the associated cultural behaviours. John is also reported as saying that his attraction to the Gestalt Therapy group that Richard was running on the campus was because it closely fitted with his own interest in the psychological function of linguistics.

Bandler and Grinder, finding that they shared common interests, decided to combine their respective skills in Gestalt Therapy, computer science and linguistics along with their abilities to copy non-verbal behaviour. Their objective in so doing was to develop a new "language of change". In order to achieve this they carried out a considerable amount of research and experimentation in an effort to unlock the secret that they knew must be there somewhere.

Their research was influenced by many contributors to the fields of communication and language but in particular by the works of Gregory Bateson (1972), Noam Chomsky (1957, 1968) and Alfred Korzybski (1958). In addition they carried out a number of studies of the methods of communication used between three outstanding therapists and their clients: Milton H Erickson MD (psychiatrist and hypnotherapist); Virginia Satir (family therapist); and of course Fritz Perls MD (Gestalt Therapist and psychiatrist), who may be seen as starting all this off via the films.

The initial outcome from their studies was the publication of two books, *Structure of Magic I* and *Structure of Magic II* , published in 1975 and 1976 respectively. These books encapsulated their collective research in developing a new understanding of the human process we call communication. The model they developed is known as the Meta-model and lies at the root of all subsequent developments in NLP. The model itself provides a means for discovering the true meaning of communication which may not always be correctly conveyed in the spoken word alone. The model also provides various tools to allow more precise meanings to be derived from any communication.

The development of NLP did not cease with the publication of these two seminal works. Bandler and Grinder continued to develop their model further, and others joined them in making additional contributions during the mid/late 1970s. Many of these were students at the University of Santa Cruz who had previously been involved as human guinea pigs during the originators' experiments with Gestalt Therapy and other psychotherapies leading up to the publication of *Structure of Magic I* and *Structure of Magic II*. Among the most notable of these were Judith DeLozier (an anthropology student of Gregory Bateson), Robert Dilts (psychology and human factors in cybernetics), Leslie Cameron-Bandler (ecology), David Gordon (psychology), Byron Lewis (psychology) and Frank Pucelik (psychology). There is strong evidence to suggest that this expanded group was influenced by the works of Carl Rogers (Client-Centred Therapy), Albert Ellis (Rational-Emotive Therapy), Moshe Feldenkrais (Body and Movement Therapy) and Eric Berne (Transactional Analysis).

California in the late 1960s and early 1970s was a hotbed of experimentation in living and thinking. Every student campus of that time was affected by major changes in thinking and in culture. This was the period of experimentation with flower power, LSD and the human potential movement.

It has been reported by some members that during this formative period they experimented with many techniques which were considered to be on the fringe of, or even outside, mainstream psychotherapy. These techniques included Arthur Janov's Primal Scream Therapy and Leonard Orr's rebirthing techniques. This highly inquisitive group continued their explorations, and by the end of the 1970s a whole host of techniques had been developed associated with the modelling of human behaviour. This research and experimentation also resulted in the development of a number of specific therapeutic interventions designed to resolve individual psychological problems. Development of new therapeutic techniques has continued up to the present day, and NLP can now be seen as fitting within the wider psychotherapeutic domain known as the Cognitive Behavioural School.

Whilst much of the early work was focused on the therapeutic application of this technology to individuals, towards the end of the 1970s it was also starting to be applied to group behaviour and then to complete organisations. A move into the business field was an obvious next step in this progression.

It is interesting to observe that in the last forty years business and commerce have become increasingly interested in most of the new developments in the field of psychology. Some of the most notable of these developments have been drawn from Behavioural Modification, Gestalt Therapy, Transactional Analysis and Family Therapy. All of these can be seen as fitting within, or closely associated with, the Cognitive Behavioural School. It is therefore perhaps not surprising to see NLP being adapted in this manner. Indeed NLP was tailor-made for the modern business community as it has structures which in many ways mirror the modern "systems approach" to business which was largely brought about by the advent of Cybernetics (Bandler's first love) and Information Technology.

Since the end of the 1970s many people from a diversity of backgrounds have continued to add further material to the domain that we now know as NLP. Indeed many of the advances made during the 1980s and 1990s open up new possibilities for application to the business field far beyond those envisaged by the original co-developers of NLP. This is perhaps because many of the new developers have themselves come from business backgrounds rather than from the realms of therapy or personal change.

NLP is also being applied to areas other than business and therapy such as Accelerated Learning where many of the major developments have been made by people with backgrounds in teaching. It is interesting to note that Accelerated Learning has in turn found its way back into the business community. Similarly, much of the early work in the late 1970s and early 1980s applied to sales and marketing has now become absorbed to such an extent that the true origin of the work has already been forgotten.

Whilst to the academically orientated this may be regrettable, it follows the normal path of integration that other psychological developments have previously followed. In fact, when such absorption takes place it can perhaps be seen as the highest accolade, as at last it has become accepted practice and is no longer viewed as just some freaky fad. So if you are new to NLP, don't be surprised if you come across a few concepts within this book that already have a familiar ring about them. Such terms as building rapport, creating a compelling future, getting in state or modelling human excellence are straight from the domain of NLP.

Today NLP is at the heart of many approaches to communication and change. It has been popularised by such people as Anthony Robbins (*Unlimited Power,* 1986 and *Awaken the Giant Within,* 1991), John Bradshaw (*Healing the Shame That Binds You,* 1988) and many others besides. Various management gurus have incorporated NLP techniques into what they offer their clients. Perhaps the most notable of these are Peter Senge (*The Fifth Discipline,* 1990) and Stephen Covey (*The Seven Habits of Highly Effective People,* 1989 and *Principle-Centered Leadership,* 1992).

Change processes and change mechanisms in the business world have similarly been evolving rapidly over the last twenty years. There is nothing new about change, as change is part of the process of evolution, and little progress or growth can be achieved in a static environment. However, since the late 1970s there has been a growing passion in business for what I have termed "packaged solutions" or "packaged change". Unlike the evolutionary approach, "packaged change" nearly always involves something much closer in nature to revolution rather than evolution. This book deals to a large extent with the failures of modern packaged solutions to produce the results that their proponents so freely promise. It explains the reason for these failures and provides solutions that, when applied, can create certainty in the outcome of any change processes.

Revolutionary change is not new to business or industry. In the first half of this century alone there were several such revolutions. Perhaps the two most notable occurred between the two World Wars. These were the advent of the production line (Henry Ford), and time and motion study (Frederick Taylor). Both of these techniques, which originated in North America, eventually revolutionised production processes around the world and also had a major impact upon management theory.

The most significant effects of these technologies were to reduce production and unit/labour costs by several magnitudes whilst increasing overall output by even larger margins. They are credited as being among the five major sources of wealth creation in the USA during the first half of this century. However, whilst these technologies could be seen as revolutionary in themselves, the method of choosing, planning and finally applying the technology was not. Much longer time scales were involved in these processes compared with today's "packaged solutions". Most implementations involved a bespoke solution which was tailored in great detail to the specific needs of the client. The combination of longer time scales and detailed tailoring provided many more opportunities to correct problems as they arose, and consequently there were far fewer failures compared to today's packaged solutions.

Also coming out of America during this period were dramatic changes in the methods of running and organising our offices and businesses. I am often amused to hear people talk about the computer "revolution" in this half of the century (since 1960) when in fact "computing" or Information Technology (IT) really is only an evolution of an existing technology based on the punch card and comptometer. Both of these owe their birth to James Hollerith who invented them around 1900. The advent of the punch card and the means to process the information encoded on it had a very pronounced effect on businesses from the early 1920s onwards.

IBM's financial and technological might in the world of IT has its roots in the punch card and associated technology developed during the 1920s and 1930s. Many of the processes now undertaken by computers are in fact almost identical to those carried out with the punch card collators, sorters, accumulators and tabulators of that period. The only real difference is in speed: computers do the same job in a fraction of the time and are much more flexible due to their "soft" stored programs. It is perhaps worth remembering that even in the mid 1970s the punch-card and its cousin, punched-paper tape, were still virtually the only means of inputting data to computers.

Similarly, it was not long after the revolution engendered by Frederick Taylor's "time and motion studies" in the factories that many of his ideas were starting to be applied to the office. This gave birth to the Organisation and Management Departments (O & M) which were so popular in business during the 1950s and 1960s. These in turn fuelled new thinking on how we managed our businesses, and we saw early attempts at producing greater productivity by incenting management through techniques such as Management By Objectives.

It was also during this period that we saw major changes occurring in the structure of our businesses. It was a period when management theory made it fashionable to acquire other businesses as a means of fuelling short-term growth or to achieve diversification. Such terms as "asset stripping", "diversify or die", "merger" and "take-over" found their way into the general vernacular of that age. Inevitably when the events engendered by these terms occurred, they had more in common with revolution than evolution. Managements who embarked upon such strategies could not afford to spend four or five years assimilating a new business. Instead, integration had to be achieved in months rather than years in order to keep faith with the stakeholders who in most cases had provided the cash for the acquisition. Suddenly there was another reason to rethink how we managed our businesses, and we first see the term "management science" coming into general parlance.

Since the 1960s the computer and its related technologies such as Automation, Robotics and Communications have radically changed our manufacturing processes and the manner in which we run our businesses. However, instead of causing a revolution, computing has spread more in the manner of a forest fire through industry. Starting with a little spark in the mid 1960s, by further mechanising areas such as the payroll and accounting departments it spread rapidly into manufacturing and marketing by the mid 1970s. Since then, Information Technology (IT), as we were by now calling computing, has pervaded every aspect of modern business.

It is perhaps this further acceleration of change associated with IT in the 1970s and 1980s that has opened the door to many of the new management theories arising in the last two decades. "Confused" is a common description of how many managers and senior executives felt about IT during this period. The technology was seen as too complex for most managers to obtain a complete understanding of how it worked. Few could even get to grips with understanding whether or not it could deliver what was promised by the IT vendors. Managers quickly learned that it was far safer to employ IT experts to advise them or to call in specialist consultants. Then, if anything went wrong, they had someone to whom they could apportion the blame.

So selling a new management technique or way of organising the business to an already confused executive was not as difficult as it might have been a decade earlier. The salesman's task was made even easier when he promised a significant "competitive advantage" as a result of implementing the new technique.

There are very few companies in this age that have not embarked upon some major change programme emanating from these new management theories in recent times. Indeed, as I write this book I am aware that most large British companies have more than one such process concurrently running in their business. Many books and articles in learned journals have been written about this sudden craze for change of the packaged solution type and what has brought it about. All seem to agree that nearly all the techniques are of American origin. They are also virtually unanimous when asked what they believe has caused this explosive growth in change. Top of the list are: fear of Japanese industrial might; the almost explosive spread of computers and the packaged solutions attached to these; and perhaps associated with both of the previous two reasons, radical changes to working patterns. However, the key to all of these is the emotion "fear" in its many and varied forms.

Fear is the one thing that will either prompt us into action or freeze us like statues. Fear is about survival, and as such is our most powerful basic instinct. Fear is the driving influence of the fight or flight syndrome that if not addressed creates stress within our working lives. So it is probably not surprising in this age when psychological techniques have found their way into almost every aspect of our life that others are using our "fear of failure" to sell us something. Whether it is the housewife who is fearful of the criticism of neighbours or friends for not having "whiter than white washing" or the senior executive who is fearful of his company not staying ahead of the pack, it is our basic instincts that are driving us.

Unfortunately, all too often packaged solutions have been sold to businesses based upon fear rather than the fulfilment of a well-defined need. Often these packaged solutions have been sold to a client company when there was no genuine need for such a process. Total Quality Management (TQM) is notorious in this respect, and, although no precise statistics exist for the UK, it is known that over 85% of TQM projects in the USA have not produced the desired results. TQM is not unique in respect to having a high hit rate of failed projects. Richard Pascale in his excellent book *Managing on the Edge* (1990), identified eighteen similar techniques spawned during the 1980s, and many more have been invented since. No doubt there are even more in the pipelines of the consultants and the Business Schools because it is this "new thinking" in management theory that largely fuels their businesses.

The latest fad, Business Process Re-engineering (BPR), seems also to have its fair share of failures. Recently there have been many companies in the UK and the USA cursing BPR for downsizing them to the point of becoming "corporately anorexic". These businesses are now finding it almost impossible to respond to the upturn in the economic environment. Their competitors, on the other hand, who did not downsize, or did so with less enthusiasm, are having a field day at their expense.

The cost of these failures and those associated with IT ventures during the last decade has been assessed as amounting to a minimum of £20bn and a maximum of well in excess of double this figure, and this for the UK alone. Whilst at first figures of this magnitude are hard to believe, one has only to think of some of the more notable disasters, such as the failed New Stock Exchange System (costed at £800m in 1992), and other well-publicised disasters of similar magnitude in the public sector, to realise that this estimate is probably at least in the right ballpark. Just think for a moment what £20bn invested in industry, the public sector infrastructure or just plain research could have achieved during the same period.

So much for the public sector, but the private sector would probably have been the largest contributor to this type of failure. In 1996 a survey of the UK's top 200 companies revealed that 97% had been involved in implementing some form of packaged solution during the previous year. This is further supported by the size of the income of the top 30 or so consultancy firms who earned £19bn in 1996 alone (Ashford, 1998).

No business likes to announce bad news, and it certainly does not usually admit to a failure in management decision-making without an accompanying resignation of one or more of its senior executives, so what better reason for sweeping such mistakes quietly under the boardroom carpet! When this happens it is extremely good news to the vendors of the solution that went wrong, because no one else gets to hear about it!

Does this mean that all modern packaged solutions are in fact just good old-fashioned "snake-oil remedies"? Clearly the answer is no, but all should perhaps be forced to have a corporate health warning attached to them. Even TQM has a lot going for it, and one must remember that 15% of companies surveyed in the USA who implemented TQM claimed it had been successful for them. So the real question is what did they do to get it right and what did the other 85% do to get it so wrong? This book provides the answer to these questions, and a whole lot more besides.

Part Two

Developing Excellence In Communication And Understanding How Other People Tick

Overview

It is doubtful whether there is a single person living who does not wish they were more skilled in the art of communication. This should not be surprising as recent surveys of people working in the major professions in Great Britain and North America have shown that less than ten per cent classify themselves as good communicators. Perhaps less surprising is finding that a large number of the good communicators were either priests, politicians or lawyers. However, what is of most interest is the finding that nearly 60% of those surveyed classified themselves not just as average communicators but as poor communicators. Therefore, logically, you are likely in your role as a Change Management agent to come into contact with many poor communicators. I know that I have!

Fortunately, NLP offers you some excellent techniques which are easy to learn and, when applied correctly, can produce startling results. These techniques have also given me the advantage of knowing when I was being deliberately misled, or when someone with whom I was communicating was being economical with the truth. They have also been extremely useful in gaining an understanding of where the other person I was communicating with was coming from, and this can be vital in achieving success in Change Management projects.

The techniques used in communication and derived from NLP have often in the past been termed manipulative, and, when used to gain an unfair advantage, I would agree. However, provided that my intention is an honest one, then I have no problem in manipulating people. After all, this is what I am being paid to do for a large percentage of the time in order to bring about change. If these techniques enable me to get the right results with more consistency, then I tend to treat them like any other tool in my Change Management tool kit. Please also remember that there is an extremely fine dividing line between manipulation and gentle persuasion anyway.

Being an excellent communicator in all its various forms, but especially speaking and writing, is, of course, of great importance to anyone contemplating becoming a consultant and even more so to those who wish to work in a Change Management environment.

However, developing listening skills and other techniques which allow you to understand fully your client's needs is also of crucial importance.

It is here that NLP scores again with a number of really powerful techniques to assist the listener in gaining a complete understanding of what the speaker is saying. I have lost count of the number of times that I have been told by someone with whom I was communicating that I must be psychic, simply because it appeared to them that I was able to "read their mind". In reality it was simply employing a few NLP techniques that allowed me to gain a better understanding of what was being communicated to me.

In the introduction to this book mention was made of the causes of failure in many Change Management and IT projects. One of the principal causes of these failures has been not fully understanding the needs of the client or, in other words, lack of adequate communication skills.

Thus learning these apparently mystical techniques for improving communication in all its aspects has to be a very worthwhile investment. This is something that anyone with a little application can achieve. I know of no one who has learned these skills who would now willingly be without them.

The last chapter of this section takes the reader one stage further and commences the process of learning how to understand what makes other people tick. To a large extent this chapter deals with the "P" in NLP, which is concerned with the programmes we run in our minds all the time. This chapter provides a number of techniques for gaining a better understanding of how other people's programmes work and, more importantly, how we can assist in changing them beneficially.

Chapter Two

The Important Role Of Rapport In Communication

During their early exploratory work in communication, the origi-nators of NLP, Bandler and Grinder, discovered that in order to communicate well one first had to develop a high level of rapport with the person or persons one wished to communicate with. In instances where rapport was not established and held throughout the process of communication, the intended message would not get through. Consequently, the person attempting to communicate would have an exceedingly low chance of successfully achieving their objective.

Bandler and Grinder came to realise that even when we are not in rapport we are still communicating something, but it may not be the message we intend. It may be something of a different nature. This phenomenon has given rise to one of the early "laws" of NLP which states, "Whatever we are doing, we cannot not communi-cate". This may sound strange at first, but when we realise that a large proportion of what we are communicating is not contained in the words that we use but in our body language, facial expres-sion and tone of voice, etc., perhaps this becomes a little clearer. Various researchers over the years have looked closely at this sub-ject and have apportioned slightly different weighting to each of these functions within the process of human communication. The overall consensus is that approximately 60% of communication stems from body language including facial expression, 30% from our tone of voice and just 10% from the actual words that we choose to use.

So even when we do not wish to communicate, and have our mouths tight shut, we are still communicating a lot of information, but in a non-verbal form. A large proportion of this non-verbal information is processed by our minds at a very deep level and out of our conscious awareness. Recognising this is of prime importance, as our brains are far more likely to interpret as correct information coming from our unconscious minds, than any language input that we may be receiving via our ears.

This is a simple function of our evolution. Man has had to trust and react to his senses for many millions of years in order to survive, whereas language is a relatively recent development (McLujan and Flore, 1967). An example of this would be to welcome someone with words like, "Hello. It's great to see you again", while at the same time standing in an aggressive stance and with an angry expression on your face. In such a situation the recipient would almost certainly feel very confused and become defensive and would probably not be able to remember the words that had been spoken. Whilst such incongruence is extreme and unlikely to happen often in practice, we need to be aware that excellent communication occurs only when we are 100% congruent in all aspects of our presentation. When we have complete congruence we have started on the path of establishing rapport, but this is only the first step.

Unfortunately, we cannot just pop down the road and buy some rapport skills! Personal skills of this nature exist in us all to a greater or lesser extent but most of us have to work at them if we want to improve them. Obviously, knowing when we are in or out of rapport with other people is the most valuable skill to acquire. Fortunately, this is easy. All that is needed is, whilst involved in a conversation, to observe what happens when we change our posture in some way. If after a few moments the other person changes their posture to something approximating ours this is an indication that we are in rapport.

It is worth observing other people who are in conversation. Notice that when they are in rapport they will display similar body postures. They will tend to retain much more eye contact. They are also likely to have similar expressions on their faces. Look closely at what they are doing with their bodies, notice that when one person changes posture the other will follow, almost as though they are engaged in some form of dance, one leading and the other following. By watching other people we can quickly learn to pick out those who are in rapport and those who are not. In NLP terms this is known as increasing our "sensory acuity". In plain language this simply means we are becoming more observant of other people and taking in more detail about the way they move and use their bodies.

As with most things in life, practice makes perfect. So after observing other people for a while, and when we feel we have obtained a reasonable understanding of this dance which we call rapport, we can experiment with someone we know. This is most easily achieved by engaging the person in conversation and then observing what happens when their body language is mirrored. Then by changing our posture in some way we can see whether they imitate our new posture. In most instances they will naturally follow and move to mirror our posture in order to stay in rapport with us.

Practising this process with several people successfully will take us more than half way towards a full understanding of the subject because 60% of communication is about body language. In NLP jargon what you have been doing is referred to as "matching" or "mirroring" and then "leading" when you change your posture and they follow.

Most human beings do not have too much of a problem with building rapport because it is something we do quite naturally. However, the more we practise the better we become at it, until a point is reached when we do not have to think about it much – like any unconsciously learned skill such as driving a car or riding a bicycle.

The next level at which we can build rapport is in the language we use. By this I don't mean French, German or another foreign language; it is more about the words we choose to use and the tonality and expression that we put into delivering them.

Let us start with tonality, which research suggests is 30% of communication. We are all very aware of the major differences that exist in the forms of expression that we put into what we say, which are controlled by our emotions. When we are excited we tend to talk more quickly, and often our voice goes up in tone slightly. If we are angry the tone of our voice will often be louder than normal, and if we are sad our voice tends to be quieter and the words delivered more slowly than usual. However, all our language is affected to some degree by our emotions all the time. With a little practice we can learn to become more aware of the changes in rhythm, pitch, volume and speed of delivery of the voice of the people we are communicating with. Again, we can match and mirror this in order to further build rapport.

We can also use this on the telephone to great effect. Then, because there is no body language present, a large proportion of what is being communicated will be locked up in voice tonality. A little effort in matching the speed, volume and rhythm of the other person on the end of the line can pay enormous dividends. On occasions when I have had to make a difficult phone call to a client I have put a lot more effort into matching and mirroring tonality, and many times this has, I am sure, assisted me in achieving the outcome that I wanted.

Finally, to the language that we choose to use, always remembering that this accounts for only a very small proportion of our intended communication. Much of language is sensory-based, i.e. we tend to use words that give some expression of our senses. Words such as: seeing, picture, outlook, focus, horizon, vision, hindsight, reflect, are all words associated with our sense of seeing. Similarly, words such as: sound, hear, wavelength, loud, tone, music, are words associated with our sense of hearing. Words associated with our sense of feeling include words such as: touch, feel, pressure, sharp, tight, hassle, weight. All of us have a preference for using one of our senses more than the others. The most common preference seems to be vision, with hearing second and feeling last.

There is one further group of people who have a preference for what is termed digital or logical language. In this group we often find people who work in or with IT, but we also come across its use very commonly with people who work with the hard sciences: chemists, physicists, engineers, etc. This group uses words like: analyse, think, review, balance, judge, surmise, rationalise, perceive.

Mirroring and matching the type of language used by your client can be a very powerful way of building rapport. Do not, however, attempt to copy regional accents, speech impediments or other more personal attributes as it could be seen as mimicking, and that is not likely to assist you in achieving your goal.

Most of us in this day and age are familiar with "computer jargon" and we have some understanding of many of the terms peculiar to the world of computing and Information Technology. However, almost every branch of industry and many commercial sectors have also developed their own particular sets of jargon which are unique. Therefore, before taking up any work in an unfamiliar sector it makes good sense to find out what terms are used, what their meaning is, and how, specifically, they are applied. I will always remember being told by a director of a large supermarket chain that we had failed to win a contract worth several million pounds because a key member of my team was not familiar with the term "shrinkage" (a polite term for theft). This was particularly galling as he went on to tell me that our price was the most competitive and our final presentation was by far the best. The lesson in this instance was if you can't walk the talk you don't get the business.

Liking the other person is not a prerequisite for establishing rapport, but mutual confidence in your competence for the task in hand *is*. So personal credibility is likely to play a key role at an early point in establishing rapport. Turning up to address a Top 100 Companies Board meeting in a pair of jeans and a T-shirt is not likely to do very much for your credibility unless the meeting happens to be with Richard Branson! Even then I am sure I would have to think very hard before donning this gear. The simple message is: never do anything which creates a mismatch with your audience's expectations of your behaviour or of their expectations of your capabilities.

Before making contact with a new or prospective client, invest some effort into finding out as much as you can about their business. One of the best sources of information can be obtained from the published company accounts. These are usually freely available from all public companies and many other institutions. To obtain a copy, just pick up the phone and call the switchboard of the head office or call the company secretary's department. They are usually only too happy to oblige. Many companies also have a potted history available and other promotional material such as sales literature, just for the asking. All of these are mines of useful information.

If you do not wish to approach a company directly you can always use the Free Annual Reports Service provided by the *Financial Times*. This service covers all the major UK quoted companies and they will send the latest set of accounts of any of these companies. They can be contacted by phone on 0208 770 0770, or fax on 0208 770 3822, or via the Internet at www.worldinvestorlink.com. All reports are sent out by second class post and take two to three days to arrive.

For more detailed information about UK companies, the *Financial Times* offers another excellent service known as FT Company Focus, currently at a cost of £8.45. This provides a very comprehensive 10 to 18 page report. This contains: key news stories from the last year; the latest survey of City profit forecasts and investment recommendations; 5-year financial and share price performance review, balance sheet and profit and loss account data; all recent Stock Exchange announcements.

For even more information in addition to that above, another service known as FT Company Focus Plus is available at a total cost of £10.95. This provides further information derived from *The Investors Chronicle*.

All of these FT services provide excellent value for money, particularly when you consider how much time needs to be expended in researching such information.

If you are going to be working for a company quoted on the London Stock Exchange, do find out what the share price is and whether it is rising or falling. All of the above can give you a multitude of ideas for starting a conversation and will permit you to demonstrate to your client your interest in his/her company. Most senior members of staff will chat on for quite a while about "their" company whilst you can just sit nodding appreciatively and asking the occasional appropriate question. This is a great way to "break the ice" and to build instant rapport. It is also a great way for you to gather information about the particular characteristics of how the person talks and what their language preferences are, etc.

It is also vital that you understand precisely what the client is expecting of you. It helps a great deal if you can develop a high degree of behavioural flexibility, but this doesn't require you to develop schizophrenia or the skills of a "method actor". Remember that your client will have a model in his or her mind of what the perfect consultant might be. This could be someone such as Sir John Harvey Jones with his love of brightly coloured ties, his soft, slow but deliberate tone of voice and his total concentration on what the client has to say. Conversely, the client may expect a typical management consultancy prodigy, straight out of business school, very assertive, boiling over with self-confidence and having all the answers to every possible question before they are asked. Clearly these two examples are poles apart. However, the point to remember is that your client will have a preconceived idea of what "a good consultant" should be. If you can closely match their expectations you are already halfway towards establishing rapport.

Perhaps the most important aspect of behavioural flexibility involves the actual role that you are fulfilling. By this I mean the way you are to be perceived by those around you. Sometimes a client will expect you to take charge of a situation, and this places you in a leadership or guiding role where you are seen as the expert and are expected to tell people what to do. In other situations you may be seen as playing an advisory role where you will offer your opinions which the client may or may not act upon. In yet other situations you may be seen as a more junior member of a team consisting mainly of the client's staff and taking instructions from the team leader. All these situations require you to behave in different ways, and you will come across many more besides. Having the ability to react like a chameleon in changing circumstances instead of having one limited mode of behaviour can certainly pay huge dividends.

In the early days of NLP much was made of building and maintaining rapport, and large amounts of time (several days) were devoted to learning and practising the skills associated with the subject. Over the last decade less time has been devoted to the subject, but it still forms an important part of NLP courses. Many of the items above are not taken from NLP but are based on simple common sense. I have concentrated upon those elements that I have found to work well for me and that I have seen others use to effect.

Possessing excellent rapport skills is vital for effective communication in this day and age. Without them in a consultancy setting you are as good as dead. Operating as a Change Management consultant nearly always means handling resistance to change and resolving conflict. Become excellent in your use of rapport skills and you will have a much easier and more successful life as a consultant.

This chapter is not intended to be a definitive study of the subject of rapport but more a reminder of the vital function played by rapport in high-quality communication. Should you feel the need to hone your skills or would like to find out more about this intriguing subject, I can recommend two excellent books, *Influencing With Integrity* (1987) by Genie Laborde and *The Magic of Rapport* (1987) by Jerry Richardson.

Chapter Three

Developing Precision In The Language We Use

NLP has another "law" which states, "The meaning of the communication is the response it elicits, regardless of the intent of the communicator". An obvious truism when we stop to think about it, but nevertheless one that is often overlooked in the course of attempting to get our message across. We see examples of this in all aspects of life.

So often does this occur that we find it embedded at the core of much of our humour. Good examples can be found in the classic television series *Fawlty Towers*, where exchanges occur between Basil the hotel owner and his wife Sybil, Basil and his guests, and Basil and his staff. But perhaps the most significant occur when Basil attempts to communicate with Manuel, his Spanish waiter, who has a severely limited understanding of the English language. A typical scene involves Manuel's failing to understand precisely what Basil is trying to tell him. When the initial attempt at communication fails, Basil resorts to speaking much more slowly but with a slightly louder voice. When this fails, he speaks even more slowly and loudly and he continues to repeat the process until he is screaming at the top of his voice and using or threatening violence. The scene usually ends with the whole situation backfiring on Basil, and he becomes the victim.

In *Fawlty Towers* the problem lies primarily in the language differences which exist between the two individuals. Basil, who is English, speaks in his mother tongue whilst Manuel, who is Spanish, attempts to communicate in English which he speaks and understands poorly. Clearly the intention of this comedy programme is to parody some of the worst aspects of bad communication.

I cannot claim to have experienced anything happening in the business world that comes close to what occurs in *Fawlty Towers*. However, the underlying problems associated with poor communication are no strangers to the business world, and I have had far too many personal experiences of these. In the past, many catastrophic events have occurred where the root cause was attributed to poor communication. I am sure that you, whilst reading this, will recall many examples from your own personal experiences.

Does this happen in Change Management consultancy? Yes, I am afraid it does, and with monotonous regularity. Frequently I have found myself sitting through a highly complex presentation about a technology that I have barely understood and which has contained words that I knew I could not spell. Often the presentation was being made by a very keen and able young person who knew their subject extremely well. However, they were simply unaware that their audience did not share their knowledge or enthusiasm for the subject. All their listeners really wanted to know was, "Does what you are offering work and can it produce results for us?"

So, as consultants, we know that such behaviour is likely to lead us nowhere but out of the door. However, I have often observed some of my more mature colleagues, whom one would imagine would know better, boring the pants off someone and not realising they are doing it. So we must develop skills that help us to magnetise the attention of our audience whilst ensuring that they fully understand the content of what we are saying to them. Two checks are then implicit. The first is to develop a high level of sensory acuity. This is a process that we started to address in the previous chapter when we were looking for signs of rapport in the person with whom we were attempting to communicate. The second is to check constantly for understanding from your audience.

Sensory acuity is acquired by watching your audience closely just as you would in one-to-one communication. It is relatively easy to detect straying concentration in a single person or a small group of people but it is more difficult with a large audience. With individuals, straying concentration often takes the form of a stifled yawn, their attention being focused away from you, perhaps even outside the room, a glazed expression on their face or a fixed focus of their eyes. Fidgeting can also be a sign of boredom on the part of your listener and is well worth watching for.

With larger audiences there are many techniques that can be used but perhaps the best involves your moving about. This can be achieved in many ways. If you are talking on a stage or in a large room you are likely to be standing up to do a presentation and moving is easy, provided you are not tied to a static microphone. In smaller meetings, where you are more likely to be sitting down, do make use of aids such as white boards or flip charts to create movement. But perhaps the best technique of all is frequently to ask questions of your audience. This keeps most people on their mental toes and stops their concentration from drifting off elsewhere.

My intention in introducing this subject is to make you aware of the importance of the need to check constantly to ensure that you still have the attention of your audience. I cannot do anything other than scratch the surface of this important subject in a single chapter. For further information I recommend you read *Effective Presentation Skills* (1994) by Robert Dilts.

The Meta-model – The first NLP Tool

I have found this tool to be the most valuable of all the techniques that I have borrowed from NLP. This is because it is the tool I have used most frequently in a business setting and which has had the most consistent and often amazing results. However, when I first began using it I found that it required sensitive adaptation to every new environment if it was to be effective. So perhaps a word or two of caution would not go amiss if you wish to avoid some of the pitfalls that I encountered:

1. Do not attempt to apply the techniques involved until you know them thoroughly. Learn a few simple ones well to start with and add to them as your confidence increases.

2. Do practise the techniques involved on a benign audience before you use them in a "real" setting.

3. Remember that to be really effective with these techniques the person with whom you are using them should not be aware that you are doing anything out of the ordinary.

Before I outline the model itself and the techniques for its successful application, it is worth knowing how it was developed and also a little bit about the psychology behind it.

Bandler and Grinder's original research was fuelled by the desire to develop an understanding of how three notable psychotherapists, Fritz Perls, Virginia Satir and Milton H Erickson MD, achieved seemingly *magical* results with their clients. Early in their study it became apparent that much of the magic seemed to be contained in the way that the therapists or "wizards", as Bandler and Grinder referred to them, used language to obtain a highly insightful understanding of the client's problem. So effective were these techniques that the wizards often appeared to fix their clients' problems by just asking a number of questions. Thus the illusion came about that something *magical* was going on, and thus the logic behind the choice of title of Bandler and Grinder's books on the subject, *The Structure of Magic Vol. I* and *The Structure of Magic Vol. II*.

What was really happening was that the questions being asked were constructed in such a specific way as to reveal the true or underlying nature of the client's problem, and then acceptable alternative options for change could be offered. The two authors wrote:

> *The therapeutic "wizards" we described earlier come from various approaches to psychotherapy and use techniques that appear to be dramatically different. They describe the wonders they perform with terminologies so distinctive that their perceptions of what they do seem to have nothing in common. Many times we have watched these people working with someone and heard comments from onlookers which implied that these wizards of therapy make fantastic intuitive leaps which make their work incomprehensible. Yet, while the techniques of these wizards are different, they share one thing: they introduce changes in their clients' models which allow their clients more options in their behavior. What we see is that each of these wizards has a map or model for changing their clients' models of the world; i.e., a Meta-model which allows them to effectively expand and enrich their clients'*

> models in some way that makes the clients' lives richer
> and more worth living.
>
> *Bandler and Grinder (1975)*

This was a radically different approach from the techniques then in use by the conventional medical fraternity and by psychologists in general. They preferred to largely ignore what their clients told them about their illness or problem, believing that they were better equipped to understand the client's needs than the client was.

The techniques used by Bandler and Grinder to unravel how the wizards were achieving their results were mainly drawn from the fields of General Semantics, Transformational Grammar and Cognitive Behavioural Science. It is in General Semantics that the key can be found as to what the Meta-model is all about. The phrase frequently quoted by the NLP community, "The map is not the territory", originated in a seminal work on General Semantics by Alfred Korzybski entitled *Science and Sanity* (1943). The concept behind the metaphor states that there is no one, true objective reality. Instead each individual constructs his/her own reality and there are therefore multiple possible constructions of reality. Individuals' concepts of reality are like maps. Maps are representations of reality but no map reproduces reality. Furthermore, different maps of the same territory can be drawn, each equally accurate and useful in its own way. For example, a map of the geology of a particular area is not likely to have many of the same characteristics on it as a road map of the same area.

This does not mean that any construction of reality has to be equally acceptable. While we may not be able to say that any one map or view is any better than any other, we can say that some constructions work better than others. Watzlawick (1984) gives the example of the captain of a boat navigating a narrow channel at night. There may be multiple "correct" routes that will get him through the channel safely. However, there are also clearly wrong routes that will certainly lead to shipwreck and disaster.

Watzlawick goes on to say that people are very adept at attempting to match reality to the wrong or out-of-date maps stored in their mind. Often psychological problems occur when people attempt to solve new life problems with a solution (map) that has worked well in the past for old problems but that does not work now. Frequently, when the old solution does not work, they compound the problem by "raising the dosage". Finally, when they are completely confused they "break down". Such a situation is often paralleled in the world of business, and the Meta-model can be a great asset in unscrambling the resulting mess.

Language is of course the main medium which we use to communicate our views of reality to others. Therefore, it is but a small step to realising that the way we use language can provide much more information than just the content of the words themselves. In fact, knowledge about the underlying maps often can tell us far more than the person communicating with us would wish us to know. Clearly our maps also work in the other direction when we are receiving information. Our maps act as a filter for incoming information. Thus, if the information we are receiving does not match our maps, we have three choices: reject the information, modify the information to suit our maps, or update our maps.

All this was known long before Bandler and Grinder started their journey of discovery. Their contribution came when first they realised that the magic of the three wizards had structure and was governed by relatively easy-to-understand rules. Using the map/territory distinction from Korzybski (1943) that we do not operate upon the world directly, but indirectly through our maps of the world, Bandler and Grinder had discovered the magic formula: change the map and you change your perception of the world. Once this had become clear it was a relatively easy step to realising that the wizards did not attempt to change the client's world, only their model of the world.

The next stage of the study was to understand precisely the key aspects of the strategies made by the wizards. These fall into two groups:

1. Non-verbal actions, such as building a high level of rapport with the client and active listening techniques. These have been mentioned previously, and trying to work without applying them will limit your effectiveness with the rest of the model.

2. A set of verbal or linguistic tools which are the very core of the Meta-model. These are designed to increase understanding of the clients' maps or models of reality, expand their model or the boundaries of the model, and create possibilities and opportunities for enrichment of the model, or the creation of a new and more appropriate model.

Clearly the Meta-model was developed with the intention of enabling other therapists to perform the same apparent magic as that of the wizards. Much of the early writing and teaching of the model had a heavy bias towards its therapeutic application. However, by the late 1980s the teaching of the model was becoming more generalised and many individuals began to experiment with its applications to fields other than therapy.

The version of the Meta-model presented in this book reflects its application primarily in the business field and as such is a sub-set of the therapeutic model. However, this does not mean that you have to restrict its use just to the business world. It is worth exploring its use in other areas of life as well.

When I first started to teach these techniques to my team, I told them that the techniques had been derived from the world of therapy. That immediately appeared to be a mistake, because those members who had hard scientific backgrounds instantly became resistant to what they thought of as "touchy-feely ideas" which, for them, had no place in the hard, logic-orientated world of business. However, when they saw how successful their colleagues became in using these techniques, they changed their minds and rapidly started learning to apply the model for themselves. Funny, really, as that is precisely what this technique is all about – changing or opening up people's minds to new ideas, and, after all, consultants are in the main employed as "change agents".

In the model presented here some of the elements of the original 1975 model have been developed further, others have been modified to suit the specific needs of the business environment, and a few have been discarded. For those who wish to gain a deeper understanding of the model I recommend *The Secrets of Magic* (Hall, 1998). This book provides a complete explanation of the original model and adds many more recent extensions.

The content and structure of Dr Michael Hall's revised and updated model is contained in Appendix One of this book.

The Meta-model as presented here is a set of eight linguistic distinctions which have direct application in the business world. These are grouped into three categories and are:

1. *Gathering Information.* The process of uncovering and exploring more deeply specific elements of the spoken words or phrases used by the person we are communicating with. We are seeking specific information concerning deletions, generalisations and distortions which distort the individual's maps of reality. These are known as Meta-model violations as they violate or corrupt in some way the intended message of the communicator. Our task in this phase is to clean up the communicator's language, removing any ambiguities and in so doing obtaining a better understanding of the real meaning intended by the client.

2. *Expanding Limits and Constraints.* This provides us with tools to assist the person we are communicating with by defining and then expanding the boundaries or limitations of his/her maps or models of the world. The intention behind this is to assist in helping the person to gain more choices in his/her behaviour and perception.

3. *Changing Meanings.* This builds upon the process of expansion which was started above and encourages the speaker to explore his/her relationship with other people with whom he/she interacts. It also encourages exploration of the world in general.

These three categories form a series of steps or processes through which we proceed in order to achieve our objective of obtaining high-quality information from our source subject. However, we may loop around each category a number of times before we move on to the next one. Similarly, we may loop through all the categories a number of times during the course of a relatively short conversation in order to extract all the information that we need. All this will become much more apparent as we proceed through some examples which will demonstrate the components of each category.

Gathering Information

Within this category there are three elements: deletions, generalisations and distortions. For ease of understanding, each element is dealt with separately.

1a. Deletions. These are neither good nor bad things. We delete a certain amount of information in nearly all our conversations and for a variety of different reasons. Sometimes these are entirely valid as they would add information that would largely be redundant. So by deleting we are being economical with our communication and saving it from being over-cluttered with surplus words. However, all too often when we delete important information we are tacitly assuming that the person we are communicating with possesses the identical maps of reality to those of ourselves. Take the following example, "They don't listen to me". There is nothing wrong with this sentence if you, as the listener, are certain who "they" are. However, in a business setting it makes sense, even when you think you know who "they" are, to check your understanding. So you would ask the following question, "Who specifically doesn't listen to you?" The reply you receive is likely to enable you to expand your maps quickly and accurately. In some instances it will stop you from jumping to the wrong conclusion about the identity of "they" and save you both time and aggravation.

The form of deletion above involves an unspecified pronoun, but the missing element can also be a verb, as in the following sentence, "I *feel* really manipulated." These are known in linguistics by the term "Unspecified Referential Indices". The correct challenge in this instance would be, "By whom are you being manipulated?"

The above example, used to extract the true identity of "they", utilises a phrase *"who specifically"*, which is intended to force a precise reply from the speaker. There are many other linguistic "challenges" contained within the Metamodel which we can use to obtain better quality information. These include *what, where, when, how*. Questions that utilise these words usually elicit more detailed information and enlarge the maps of the person who is communicating with us. However, it is advisable to avoid using the word *why* in any Meta-model challenge as you are likely to receive a poor-quality reply which will not provide you with the information you are seeking.

Close to the situation above is another group of statements which are evaluative in nature and which either delete the identity of the speaker or do not specify who the speaker is. These are known as "Lost Performatives" and often refer to judgments, beliefs or standards expressed by the speaker in such a way that the person making the judgment or setting the standard is not identified by the speaker.

These can be really dangerous in a business setting as they can often be extremely misleading and can imply an absolute truth which stands for all time, places and people, etc. Consider the following statement, "It's bad to be indecisive". Probably most of us would agree with a statement of this kind. That is until you begin to evaluate it thoroughly. Then you may discover the underlying map as offering something else. So let us do a couple of tests by asking the following questions, *"Who* makes the decision that it is bad?" or, alternatively, "According to *what* standard is it bad?" or, *"How* do you decide bad is a good label for indecisiveness?" It is highly likely you will have enriched your model of what your informant is telling you when you have obtained answers to these questions.

There is another more subtle form of deletion which comes in the form of the word *but.* The purpose of this word in any sentence is to delete or devalue anything that precedes it in the sentence. This may sound a hard interpretation until you think about it for a moment. If you still doubt it, think about this sentence for a moment, "You are the most wonderful and adorable person I have met in my entire life but you smell". The only message that carries real power in this sentence is *"you smell".* So be on your guard for these "get-out clauses" prefaced by the word *but.* So how would you reply to the following sentence? "I like everything you have told me and I would love to buy it from you *but* I don't have the budget." Perhaps you could say, *"What* would happen if you did?" Alternatively, *"How* can you obtain more budget?" or, *"When* will you have more budget?" These challenges do not necessarily get you the instant sale you may be keen to obtain. However, they take you in that direction and open up a range of possibilities for your client.

When we first started looking at the effect of deletions on our understanding of what was being communicated to us, we considered unspecified nouns and verbs. There are two other classes of deletion which are closely coupled, and these are known as "Unspecified Processes". These are either adverbs modifying verbs or adjectives modifying nouns. The following is an example of a sentence containing an adverb which modifies the verb: *"Surprisingly,* I enjoyed learning something new." An appropriate challenge here would be, "What made you feel surprised about that?" The intent here is to uncover more about the person's feelings about learning. An example of an adjective modifying a noun could be, "I don't like *unclear* people". The challenge in this instance could be, "Unclear about what and in what way?" This is intended to recover from the speaker his/her sense of feeling "unclear".

1b. *Generalisations.* The structure of the English language encourages us to use generalisations and this is apparent in many popular idioms such as, "Women are bad drivers," and "Men are aggressive". In these two examples "women" and "men" are the generalised terms. Generalisations take the form of either a noun or pronoun which refers to a nonspecific group or category. Occasionally, the generalisation is further compounded, modified or reinforced by the addition of adjectives such as *all* and *every*, etc. The Meta-model challenge to generalisations such as the examples above is simply, "What, *all* women/men?" The reply you receive is likely to be more specific than the generalisation first offered. If the answer is not specific enough for your requirements then follow it up with further questions until you are satisfied.

Generalisations go so deep into our language that it is easy to miss some of the more complex and subtle uses of them during a conversation. It is worth considering the following examples, "There are *those* who would not agree with you", or "*One* who objected to your proposals could be seen as being disloyal", or "*Employees* who do these things should not be rewarded". In these three examples we are being offered a "cop-out" instead of identifying the person or persons involved. So, armed with *who, what, where, when, how,* we can gain more precise information about the identity of the people involved. However, be careful in your approach as these types of comment can sometimes be used by informants to provide a cover-up for their own involvement.

Another subtle way of forming a generalisation is to pluralise nouns so removing specificity. An example of this could be, "Computers are anti-social". A suitable response could be, "You mean every computer is anti-social?" A response like this inevitably forces specificity and gets you the answer that you need.

In my personal experience, breaking down generalisations has been my most frequently used tool from the Metamodel. Time and again I have been able to look back on an interview and realise that my understanding of a particular problem increased by several magnitudes just by breaking down a few generalisations. But perhaps even greater endorsement has come from many hundreds of clients who, at the end of an interview, would compliment me on my insightfulness. In fact, all that I had done was to reduce their vague generalisations to a more specific understanding of the problems in hand.

Be aware that generalisations can become part of the descriptive mythology surrounding a business and that these can become highly restrictive in respect of the opportunities of the organisation to make changes. One notable instance that stands out in my experience concerned an evaluation I carried out of a large public company's five-year corporate strategy. When I am given the supporting information for review, the part that I nearly always read first is the pages with the numbers on them. In this instance I was surprised to find that they were showing growth rates barely above forecast inflation rates and way below what was considered average for this business sector. This made no sense to me whatsoever, so I turned my attention to the accompanying script. There I was confronted by a series of statements of apparent great importance, but on closer analysis nearly every sentence contained a generalisation, with many being quoted as fact. Worse still it actually contained generalisations supporting other generalisations. In an age of accelerating change it is certainly difficult to forecast very far ahead with great precision. However, this was a case where the strategic planners had nearly generalised themselves out of existence. By turning generalisations into specific, non-generalised statements the company was forced to contemplate several important issues, many of a painful nature. Some involved divestment and downsizing, others involved acquisition, but many were simple issues that were getting in the way of progress and holding back growth. It is quite amazing what you cannot achieve if you choose to generalise everything in life!

1c. *Distortions.* These have several different forms and are natural parts of our communications patterns, just like the previous two groups. Many distortions stem from a linguistic term known as "Nominalisation" which is attributed to our use of abstract nouns. These are words like strategy, productivity, tension, decision and frustration. The business world loves to use them and has in fact invented many of its own. These words can be particularly dangerous in the business field as they tend to freeze ongoing situations into static events, just as in a photograph. Doing this creates a model of the world which is fixed, static, inflexible, unmoving, permanent, and finished. This in turn creates a situation where the possibility of change becomes excluded – not a healthy situation in which any self-respecting consultant would wish to find him/herself.

So are nominalisations "bad" words? Clearly the answer is no, as they form a large part of the vernacular and help us to understand complex and abstract concepts. They become "bad" only when they delete the action and process of the territory and create a distorted map of reality. The word "strategy" is a good example. Often we spend many thousands of management man hours constructing a plan for moving from one business position to another. Once we have completed the task of mapping the steps involved in the process, assessed the risks and opportunities and done a million-and-one other things, we commence implementation. It is at this point that we often start to refer to our plan as our strategy, as if to reinforce its fixed status. However, if we had used the term "strategic direction" instead of the word strategy, we would have retained the essence of resilience and flexibility.

From a linguistic point of view, perhaps a better way of understanding nominalisation involves the process of changing a verb which is active in time into a noun which is passive, static or unchanging in time. Since a verb is a process word, it implies activity by one or more elements. On the other hand a noun is static and unchanging.

To test for nominalisation, check to see whether a noun will fit into the following phrase, "an ongoing ..." True nouns indicating a person, place or thing will not. However, pseudo-nouns signifying a process will fit. For example the term "an ongoing door (house, car, office, etc.)" just does not sound good English, whereas "an ongoing decision (failure, motivation, merger)" makes much more sense. If you are not sure from applying this test there is a second one, which is known as the wheelbarrow test, and involves asking a simple question. Can you put the referent of the word in a wheelbarrow? Ignore for a moment how stupid such an act might be or how large your wheelbarrow would have to be! If it is possible, then it is a proper noun and is okay. If it is not, then it is a nominalisation and is likely to need your attention.

In order to de-nominalise we can again turn to the Meta-model challenges, *who, what, where, when, how,* for assistance. The following examples show how to deal with a nominalisation contained within an apparent statement of hard fact: "I regret my *decision*". This can be challenged with, "*What* stops you from changing your decision?" or "*Who* would object if you changed your decision?" or "*How* would changing your decision affect you now?"

Here are some more examples with the relevant response:

"Frustration" ....Who or what frustrates whom?
"Productivity"...................Who produces what?
"Relationship"..................Who relates to whom,
                                               and how and when, and under
                                               what conditions?
"Skill level".......................Who demonstrates skills,
                                               towards what subject?

It is true to say that the more abstract nominalisations are, the more difficult they can be to detect. However, fortunately, taming them remains relatively easy and is achieved by use of the same techniques. Here are a few by way of demonstration:

"Self-Esteem" ....In what way do you value yourself?
                                               According to what standard?
"Mind" ....What is "mind" or how do you
                                               entertain thought?
"Wind" ....How does the air move?

We have now completed our look at the process of gathering high quality information and the tools that are available to assist us in achieving our goal. Clearly, during the course of any conversation we are likely to be presented with a mixture of statements by our clients which will contain a number of Meta-model violations. How we handle these will depend upon our relationship with our client and the information that we are seeking. In nearly every conversation there is a large amount of information which need not concern us. Making a challenge of, "How specifically?" when your client welcomes you with, "It's a lovely day today" is not likely to start your conversation off on the right footing. Similarly, over-use of the challenges can make you seem overbearing, and, used to the extreme, something akin to a Gestapo interrogator. So a degree of diplomacy is recommended in the application of these tools!

Expanding Limits and Constraints

As the title of this category suggests, its purpose is to enrich the client's maps of the world. The category has two elements, known as "Modal Operators" and "Universal Quantifiers".

> *2a. Modal Operators.* This is a linguistic term meaning "mode of operation". We may characterise these modes of operation in terms of necessity, desire, possibility and impossibility. These define the boundary of the person's model of the world. The speaker would believe that to extend beyond these boundaries would be to invite a problem or even a disaster over which they would have no control. Bringing this expectation into the conscious awareness of the speaker enables him/her to test and evaluate it more accurately. If the limit is found to be unreasonable, the speaker can be invited to expand or remove the boundaries altogether, thus increasing choice and opportunity.
>
> Modal operators appear in two different forms. The first is exemplified by the word *should* and is known as a "Modal Operator of Necessity". The presence of the word *should* within a sentence implies that a hidden rule exists which in some way governs or restricts the maps of the speaker. Take the following example: "I really *should* be more flexible at times like this." To this the appropriate Meta-model response is, "What do you think would happen if you weren't more flexible?" This causes the rule or rules to be challenged and is likely to bring out the underlying catastrophic expectation that caused the original response, such as "I'll be fired (demoted, admonished, etc.)". Now you know what the underlying fear is, you can challenge the associated assumptions (rules) and establish what or where the speaker's boundaries are in this instance. At this point you will discover whether or not the boundaries are appropriate and functional (to the speaker, not yourself). If they are, honour your speaker's view, and move to the next point on which you need clarification. If not, new options or choices can be explored, and the boundaries either expanded or discarded accordingly.

There are other words besides *should* that are classified as Modal Operators of Necessity, all of which indicate a lack of choice or a lack of awareness of other possibilities on the part of the speaker. These include *must, ought, have to* and their opposites *must not, ought not,* etc.

The other form of Modal Operator is that of Possibility and the most common form is wrapped up in the word *can't.* When someone uses this word in a phrase or sentence they are saying that whatever is required is outside their ability or sphere of influence to provide or do. However, this is frequently not the case. It is simply the person's perception of what is possible for them which is limited. Often they have the ability or the resources needed, but either they do not realise it, or some belief based on past experience is restricting them from seeing what is possible. Being presented with a *can't/not possible/may not* is an opportunity for you to explore with the speaker to find the limitation or boundary in the speaker's model of the world. Being presented with these words in a sentence the two most powerful questions you can ask are, "What stops you?" or, "What would happen if you did?" By using these challenges you invite your speaker to examine the validity of the limit and how functional or dysfunctional this is for them.

Being able to deal effectively with Modal Operators is a very powerful technique to have available in any scenario and particularly so with those involving change. Many people, including senior managers, are reluctant to change, and often this is seen as stubbornness. However, the reluctance to change often stems from insecurity created by their own self-imposed boundaries, more often imagined than real. Being able to move or remove the boundaries is a highly empowering process, and sometimes in the business world this can seem to work almost like magic.

2b. **Universal Quantifiers.** These are words that describe things in extremes of *all* or *nothing, black or white* or absolutes. Other examples include *always, never, absolutely, totally, everyone,* etc. They often indicate that a generalisation has been made from a specific experience in the speaker's life. Often these words find their way into phrases that become built into the culture of organisations. These are then repeated and reinforced by members of that organisation as though they have been handed down in tablets of stone. Eventually, if not challenged, they can become part of the core beliefs of the company as a whole. Having beliefs built around universal quantifiers is a very dangerous strategy to pursue, as they create restrictions which can have a profound effect upon a company's ability to grow and to effectively manage change.

I remember an occasion when I was visiting a company for the first time and was waiting to meet a senior director. I had arrived on time, but the director's meeting was over-running. After waiting twenty minutes or so and having read the *Financial Times* and looked at the various advertising brochures on the coffee table in front of me, my eyes were drawn to something in an elaborate frame on the opposite wall. Closer examination revealed that it contained a list of eight "Guiding Principles" upon which the company claimed to pin its faith and future direction. Only two did not contain at least one Universal Quantifier. With a slight stretch of the imagination another two could be seen as valid but the remaining four certainly would not withstand our test for linguistic accuracy. Eventually when I was admitted to the great man's office, I did not receive an apology for the delay but instead he told me that he would have to keep our meeting short as he had an important lunch appointment to keep. It was at this moment that I remembered that part of one of their guiding principles had something to say about "being on time every time". I decided that, whilst I loved a challenge, managing change in that environment would be like entering a long dark tunnel with no light at the other end. I was glad that my meeting was destined to be a short one. Within two years of this meeting the company had been acquired by a foreign competitor and the old management team was swept away, along with their "Guiding Principles".

The most effective way of testing specific Universal Quantifiers is to invite clarification by repeating them back to the speaker in the form of a question. The speaker says, "I *always* get the rotten jobs to do." The challenge is, "What, *always*? Are there not occasions when others are given rotten jobs?"

Be aware that many statements are also made that only imply universalisation and do not actually contain a Universal Quantifier. Statements such as, "You just can't believe people" can be challenged with, "Nobody? You just can't believe any other person?" or, "Have you ever believed anyone in the past?" Or perhaps more directly, "Does that mean that you do not believe me right now?" Questions like these invite your speaker to re-examine their map and encourage them to re-map their experience more appropriately.

Changing Meanings

This is the final section of the Meta-model which is concerned with a number of violations all of which have the common characteristics of either incompleteness or logical impossibility. The words and phrases in this category provide many opportunities for enriching your clients' maps of reality and thereby improving your understanding of them.

3a. *Mind Reading.* This occurs when we make a statement that claims, or assumes, that we know what other people are feeling or thinking without verifying our claims with them. This can be applied to thoughts, emotions, values, beliefs, intentions, etc. For example, take the statement, "Everybody in the team thinks I'm arrogant". Here the speaker presupposes that he/she can directly read the minds of all the members of the team or is entitled to jump to such a conclusion. The Meta-model challenge to such statements is simply, *"How do you know?"* Often this simple question will provide you with a surprising amount of information about how the person perceives the world about them.

Sometimes it is also possible to gain an indication of the personal rules which the speaker uses in building and maintaining their model of reality. Take the following example: "The boss doesn't really respect my views". Following your challenge of, *"How do you know that?"* you may obtain an answer such as, "Well, he doesn't seem to look me in the eye when we are discussing my proposals. And he doesn't seem to notice all the extra work I put in to get them right". With this information we know that the speaker values being looked in the eye and being appreciated for extra effort. So armed with this information we make sure we are looking them in the eye and are coaching them with statements such as, "That really helps my understanding", or "I know you are busy but I really value your input".

There is another version of mind reading which works in the opposite direction and tends to come out as, "She knows what I'm thinking." or, "He should know better". Examples like this are dealt with using the same form of challenge as the previous examples but in a slightly modified form by asking, "How does she know what you are thinking?" or, "How should he know not to do that?"

3b. *Cause and Effect*. These statements assert that one thing causes another thing to occur. They appear in many different forms from very simple phrasing such as "If x then y", to far more complex covert statements that add up to the same implied meaning. Commonly cause-and-effect statements indicate the speaker's beliefs and presuppositions about causation. Normally the cause is attributed to an outside source when in fact the cause is within. Frequently the words involved in such cases appear with unspecified causal verbs, such as *make, cause, force*, etc., or almost any active verb. For instance, there is a lot of material missing from the complete map when someone says, "She forces me to make mistakes". To challenge this statement we could say, "What specifically does she do that causes you to make mistakes?" This would clarify the action(s) that the speaker attributes to causing the problem.

More frequently we are likely to come across this type of Meta-model violation when it involves internal states or emotions. "Their behaviour makes me furious" implies that others have control over the emotions of the speaker. This can be challenged with, "How does their behaviour cause you to be furious?" Often a simple challenge like this can have a profound effect upon the speaker by forcing them to consider exactly what precisely it is that causes them to be "furious".

Another form of cause and effect occurs when the cause is not stated but simply implied. This is often associated with the use of words such as *since, that, because,* etc. If these words are substituted for other more specific words, we can get at the true meaning intended by the speaker. This can also show up in conjunction with the word *but* which we came across earlier. However, in this instance *but* forms the bridge between the cause and the effect as in the following example, "I don't enjoy being uptight, *but* my job demands it". In response to these cause-and-effect statements, we can enrich the person's model and his or her sense of choice by questioning the statement as follows, "How specifically does your job demand that you feel uptight?" There are, of course, many more questions you could ask about the cause and the effect in this type of situation.

This brings us to the end of the explanation of the methods defined by the Meta-model for obtaining higher quality information from our speaker. It is worth remembering that nearly all the *challenges* contained within the model are composed of questions using the words *what, when, which, who* and *how.* Using these questions enables us to maintain a state of sensory awareness whilst gathering information. It assists us in avoiding the common pitfall of using our own model of the world to fill in the missing pieces presented by our speaker. In the place where we might have previously made reference to our own experience (e.g. "I know what you mean. Back in 1992 I had a similar experience..."), we can now use the Meta-model challenges. When we do this, we meet the other person *at their own model of the world* rather than attempting to invoke or impose our own model.

Questions prefixed with a *why* are not used as they tend to evoke *because* type answers followed by explanations, reasons, history, rationalisations, excuses, defences, etc. However, the very reasons we don't use *why* questions as challenges whilst obtaining "clean" information can have beneficial uses at other times. These situations will be explored later when we look at the "Well-formed Problem".

Chapter Four

Bringing It All Together

Whilst we have largely been looking at the use of the Meta-model in communication through the medium of conversation, the model clearly presents major opportunities for its application when reviewing written material and in particular reports produced by others. I have found it to be of great value when reading the Chairman's Report which normally forms part of a company's annual report to shareholders. Reports of this nature are rarely produced by the chairman alone. Usually other directors and senior staff have contributed to it, with the corporate "spin doctors" also having their say. Occasionally, with a little careful Meta-model analysis, one can come to realise that the "Chairman's map" is almost certainly a very highly embellished version of the real territory.

I recommend that anyone who wishes to learn and apply the Meta-model should read through the whole process at least twice to obtain a general feel for what it is all about. Once this has been completed, return to the beginning and start with the first of the eight distinctions which is about *deletions*. Review what deletions are, how they cloud the real territory and the associated Meta-model challenges that can be used to obtain higher quality information. Then attune to other people's language and learn to listen for the deletions which will no doubt occur.

A method that I found useful in learning these techniques was to listen to talk shows on the television. Better still, record them and then go over them several times. I can guarantee that doing this will improve understanding of the language patterns used each time the video is viewed. When this is mastered, listen for a particular deletion whilst in a conversation and start to use the appropriate challenge. Once success is obtained, repeat the process with the next element of the model, which is *generalisation*, and so on until all elements have been covered. Once this point is reached most people rapidly incorporate the challenge techniques into their everyday language and start to discover things about friends, colleagues and co-workers that they never knew before. At this stage you are ready, if you have not already started, to use it in active consultancy work.

If any scepticism remains about the efficacy of these techniques and why they are necessary in Change Management consultancy work, take a short time-out from reading the book and carry out the following simple test. It works best with a group of three or more individuals and can be carried out with friends or work colleagues.

Fuzzy Meanings Test

Provide each person with the following list of words.

a. Often   b. Always   c. Sometimes

d. Never   e. Usually   f. Most of the time

g. Occasionally   h. Seldom   i. A lot

j. Almost always   k. Rarely   l. Frequently

m. Quite often

Task: Rank the above list of words in order of the amount of time that each word or phrase represents and award a percentage score for each one. For example if you believe that item e. means about half the time then award it 50% and so on.

When all the words have been given a percentage, rank them in order from 100% to 0%.

Allow from five to ten minutes to complete the task and then compare results from each person or group of people and note the differences.

I have conducted this test many times with a variety of different groups ranging in number from three to over a hundred and I have never seen all groups or individuals produce the same answer. Indeed it has been rare to see anything even approaching a close similarity in all the resulting answers. The implications of such diversity of meaning when extrapolated to real-life situations can be enormous, particularly for anyone involved in attempting to understand another person's viewpoint. How, for instance, do you rank the words *occasionally*, *rarely* or *sometimes*? Do they all mean the same thing or do they have different meanings for you? If so, how far apart should they be ranked?

In an exercise of this nature the meanings are of academic interest only. However, if applied to information needed for designing an aircraft, a bridge or a simple computer system, they could be of very profound significance indeed. Many man-made disasters have their root in the failure to correctly understand the words of others. The London Stock Exchange System mentioned earlier, the crash of the space shuttle Challenger, and the nuclear accident at Chernobyl are all believed to have had their roots in misunderstandings of this nature. Therefore, applying our own meaning to other people's words is a potential recipe for disaster.

Finally, do not overdo it. Use the Meta-model and its associated challenges only when they are really needed to uncover lost information or clarify ambiguity. Success with these techniques is achieved when the person with whom you are in conversation is not aware of your methods. If these techniques are overused there is a real risk of isolation from colleagues, friends and family. If, on the other hand, they are used sparingly and wisely they will improve success rates with your clients by many magnitudes, and who knows where this may then lead?

Part Three

Developing Excellence In Change Management

Overview

Everything that has been learned in the previous chapters has provided a basis on which this part of the book is built. However, much of the work in this section is not based on what is often termed "conventional NLP". Instead this section is about taking existing techniques and ideas from several different disciplines, including NLP, and adapting and developing them to suit the requirements of Change Management.

Similarly, there are several well-established methodologies for the management of change in organisational settings. The underlying approach used in this section is largely built upon an amalgamation of two approaches: the Systems Engineering version which is often referred to as a "hard systems" approach, which, as the term implies, is largely derived from computing and engineering methods where the focus is on tangible things, and a "soft systems" approach where the focus is more on people, their activities and motivations. The basic Change Management techniques used in this book closely parallel Dr Bill Mayon-White's highly effective approach which can be found in his book *Systems Thinking For Managing Change*. Appendix Two provides an overview of Change Management Strategy (CMS) which forms the core of Dr Mayon-White's approach to this subject.

All the work in this section has been developed as a result of bringing about change in live situations, together with feedback from clients with whom my colleagues and I worked. Many of the techniques described started to be developed as a result of research carried out under the umbrella of the International Ecotechnology Research Centre (Ecotech), which forms part of Cranfield University in Bedfordshire.

Much of the early research focused upon Change Management projects that had failed or were failing. Later, successful projects were drawn into the study in order to provide a comparison. When the comparison was made, the real causes of failure started to become apparent. Only then were we able to identify the shortcomings and produce solutions to the problems that our clients had encountered.

This was only the starting point, as we were determined to develop a set of models and procedures which if implemented correctly would avoid any such failures occurring in the future. This section is about these models and procedures.

Chapter Five

Thinking And Understanding With Greater Precision

In the preceding chapters we have discovered that our internal maps of the world are at best poor representations of reality. Therefore there is no such thing as a perfect map of reality, and each individual's map is unique to that person. We have also discovered that the language we use represents our attempt to express our internal maps externally. Thus our language provides an indication of the boundaries or limitations placed on us by our maps. The Meta-model provides us with techniques that allow us to challenge other people's maps in order to gain a better understanding of their world. The model also provides us with techniques which enable us to enrich their maps of reality by the expansion of boundaries and removal of limitations. In this chapter we take our understanding of the structure of our internal maps a stage further and learn how they can be changed or, in NLP terms, re-programmed.

The process of creating and modifying our maps is known to start at a very early age. Many paediatricians believe that the process starts well before we are born. Clearly the early part of our lives is the time when we create most of our maps, the majority being established long before we reach the age of six. It is also known that our ability to create new maps or indeed to update our existing ones slowly decreases with age. It is likely therefore that the old saw, "You can't teach an old dog new tricks" has an element of truth about it. This, however, is of no practical concern to us as only a small minority of people are affected in this way before reaching their late sixties.

Anyone who is able to read the words on this page must be in possession of a map which facilitates the task of reading. It is certain that none of us possessed this skill at the time of our birth because then we did not have the many different maps necessary to enable us to make sense of language. Therefore we must have acquired this skill at a later stage in our lives, at a time when all the maps required to form an understanding of language had been established. If we can turn what we have read into some form of understanding as well, we must also possess other maps that enable us to reason, form judgments, and do whatever we find necessary to assimilate this information. While all this may sound a little convoluted, it demonstrates just how complex our mapping processes are.

Whilst reading this we are building a new map or modifying old maps as part of the process of learning something new or different. Such a process is normal and healthy as all our maps are based on, or modified by, events which have provided a learning experience for us at some time in the past. This does not necessarily mean that all the maps we possess actually serve us well. In the previous chapter we became aware that part of the normal human process is to delete, distort and generalise, and all our maps are to a greater or lesser extent affected by these self-imposed limitations. So some of our maps are empowering, some inhibiting, whilst the majority just serve us well.

Similarly, some of our maps are capable of being updated and some are not, those in the latter category being known as "frozen" or "locked". Those concerned with our personal survival are highest in the hierarchy of our frozen maps. In most instances these serve us well because they protect us and keep us alive. At a slightly lower hierarchical level we have many other maps associated with our moral code or those that have attached to them strongly held personal beliefs. These have slightly more flexibility. Fitting into this group would be our beliefs about such things as religion, murder, theft, infidelity, etc. However, lower in the order other maps of more general nature can also become frozen and reduce our opportunities for choice. The causes for this can usually be traced to a bad experience or a series of bad experiences which have imprinted on us in a powerful but limiting way. Such a situation is often referred to in psychological circles as a "stuck state" and lies at the root cause of many personal limitations and behavioural difficulties.

I have experienced hundreds of examples of stuck states in clients whilst using the Meta-model in business situations. In many of these cases I have used all the appropriate challenges, rephrased my questions, and have still failed to persuade my client to examine other possible views of reality. The key to change in these cases lies in being able to assist the client in modifying or changing the content and structure of their maps of reality. These changes are made in such a way as to make other options at least a possibility, thus breaking out of the restrictions imposed by the stuck state.

At this point it is worth considering how our maps operate on our lives and what they consist of. It is also worth remembering that the term "map" is just a useful metaphor which has been adopted to describe the highly complex process by which we store and retrieve information concerning the world about us. Thus the term we are using is in fact a gross generalisation. However, it is widely accepted by the scientific community that internal maps exist and each has associated with it a number of discrete behaviours to suit most situations that we are likely to meet in life.

These maps and their associated behaviours seem to operate in a manner somewhat analogous to a suite of computer programs where each program has a designated task to fulfil. However, each separate behaviour or program can be selected and then called into action only by some specific stimulus which closely matches an internal map. It is worth recognising that many of these programs operate outside our conscious control or general awareness. In other words, they are run by our own internal autopilot which we usually refer to as our subconscious or unconscious mind.

The steps in this model are: receive stimulus; search for appropriate maps; compare the maps with the external environment; select the map that best fits the situation; and "do" the behaviour associated with the map.

Here is a simple example which demonstrates the concept.

Scenario: A person is out walking in the country on a bright summer day and enjoying the experience.

Stimulus: Suddenly a large bear jumps out from behind a tree.

Select appropriate internal map:
1. Five years old, watching a cartoon of Yogi Bear on the television.
2. Ten years old, having fun visiting a zoo and watching bears playing.
3. Adult, watching a film in which a bear attacks a man but he succeeds in fighting it off with a stick.
4. Reading about how dangerous the bears can be in Yellowstone Park and what to do if you come face to face with one.
5. Being chased by a wild and dangerous bull only to find out afterwards it was just a friendly cow.
6. A close friend fooling about dressed up as a bear at a party.

Compare maps with environment:
Discount maps 1, 2 and 6. Consider maps 3, 4 and 5 as possible best fit.

Consider behaviours of maps 3,4 and 5:
Discount map 5 as the person felt such a fool after the event.
Discount map 3 as it was just a film and not a real experience.

Do behaviour associated with 4:
Run.

This example is obviously a highly simplified version of what would happen in real life. Events of this nature involve us making many hundreds of comparisons between our internal maps and the reality on the outside in the space of only a few seconds. Here we have seen that there were six maps available to choose from. The choice is made only when all possible options have been considered. A person in a stuck state does not do this. Instead, while they may possess all the maps, all but one are excluded from consideration. Thus their choice is really no choice and may be totally inappropriate for the given situation.

So if we are presented with a situation where we are forced to work with just a single map, how do we set about changing it? The first step is to understand the composition of the map. Our maps are made up almost exclusively of pictures, sounds, physical feelings and emotions, and in NLP terminology they are referred to as the visual, auditory and kinaesthetic modalities. The reason we store information in this way is that our maps relate directly to our primary senses – seeing, hearing, touching, smelling and tasting. If we were to be deprived of these, we would have very little means of making sense of the world which exists outside our bodies.

As with most things in life we all have preferences, and this applies to which modalities we use to construct our maps. Some of us use predominantly one modality more than the other two and we often vary the mix dependent upon circumstances. The NLP community claims that most of us have a preference for using the visual modality, with auditory being the next choice and kinaesthetic last. However, normal people make use of all the modalities some of the time.

Each modality also has associated with it a number of component parts which provide us with the detailed content of our maps. These individual elements are known as sub-modalities. The following shortened list provides some examples of sub-modalities from each modality.

VISUAL
Colour, or black and white
Location, left, right, up or down
Size, large or small
Movement, still or moving picture
Brightness
Contrast
Clarity, crystal clear or blurred
Framed or without distinct edges
Two- or three-dimensional
Associated (as seen through our own eyes as though we are part of the picture)
Dissociated (just as though we are watching a film of ourselves)
Speed, faster or slower than normal

AUDITORY
Volume, loud or soft
Content, words or sounds or a mixture
Tone, harsh or soft
Stereo or mono
Clarity, clear or muffled
Location of sound
Distance from the sound source
Speed faster or slower than normal

KINAESTHETIC
Intensity
Location, inside or on the surface
Duration
Temperature
Feeling or emotion
Texture, rough or smooth

At this point it is worthwhile spending a moment or two familiarising yourself with the list of sub-modalities above. There are many more besides, and it is useful to think about these as well. You may have some personal preferences of your own which are not on the list.

The secret to opening up new possibilities is a simple one, and involves changing some of the sub-modalities within a particular map. To understand how to do this, it is worth first carrying out some experiments. The following steps provide a framework for further exploration:

1. Find a place where you can be alone and will not be disturbed for a minimum of ten minutes. Make yourself comfortable in a chair and allow yourself to relax for a moment or two. You may find it helpful to close your eyes.

2. Cast your mind back to some occasion in the past when you were feeling really good, perhaps at a party when you were a child, a happy family event, when you were on holiday or any other occasion when you were feeling really good.

3. With your chosen event clearly in you mind, start to take notice of the sights, sounds and feelings that are associated with your memories of that event. Perhaps you have a picture of that occasion or maybe you can hear music playing or the sound of a voice or voices. Notice how you feel. Remember the list above and pick two or three of the sub-modalities that seem important to you about your memory from the past.

4. Take one of the sub-modalities that you have chosen and increase its intensity. If it is a still picture, you could make it into a movie, or if it is in colour you could turn up the intensity of the colours or speed up or slow down the picture. If it is a sound, what happens if you increase or decrease the volume or perhaps change the tone? If it is a feeling, what happens if you intensify this or change it in some way that increases your pleasure?

Once you have experimented with changing a number of the components of your past pleasant experience in a positive or enhancing way, leave this experience and continue to allow yourself to relax.

Now allow your mind to remember one of your favourite songs or a piece of music from the past which seems to have special meaning for you. Note the memories which are associated with the sound of the music, or perhaps the lyrics contain special meaning for you. You will almost certainly find that the music has some emotional attachment. Perhaps it makes you feel happy, sad or reminds you of some person or event which has a special meaning for you in the past. Maybe you are reminded of a particular event and can see this as a picture in your mind's eye. Possibly you do not have a picture, but other sounds such as voices may form part of your memory. Explore some of the sub-modalities associated with this experience for a moment or two. You could start by turning up the sound of the music, or play it more slowly, or change it in some other way. If there is a picture or an emotion associated with the music or lyrics you could experiment by changing some of the sub-modalities associated with these. Notice how changing sounds or pictures can affect your feelings or emotions.

When you have explored this to your own satisfaction you can leave this example and move on to experiment with other powerful experiences which form part of your past. In my own experience some smells have powerful memories attached to them. The wafted aroma of either of the perfumes Chanel No 5 or Rive Gauche can send my mind instantly regressing way back into the past to some very enjoyable but private memories. The smells associated with certain foods cooking are known to have a similar effect upon a good friend of mine. Photograph albums can be a mine of memories for those who believe they have problems with visualising past memories.

If you happen to be one of a small minority of people who find some initial difficulty in visualising or in accessing the component parts of your internal maps, do not be concerned, as it is a process that is easy to learn.

First imagine a picture of some ordinary thing such as the front door of your home. Without going and looking at it, describe to yourself the colour of the door and anything else attached to the door. Perhaps it has a letter box, a door knocker, or glass set in it. When you have a clear picture of this, imagine what you have on your feet right now, again without looking first. Now perhaps imagine what you ate for your last meal and where you were at that time. When you have a good picture of this in your mind, think about what the meal smelt like and what sounds were occurring at that time. Practise eliciting this type of information from your memory until you have mastered this simple process with everyday things. You will then find your ability grows rapidly until you can just "go inside" and extract the information you need without having to think about it.

On very rare occasions I have come across people who tell me that they cannot visualise at all. They usually tell me they have tried many times to do so but have failed completely. I usually ask them a number of polite questions about their experiences and then I ask them if they use a car for going back and forth to work. I then ask them how it is that they do not get lost each day, if they cannot visualise? How do they know when they are on the route? Do they ever park their car in large car parks and if so how do they find it again? By smell?

This line of approach usually works and it really is a matter of the person simply having a different understanding of the verb to visualise. So we are back to the Meta-model questions in order to find a point at which we both can meet with a common understanding. I must admit that I have come across a couple of people who adamantly refuse to accept that they can and do visualise. Both of these individuals had other problems with relating to people and the world about them.

Perhaps you are thinking, "Why am I spending time learning how to change my own maps when all I really want is to learn how to change or affect my client's maps?" The answer is a simple one. In order for you to produce the magical change in your client that you desire, you first need to have attained a thorough understanding of sub-modalities and how they operate.

Many of the techniques that form the bulk of this book utilise your ability to gently persuade your client to access their internal maps without the need to first teach them what you have just been learning. However, when it comes to changing other people's maps, the first thing we must do is to honour their existing ones.

The reason for this is simple. All behaviour has a positive intent which forms the driving force behind it. Thus, to your client, the behaviour you are seeking to change has value of some sort. It has probably served them well in other circumstances in the past and could be an appropriate behaviour in other circumstances in the future. In most instances people do not set out to be awkward, difficult or obstructive. They are simply applying a wrong behaviour to a particular situation. Our task is to un-freeze their internal programmes so that they can have more choice in what they do.

In the first few paragraphs of this chapter I mentioned working with many hundreds of business people who were resistant to change and whom I described as being in a "stuck state". One particular client stands out as an extremely difficult character to work with, and he will serve to demonstrate the next method for changing maps using a technique associated with sub-modalities. The client was the managing director of a medium-sized family business with a turnover in excess of £100m. The company had been very successful in the past but now was beginning to show signs of needing a complete overhaul if it was to stay competitive in the future.

My client's father had formed the company in the mid 1920s and had built the business up from scratch. Apparently his father had been a very proud character with strong, autocratic tendencies and a person who did not like his ideas or decisions questioned in any way. At the age of 75 he formally retired and officially handed over the reins to his elder son, the brother of my client. However, the founder still came into the office twice a week until shortly before he died aged 84. During this nine-year period it was apparent to everyone in the business that all the major decisions were still being made by the founder and not the elder son. The business was still organised and managed very much as it had been since the mid 1960s.

Two years after the founder died the elder son retired on his 60th birthday and handed over control to his younger brother. I was called in by the new CEO about six months later. He had some ideas about changes he wished to make and sought my advice on others that had been suggested by his co-directors. He gave me a completely free rein to look at all aspects of the business, to speak to anyone I chose and to come up with any new ideas that I might have. After a short period of investigation I reported back my preliminary findings and made a number of recommendations. These were readily accepted with what appeared to be a great deal of enthusiasm. My client stated that he wished to have more time to fully digest my report and we agreed to meet a week later to discuss the matter further. It was also agreed that we would put together a draft strategy for implementing the changes which would be circulated to all the Board-level directors.

The following week we met as arranged in the company's boardroom at 9.00a.m. for what I had understood was to be at maximum a three-hour discussion. My client went over all the salient points of my report in great depth and asked a multitude of questions about my more radical suggestions. We continued to talk over lunch and into the afternoon although the meeting should have ended by midday. Eventually I began to realise that whilst my client recognised the need to make the changes that had been recommended there was something holding him back from committing to their implementation. I covered all the possible reasons that I could think of for his reluctance to make a commitment and came to the conclusion that it was none of the reasons I had ever previously encountered.

Finally, I focused on what I assessed to be the most obvious but easy-to-implement change with clearly defined, tangible financial benefits. If put into effect, my client had already agreed, it would save the company a minimum of £25m over the next five years, with a one-off cost of something in the region of £7m. I asked my client to visualise the current situation and the situation that would exist after the change had been implemented. I then asked him about the components of his two pictures and drew up a list of the sub-modalities he associated with the current and future situations.

I was not surprised to find that there were vast differences between the two lists. The current state had a dull picture running in slow motion with a slow waltz playing in the background. It felt comfortable and familiar. The future picture was bright, full of life and colour with modern upbeat music playing. There was a feeling of excitement about it. However, the most significant feature of the picture of the future was a loud, strident voice emanating from behind my client's back, saying things such as, "Who gave you the right to make changes like this?" and, "How can you possibly know it will work?"

After a little further coaching on my part, my client told me that he had identified the voice as that of his father. He was quite clearly shocked by this realisation and I had to spend some time reassuring him that we all have voices of this nature within us and that they form an integral part of our identity.

There were a number of strategies that I could have adopted to move things on but I chose to stay with my client's pictures. First I suggested reducing the volume of the voice but after a few moments the volume returned to its previous level. Then I attempted to move the source of the voice to various other positions, in front, overhead, at one side, etc. This did not work either as after a few moments it reverted to coming from behind his back. After many other suggestions which had little effect, I asked my client to change the sound of the voice from that of his father to that of a cartoon character. Within a few moments my client started to nod his head slowly. Then a knowing sort of a smile spread across his face and, without opening his eyes he said, "Got you, you old tyrant".

When I was sure that my client was now feeling comfortable with the cartoon voice, I asked him if there was anything else which would give him even greater control. He said he thought that if he had the voice coming from somewhere in front of him it would feel even better. Ultimately after a certain amount of further experimentation we had the source fixed in one spot and with the voice emanating from his right big toe.

I stayed with my client for a little while longer to ensure that he was feeling all right and then agreed that he would phone me the next day and let me know how he felt. The following morning he called me to say he had probably never felt better and the cartoon voice was still coming from his big toe. He then asked me to prepare a presentation to the company's Board outlining our joint strategy for implementing change.

Five years later I was invited to my client's retirement ceremony during which he said some kind things about me and afterwards we drank a private toast to "Bugs Bunny who lives in my big toe". His wife who was with us at the time thought that he had drunk too much and it was only after a great deal of reassurance that she accepted that it was a private joke between the two of us!

In the intervening years since my first involvement with the company it has changed in many different ways, sometimes with my assistance and sometimes with the help of others. It has grown by a factor of two, which is way above the sector's performance, and its profit margin has increased by a factor of five. In the same period I have billed the company for a very significant seven-figure sum. My client believes he had spent his company's money wisely and he has proved to be an excellent reference for my services, as well as becoming a trusted friend.

The above story may sound a little far-fetched but I can assure you it is true. Often in situations where it becomes almost impossible to obtain a decision from a client, it is all too easy to just give up. If, however, you have learned to get under your client's skin in the gentlest sort of way, anything can become possible. Do remember that to disclose specific personal details of the above nature to any other person is a gross breach of personal privilege.

The learning experience from the above I am sure is obvious. You can move the contents of people's maps around until you have in effect modified an existing programme, or you can assist in the process of creating a new programme. However, not every change of this type will work perfectly, first time, and you sometimes have to offer a number of options before you obtain the best results. In the case above I offered many options, but only when the tone and type of voice were changed was the location of the voice successfully moved to a place that the client was happy with.

The positioning and repositioning of our maps can also have a major effect upon our internal programmes and consequently upon our behaviours. There are many different ways this can be achieved, and in later chapters we will discover how we can harness this to provide other beneficial vehicles for change.

For now, though, it is worth again exploring one of the maps you have previously accessed and noting its spatial position in your mind's eye. Maybe it is immediately in front of you or maybe it is off to the side. Perhaps it is close up and panoramic, so that you can almost step into it, or maybe it is some distance away and just the size of a postage stamp. Wherever it is, note its position and then reposition it spatially in your mind. So, for example, if it is off to the left, move it to the right and note any changes in the way you feel or anything else that is significant. You may find some of the sub-modalities change, becoming more or less intense, something for instance that was blurred becoming clear or a sound that was loud becoming soft, or maybe you become aware of a feeling that you had not noticed before.

Practise this type of exercise until you have a good understanding about what works for you. Remember that we are all unique in the way that we store information about the world about us, and do not attempt to make changes in others that work for you. Always allow the person you are working with to make their own choices about changing elements of their sub-modalities.

Association and Dissociation

The last element of sub-modalities which can have a major effect in the change process involves whether or not we associate or dissociate with our map or maps. This simply means that, when we are associated with a map, it is as though we are directly involved in the story and are viewing events as through we were there. When we are dissociated, we are seeing the map as though it were a film or a video recording of us.

In the associated form, we are directly involved with the map even though it may represent events way back in the past. This is often the case when remembering instances which have left a marked imprint on our lives and on our resulting behaviour. Almost inevitably, association involves our emotions, and often we find that maps that are associated contain large elements which are directly connected to our emotional states. Emotions often form extremely powerful anchors for our maps which consequently make attempts at changing the maps in a business setting very difficult. However, if a client is encouraged to move from an associated perspective to a dissociated perspective, change becomes easier and, in the main, the involvement of the emotions is removed.

A simple device for achieving a shift from associated to dissociated is to say to your client, "How would it be if you were to view these events in the past as though you were sitting in a cinema watching a film?" If this still does not work, then move one stage further back and say to your client, "Now I want you to see yourself sitting in the auditorium watching a film of yourself on the screen but remember you are in the projection box." This technique is known as double dissociation.

Occasionally one is forced to work with the associated maps of a client. In these situations it is worth bearing in mind that the outcome is likely to be in the form of subjective observations from the client. Note these and then apply Meta-model challenges at a later stage to obtain a more objective view-point.

Dissociated maps are generally easier to work with within a business setting because of their lack of emotional association. Thus, observation of dissociated maps normally takes place in a detached, analytical and objective manner. However, be aware that emotion has a role to play in the business world. We cannot get "excited" about some new development without accessing our emotions, and much of our motivation stems from accessing internal emotional states.

There are many other elements to maps and sub-modalities from the field of NLP which we could explore further but, whilst useful to know, these would not have a direct application in the business world. I recommend reading *Persuasion Engineering* (1996) by John LaValle and Richard Bandler.

Corporate Maps

Just as we as individuals have maps, organisations also have maps. These maps are shared by the members of the organisation and form part of what is often referred to as the corporate culture. All organisations have them, and as a general rule the older the organisation the more maps it will have and the more difficult it will be to change.

The most common and also the most obvious maps are those that control or influence the modus operandi of an organisation. I have long since lost count of the number of times that I have been confronted with the expression, "It's not the way things are done around here". This phrase is a clear indication that something that I have suggested conflicts with an established map of the way things are done in that organisation. My standard Meta-model challenge in these situations is, "Yes, but what would happen if it were?", referring to what I had previously suggested. Sometimes such a challenge instantly breaks down the barriers to new thinking, but more often it produces a reply which leads to more Meta-model challenges until eventually I can begin to gain acceptance for my ideas. Sometimes the answer I obtain makes me reconsider my ideas!

In the main, corporate or shared maps that have to do with procedure or how things are done within an organisation can be successfully challenged using the Meta-model alone. However, occasionally you will come across maps that remain resistant to change. Before attempting to resort to other means to force change, check to make sure that what you are proposing is appropriate and will serve your client well.

On two occasions I have encountered what I considered to be unreasonable resistance to fairly simple changes. In both cases, had I gone ahead with my proposals in their original form, they would not have produced the results that I had predicted for my client. Instead, they could have caused chaos. Fortunately I took the resistance to be an indication that I was not in possession of all the facts surrounding these cases. So I set out to review the details of the projects concerned. In both instances, after a little searching, I discovered that some vital information was missing and that it had been withheld by my client's staff.

Once I was in possession of all the facts, I was able to modify my original proposals, and both projects were completed producing the results that we had originally predicted. Both of these events served as a useful reminder to me that the consultant is not always right and is most certainly never infallible.

Be extremely cautious about attempting to change maps that involve deeply-held beliefs about the organisation, or anything which is likely to cause the identity of the organisation or a person or group within it to be challenged. Such ventures can be akin to entering an uncharted minefield blindfolded. If it is part of your remit to make such changes, always ensure that before carrying them out you have your client's full authority and backing to do so. Make sure that your client is in full possession of all the facts, and underscore the implications of carrying out such a change.

If it is not part of your remit, and you believe that such a change is necessary for your project to succeed, inform your client of the facts, offer advice and counsel where necessary, but allow your client to decide on the appropriate line of action that needs to be taken. Your client is far more likely to respect you for this rather than if you take matters into your own hands without prior approval.

Often corporate maps have metaphors associated with, and supporting, them. Indeed, often the most obvious evidence of the existence of a corporate map is its associated metaphor. Just as with any other statement, metaphors can and should be challenged using the Meta-model. However, corporate metaphors tend to be treated, and often defended, within organisations a little like sacred cows. So watch out for some really wild responses to Meta-model challenges to things held to be sacred.

Verbal Predicates

In the past the NLP community has placed considerable relevance on the use by individuals of particular verbal predicates. I touched briefly on these in Chapter One whilst discussing rapport skills.

In the main, verbal predicates are words or phrases that are directly associated to the modalities and sub-modalities which go to make up our maps. So the use of the word *see* in the sentence, "I *see* what you mean," may in some way indicate a connection to the visual modality. Our language is littered with such words. In the visual modality we have: *look, clear, hazy, view, perspective, focus,* etc. Auditory examples include: *hear, loud, clear, sound, ring, resonate.* Some kinaesthetic examples include: *feel, grip, handle, warm, cold, touch.* The choice of verbal predicates that we use can possibly provide an indication of our preference for a particular modality in a given circumstance. However, I am far from convinced that it has much direct value in the business world. I would therefore advise you not to spend too much of your time trying to read very much into the use of predicates beyond providing a general indication of modality preferences.

Often organisations develop a mode of language which is particular to them. I know of an instance where a new executive arrived in an organisation who had a penchant for using phrases which included the word *focus*. In the space of only a couple of weeks of his arrival all his team members, numbering over a hundred, were using the word extensively and sometimes in the strangest ways. Clearly an outsider who believed that there was a connection between verbal predicates and modality preferences and who came into contact with these people could rapidly come to the conclusion that they were all visually orientated. In fact they were a very mixed bunch just like the rest of us. However, just like the rest of us, nobody wanted to be the odd one out so they adopted the new boss's language style.

Such examples are legion. However, there is a positive learning experience which can be drawn from it. Any consultant entering that environment would be well advised to adopt the use of the word *focus* where appropriate but refrain from its overuse.

Chapter Six

Understanding The Causes Of Failure

Cause and Effect

Earlier I mentioned that during the last decade many Change Management projects failed to produce the results intended and a significant proportion resulted in total failure. Many of these situations could have been avoided if a proper understanding of the client's needs had been obtained at the earliest possible stage of the project. The Meta-model provides tools for obtaining precise information from the client about their needs, and, had this tool been used properly, many a failure would have been avoided. However, while poor communication stands out as a common cause of project failure, many other causes also exist.

This was constantly reinforced during my time working on the short-course programme at Ecotech at Cranfield University in the late 1980s and the early 1990s. One of our most popular programmes was for senior executives and was concerned with new approaches to the management of change. Very frequently during the course participants would mention Change Management or IT projects within their own organisations that had failed. We received so many of these examples that after a while we started to collate and categorise them, surprised at how many there were. Initially the team felt that the problem lay primarily with poor project management, but after a while we became uncertain whether this really was the primary cause. Later, using the empirical evidence provided by our course participants we began to analyse the information further in the hope that we could find common patterns that would lead us to discovering what these causes were.

The following is the unranked list that, while not exhaustive, contains the most common problems encountered:

1. Top management being persuaded by external agencies that change is necessary but failing to ensure that the case for change is a genuine one and fully proven.

   In other words, top management falling victim to what is commonly called the "Emperor's New Clothes Syndrome" (ENCS).

2. Failure to keep the objectives of the project flexible.

   Put another way, the programme is frozen at far too early a stage in its development. This is a common problem with large and expensive projects simply because management and/or accountants demand that a cap be placed on potential project expenditure. The key failure here is not to recognise and take into account that we live in a changing world. It is a heck of a job to plan or budget for this. Similarly, those involved with projects have a tendency to fix their concentration on their change programme and fail to notice that the rest of the world is changing around them. This is rarely a cause of failure in projects of short-term duration but is a common cause of failure with projects that extend over a period of several years and involve complex technology.

3. Subcontracting the change programme to outside "experts".

   Often this occurs where a level of expertise has been sought outside the company, but the experts are not experts in that particular line of business. This is a danger with employing consultants of all types, shapes and sizes. Total Quality Management and Business Process Re-engineering consultants seem to stand out for particular criticism in this respect.

4. Encountering major resistance not previously predicted.

   A characteristic that stands out in this situation is carrying out most or all of the planning of a project in total isolation from those who will be affected by the change.

5. Implementation taking longer then planned.

"So what's new?" is the most common response that I have received when presenting this information in a seminar. Nevertheless, this bucks the question. Does it always have to be like that? Clearly the answer is no, as some projects do complete on time and a few actually succeed in completing early.

6. Senior management becoming distracted.

This is a tough nut to crack and can really only be addressed very early on in the planning stage of a project. Clearly if management's attention does become diverted, it is because they believe that other things have a greater priority.

7. Major problems surfacing during the implementation phase not identified during the planning phase.

Again a cause of failure that is nearly always avoidable. Obviously lack of research is a major contributor and many reasons exist for this. These range from ignoring major issues during the planning phase and hoping that they will go away, to simply a poor understanding of the problems involved in the project. However, often items 1 and 4 above can make significant contributions to this problem.

8. Key development/implementation tasks and activities not defined in sufficient detail.

This has been separated from 7 above because they are two different problems. In this category the problem is more often concerned with taking things for granted. This leads to assumptions being made that later prove to be incorrect. The emphasis here is very much on detailed understanding of problems.

9. "A bridge too far."

This is often associated with the introduction of new technology and its failure to live up to its expectations. However, it can also be associated with attempting radical change in an environment that is not mature enough to accept it. Frequently this is seen in projects that have attempted to achieve "competitive advantage" but failed.

We published this list in 1991 with a supporting commentary but avoided attempting to rank it as we felt we did not have sufficient detail available to support such a ranking. In any case such a ranking would have been difficult to achieve as many failed projects contained more than one attributable cause.

Within weeks of publication we were contacted by other people both in Europe and in the USA who had also come up with very similar lists. From our standpoint we found this very encouraging as now we knew that we were faced with a far more common situation than we had previously assumed.

For us in the Ecotech group, having a list of known causes of failure backed up by large amounts of supporting data was the only stimulus required to trigger us into yet further research. The objective of this, of course, was to find or invent solutions to these problems that could be implemented successfully in the field.

It is perhaps pertinent at this point to state that our group was composed of six individuals, all of whom originally had quite diverse business, management and academic backgrounds, and all earning their living from consultancy. In our team we had two engineers, a psychologist, a social scientist, a chemist and an economist. We had been drawn together through our active involvement in the IT industry, shared interests in systems theory and Change Management techniques. It was perhaps our different backgrounds and our tolerance for each others' often "off the wall ideas" that produced a synergy of thought that allowed us to view the problems from a new perspective.

This did not mean that we suddenly came across a solution to all the problems upon which we shouted, "Eureka!" in unison. Indeed, our early research threw up so many seemingly insoluble problems that we often despaired of finding answers to many of them. Sometimes our research even left us feeling more confused than when we had first started. Fortunately we did not allow ourselves to become demoralised or give up our search for solutions. Instead we battled on in the belief that there had to be answers to our questions somewhere. Eventually, during one of our brainstorming sessions our thinking about the problems seemed to shift. Suddenly we realised that there must be problems lying behind the problems. In other words, what we were seeing and trying to solve were just the symptoms and not the causes.

At this point we also took a lead from Tom Peters and the theme of his book *In Search of Excellence* (1982). We stopped looking just at failed projects and started to look at successful ones as well. After a little further research we began to be reasonably certain that we could identify the differences that made the difference between the successful projects and the failed ones. Please note that we were looking at the *differences* and not what contributed to success or failure alone. All the members of the team have been asked many times why we did not just simply build our methodology around adopting best practice from the successful projects and ignore the failed ones. The answer is simple: this approach had not worked for others so why should it work for us? We also firmly believed that we could learn much from the failed projects, and so it proved.

All of us at this time were involved in real-life change programmes in a variety of companies. This provided us with the opportunity to carefully test some of our ideas. After about six months of trialing these with our clients we felt that we had a better understanding of how to solve the problems. So it was back to Cranfield to share with one another our individual thoughts and ideas. After many more brain-storming sessions, several false starts, lots of hard work and yet more research, we came up with a list of what we felt certain were the principal causes of failure in change projects. In this instance we ranked the causes in order of precedence in order to indicate which were the most frequent causes of failure in our research sample. However, as with the previous list, multiple causes can often be identified in failed projects, and identifying the prime cause becomes a highly subjective exercise. Thus in terms of frequency this list (Figure 1) should be treated with just a little caution.

Causes of UK Management Failures

1. Not conclusively identifying the problem to be solved.

2. The organisation adopting an inappropriate change mechanism.

3. The change agents not identifying and understanding the cultural implications of the change upon the subject of the change or those closely associated with it.

4. Underestimating the time and effort required successfully to change beliefs and values closely associated with the change process.

5. Not developing a **genuine** "shared vision" by all those involved in the change process.

6. Not establishing the Critical Success Factors associated with the overall goal of the change programme.

7. Not taking a holistic view of the organisation and attempting to implement change in isolation from other parts of the business.

8. Not identifying the "human factors" implicit in the process of bringing about change.

Figure 1

Armed with this information we now just needed supporting methodologies that would be easy to learn and use. This was when the really hard work began. Over the next year many techniques were borrowed from other sources. In some cases they were modified or adapted to suit our purposes. During this period some totally new techniques were also developed by members of the group. The process of trialing these methodologies and techniques in the real world continued. Similarly, no opportunity was lost in introducing these ideas to our short-course candidates.

The short-course programmes went from strength to strength as senior executives were attracted towards what was seen as revolutionary thinking on the subject of change. Most of the major consultancy firms also sent candidates on the courses, and it was not long before our ideas and concepts were being disseminated through them to a wider audience.

The sad death of both Dr Roger Crane and Jim Stuart in 1993 effectively marked the end of this highly innovative and collaborative project. A little while later, Dr Bill Mayon-White left Cranfield to take up a senior appointment at another university. The remaining team members then went their separate ways.

The techniques that now follow form part of the legacy of that highly inventive group of individuals who had been drawn together under the umbrella of the Ecotech Centre. In the five years that have passed since then I have continued to adapt and develop many of these techniques in the light of the experiences gained in the real world. Where I have been able positively to identify the original sources of material I have done so. Otherwise, assuming that it originated through a joint effort of the members of the group is a safe course.

Precise Problem Definition

Definition of the problem is probably the most difficult phase of any investigation to get absolutely right. Most people involved in a project (be they client or consultant) do not take adequate time to ensure that they conclusively know the nature of the problem and how it has been caused, and, because so little time and effort are invested in this stage of a project, failures are high. Not surprisingly, therefore, this was seen as a major cause or contributor to many failures in our survey. Conversely, it was not seen as causing a difficulty in most of the successful projects that we studied. Comparison between the two groups failed to produce any clear indications of the differences between them regarding problem definition, although statistically the failures group had less of what we had categorised as the "easy-to-solve" or "clear-cut" problems within its population. If it had been otherwise, I think we would have been extremely surprised.

Eventually we came to realise that our thinking was being swayed by the complexity of the solution to the problem rather than the complexity of the problem itself. Perhaps the biggest break-through occurred when we recognised that complex solutions were not always associated with complex problems, and vice versa. Once we were detached completely from contemplation of the solutions, we could achieve a better understanding of the underlying causes of the problems themselves. Soon the answers we were seeking started to became apparent, or clues to the existence of other, or underlying, causes surfaced. It was then only a short while before we could categorise the causes of many failures attributed to problem definition. We named these "badly-formed problems" and those associated with successful projects we called "well-formed problems". Each of these groups had their own set of characteristics associated with them, and many (as often happens in these situations) were the inverse of the others.

Features of Badly-formed Problems

1. Being poorly defined and often described in generalisations.

2. Having indistinct boundaries.

3. Often having a long history.

4. Frequently seen as having multiple causes.

5. Containing an unaddressed "political" dimension.

6. Having many symptoms but no/few identifiable causes.

7. Lacking ownership.

Figure 2

Badly-formed problems generally have one or more of the characteristics listed in Figure 2. However, being aware of them and avoiding repeating them in future projects are two different things. Obviously more attention to detail during the problem definition phase of a project would be a step in the right direction. However, for over half the failures in our survey this simply would not have been enough. Some causes, while quite easy to identify with twenty-twenty hindsight, would not have been anywhere nearly so obvious when carrying out the original research.

Of the seven items listed in Figure 2, only three are normally easy to identify and the remaining four are more complex.

1. Problems poorly defined and described in generalisations

More often than not this is caused by communications failure at one level or another, although poor definition can be caused for many other reasons. These range from attempting to cover up for the person responsible for the problem, to sheer laziness on the part of the person carrying out the investigation. A word of caution here would not go amiss regarding my use of the word "poorly". I could have used other words instead of "poorly", but these would have added specificity which is not appropriate here.

"Poorly" is a generalisation and is intended as such in order to cover many different problems. However, the essence is that from the material supplied it is not easy to find out what the problem is. I have come across projects that contained inadequate detail, and others where there was so much that it was difficult to understand what the problem was. Often problem definitions focus on the symptoms and not the causes. Occasionally definitions are written with a heavy bias towards obtaining budget for the project rather than identifying the problem clearly. A few are constructed with the intention of introducing something new and almost ignore the original reason for so doing. Many contain ambiguities. The word "poorly" therefore covers a multitude of sins that I am aware of, and possibly many more that I do not know about. Put more simply, it implies "not fit for the purpose intended".

Generalisations often appear in problem definitions. Sometimes they are inserted deliberately and semi-covertly to broaden the scope of a project or to create ambiguity. Occasionally they slip in either through poor workmanship or by accident. The method for dealing with generalisations is covered in Chapter One, and the main method for breaking these down is to use questions such as,

"How specifically…?" Most of the project failures of this type in the Ecotech study were associated with a generalisation that had not been challenged until something went seriously wrong.

Case Study

A few years ago I was called in to a large international conglomerate to identify what had gone wrong in the development of a new integrated group accounting system. The group was composed of three main divisions and seventeen separate operating companies. Previously a small team of accountants based in the head office had manually extracted information from the accounts of the component parts of the group to produce a set of consolidated reports for the group as a whole. The company's auditors had stated that they did not think this was adequate and requested that a modern approach be sought.

An independent firm of consultants had then been engaged by the group Board to produce a Strategic Information Systems Study that was duly accepted. The plan had identified the need for an integrated accounting system covering the whole group, and the consultants were commissioned to produce a feasibility study with associated costings. This was also accepted by the Board, and the consultants then went on to design and build a group database.

Just over a year later I was called in to review the system when it was found that it was not producing the intended results. By this time the direct costs incurred by the company had amounted to over £3m. The indirect cost, largely associated with the staff of the conglomerate who were involved with the project, was assessed at around £2m. The overall costs when intangibles were added increased the total cost to a figure close to £6m.

A major cause of the problem was generalisation, a simple example of which involved the term "sales", a common generalisation used by every business. In this instance the word had many different uses, and its meaning was interpreted differently in the many different component parts of the business. This was further compounded by disparate interpretations of the word "order" being used by some units. Sometimes one part of the company called an order a sale. Some parts of the company had made a sale only when they had received payment for the goods. To others it was when they received an order from a customer. When my team had completed its investigation, we found twenty-nine different variations on this theme! However, only seventeen of these had been identified by the consultants designing the database.

My task was to prepare a report for my client identifying the problems and recommending solutions. My client's intention was to use the report to persuade the consultants to fix the problems at their own cost or, if they were not prepared to do this, ultimately to sue them. Fortunately a compromise was reached which was acceptable to both parties. However, it left the consultants with the task of carrying out a major reconstruction of the system at their own expense, which was not inconsiderable, and my client feeling badly bruised by the experience, all for the sake of not dealing properly with a few generalisations!

2. Problems with indistinct boundaries

This is a frequent problem in change programmes and seems to become more common as projects become larger and more complex. However, this does not mean that even a low-budget, single-department project cannot be affected by this type of difficulty.

When the Ecotech group first identified this as a cause of failure, we thought it was part of a larger problem closely associated with items 4 and 7 on the list – having multiple causes and ownership problems. Subsequently we realised that a significant number of projects had failed where the cause was directly attributable to boundary problems. Therefore, it warranted its own heading, and my own personal experiences since that time have reinforced this view.

The trouble usually starts because we all have the tendency to think that every problem has boundaries. This, though, is rarely the case. Many things have only the vaguest of boundaries, and some things that we assume have boundaries in reality have no boundaries at all. This is because our brain has developed in such a way that it is used to coping with imprecision. This is reflected in the way we describe the world around us. Examples are all around us. They are quite familiar to us and form part of our everyday life. Consider for a moment what divides day from night, tall from short, beautiful from ugly, true from false and perhaps another ten-thousand or more other dichotomies that are part of our everyday life. They don't give us too may problems because if they did we would not use them, would we?

Solving these types of problem will again take us back to the Meta-model in our search for specificity, and in fact this is a very good place to start. Many will yield to skilful questioning using the Meta-model challenges. Take for example *tall* and *short*. In this example questions such as, "How specifically different is tall from short?", followed by other challenges, may eventually yield an absolute answer, or one at least suitable for our needs, though a similar result is not likely to occur with *beautiful* and *ugly*.

The Meta-model will not clarify all the dichotomies or ambiguities that we encounter. Neither is it capable of solving a host of other problem words and descriptive expressions in common use which lack obvious specificity or boundaries. Take for example something like a heap of sand. If we take one grain of sand away from the heap, and then another, and another and so on, at what point will the heap cease being a heap? If a point is reached where it ceases to be a heap, what then does it become?

You may have a view as to when a heap ceases being a heap. However, if you asked several other people the same question, they would probably give you answers that were different from your own. So again we are back to the problem of ambiguity. The example of the heap of sand is far from unique. Many thousands of similar vague expressions exist and enrich our lives and give added meaning to the world around us. Our problem here is that they also exist in the world of business and commerce, where they can cause major problems.

Business operates on sets of precise rules, laws and governances, most of which obey the laws of logic and mathematics which were laid down by Aristotle 2300 years ago. Computers and their associated systems lie at the heart of nearly every business and they are constructed on the rules of Boolean Algebra where things are either true or false, with no possibility of a grey area in between. Consequently vagueness has no place in the systems currently used by business. However, in the next decade or so this may begin to change as a new domain known as "Fuzzy Logic" is further developed. Fuzzy Logic works in much the same way as our brains work and is happy coping with vagueness and imprecision.

The example of the heap of sand is, I understand, a favourite example used by Professor Lotfi Zedeh of the University of California at Berkeley when explaining the concepts behind Fuzzy Logic. It was he who, as early as 1965, published a paper on fuzzy set theory which gave rise to the name Fuzzy Logic. He is the same genius who, whilst working as an assistant professor in electrical engineering at Columbia University in 1954, is credited with coining the term "Systems Theory". Since the publication of Professor Zedeh's seminal work on Fuzzy Logic considerable progress has been made in researching and developing our understanding of this intriguing subject. The point has now been reached where so many inventions have been based upon the concepts that there are far too many to count. Most are not seen at a surface level but buried deep within some other technology. We could not have truly intelligent washing machines, microwaves, cameras, camcorders or even high levels of fuel efficiency in automobiles without Fuzzy Logic.

Fuzzy Logic is a charming name and also a wild misnomer. Fuzzy Logic is not logic that is fuzzy but logic that describes and tames fuzziness like the heap of sand that we considered. However, even that description is not complete, for most of the theory is not logic at all. It is a theory of fuzzy sets, sets that calibrate vagueness. Fuzzy Logic rests on the idea that all things admit of degrees. Temperature, distance, beauty, friendliness, colour, pleasure – all come on a sliding scale. The Swiss Alps are *very beautiful*. My next-door neighbour is *fairly lazy*. Heathrow Airport is *quite close* to London.

Whilst Fuzzy Logic is a very interesting subject to explore and of growing importance when dealing with some problems, it is largely a side issue as far as this book is concerned. Thus we are forced to deal with heaps of sand in other far more basic ways by using descriptions other than heap. A ton of sand or a cubic yard of sand or even 100,000,000 grains of sand is far more specific (though not perfect) than a heap or a pile or any other vague description. If you wish to know more about Fuzzy Logic then read the book of the same name by McNeill and Freiberger, published in 1993.

So not all boundary problems are directly associated with fuzzy thinking or fuzzy words. Within the statistics gathered by the Ecotech group there were a number of failures that could clearly be attributed to problems resulting from what we had first ascribed to "problem complexity". I believe it was Dr Mayon-White who first named these "messy problems", although for some strange reason the press at the time credited me with it. In fact, the originator of the term was Benoit Mandelbrot, Nobel Laureate and the father of another fascinating subject, fractals. However, having originally borrowed the name I remain at a loss to think of a better one to describe a whole population of problems that we find hard to define and almost impossible to describe. As another member of the team suggested, it is almost like trying to unravel a bowl of boiling spaghetti with no tools and without burning your fingers. So we could have been stuck with a term like "the boiling spaghetti conundrum" instead!

Our group was not the first to discover that problems of this nature existed. Many people had previously become aware of failures occurring in developing computer systems which had causes apparently similar to those of our own study subjects. However, our team was probably the first to discover that when you broke "complex" projects down to their component parts it was more often than not boundary problems and not complexity that had caused failure. Often problems occur in clusters within organisations. Thus it is not unusual for one problem to overlap onto another. Sometimes one problem feeds another, forming a knock-on or chaining effect so, when you solve one problem, another one goes away. Of course the inverse of this is also true: you can solve one problem only to create another.

In all cases like these we have to focus our attention on the causes of the problems and then think through carefully the implications of the changes we make. Problems like these have much in common with playing a game of chess. Often it is not the next move you or your opponent makes that matters but one several moves later. Therefore it is vitally important to think through the consequences of any changes made in order to avoid problems later.

The single most frequent problem with boundaries beyond the relatively straightforward ambiguities discussed earlier involves what is known as "project creep". This most often happens when the project expands into areas where it was not originally intended to go. Often more work is done than was contracted or originally intended, and overruns on budget or time are other examples of creep. Most problems of this type can be attributed to bad project management, poorly managed changes to specification or simply to an inadequate project specification. Often the causes for these types of problem are placed at the door of the people actually engaged in developing the project. This is rarely the real cause and more often than not it is a case of placing the blame on the symptoms and not the cause.

Boundary problems can occur in many other areas as well, so many in fact, that probably a book could be written exclusively about them. Most boundary problems can be avoided by following a few simple rules. The extent of the project itself should have clear-cut boundaries agreed by all parties involved and which are not open to dispute. The boundaries here are those principally defined as measurements of time, resource, expense and the critical success factors (CSFs) of the project as a whole. CSFs are, as the term implies, the factors which must be achieved if the project is to be judged as successful. It is interesting to note that few of the failed projects that were examined by the Ecotech group had clearly defined CSFs but most of the successful ones did. We will look more closely at this later.

All these items should be contained within a document or set of documents detailing the specification with no ambiguities. Finally, when all elements of a project are agreed it should be supported by a relevant and enforceable contract between the parties involved. I have often been asked whether or not a contract is really necessary when the project is entirely an "in-house" one. Clearly the answer has to be that this depends on the size and the importance of the project, but, if there is any potential for boundary problems (and there nearly always is), then I believe it makes eminent sense to have a contract.

Finally, all those affected by the project should be made aware of the existence of the project specification and what implicitly is expected of them. There should also be a procedure for administering and controlling progress on the project as well as a procedure for managing any change to the specification or contract.

3. Problems with a long history

This may seem at first sight to be a slightly strange heading. It is used because when examining the original statistics at the Ecotech this was the only obvious characteristic that we could positively identify associated with one particular group of failures. Initially, we did not think too much about this and treated the long histories as purely a symptom and not a contributory cause of failure. Later, when we looked more closely at this group and sought more information about them, we discovered that a history of past failure(s) had a particularly powerful influence on projects.

As someone with a little knowledge of psychology I began to realise that what we were up against here was what is known as "the power of presupposition". Presupposition has a very powerful influence on our lives and works in the following way. If we commence a task with a particular mind-set or belief concerning success or failure, this will have a powerful influence on the outcome. This effect has been demonstrated many times in the past in a vast number of experiments. Put simply, if you start out by thinking you will not succeed (presupposition: we will fail) then the most likely outcome will be failure. Similarly the reverse is the case. When we presuppose success, success becomes the most likely outcome.

The problem here concerns past history which, as we know from discussing our internal maps, can have a very powerful effect on our behaviour. Problems and the associated projects intended to solve them are no different from individuals in this respect. Often a group of people working together will share similar maps with respect to the problem. This is particularly so where a problem has been around for a long time and has failed to be resolved. The presupposition of failure grows on an exponential scale with each failed attempt to fix the problem. This then fuels demotivation and other similar behavioural factors which will then, if left unchecked, bring the project down.

In those projects which were judged as successful but had long past histories of previous failure, considerable effort was put into understanding what caused the earlier failures. Effort was also directed towards making sure that the previous problems could not be replicated again. The first step on the path to resolving this type of problem was to give past failures full recognition for what they were: failures. The next was to make public what the causes of past failures had been and how they would now be addressed and avoided in future.

Finally, a programme was implemented to get everyone affected by the project committed to success. There are many ways of doing this, but using a team leader who has a reputation for leading successful projects is clearly not going to do any harm. Making information on the progress of the project public also helps to scotch the rumour-mongers who would perhaps wish to see the project fail. Keeping morale high during all stages of the project is also seen as a very important key to success in these cases.

4. Problems with multiple causes

This has a close association with "messy problems", mentioned earlier when looking at boundary problems. However, in this instance we are looking at the "boiling spaghetti" a little more closely and introducing a tool to assist in resolving the problem.

Many of the failures in our study demonstrated at least some difficulty with positive identification of the problem. Often this happened because the problem was perceived as having many different contributory causes, but the focus fell on just one of them. In several instances this gave rise to the wrong problem being identified. Consequently when the "cure" was applied the problem remained.

There are several ways of addressing issues like this but perhaps one of the easiest to understand and formulate is cluster analysis. In its simplest form, all that is required is to list all the symptoms and suspected causes and then to connect them by association. Clustering then usually occurs around a common cause or sometimes a symptom if the cause remains hidden.

Cluster analysis works well in most situations and can be considerably enhanced by the use of diagrams (see Figure 3). Drawings or diagrams often draw out information that cannot be obtained easily by any other method. A familiar metaphor suggests that "a picture is worth a thousand words". A good example of this could be taken from our metaphor of the "boiling spaghetti". It would obviously be much easier to identify and trace one complete strand of spaghetti from a picture than by just using words to describe it.

Multiple Cause Diagram for the XYZ Company

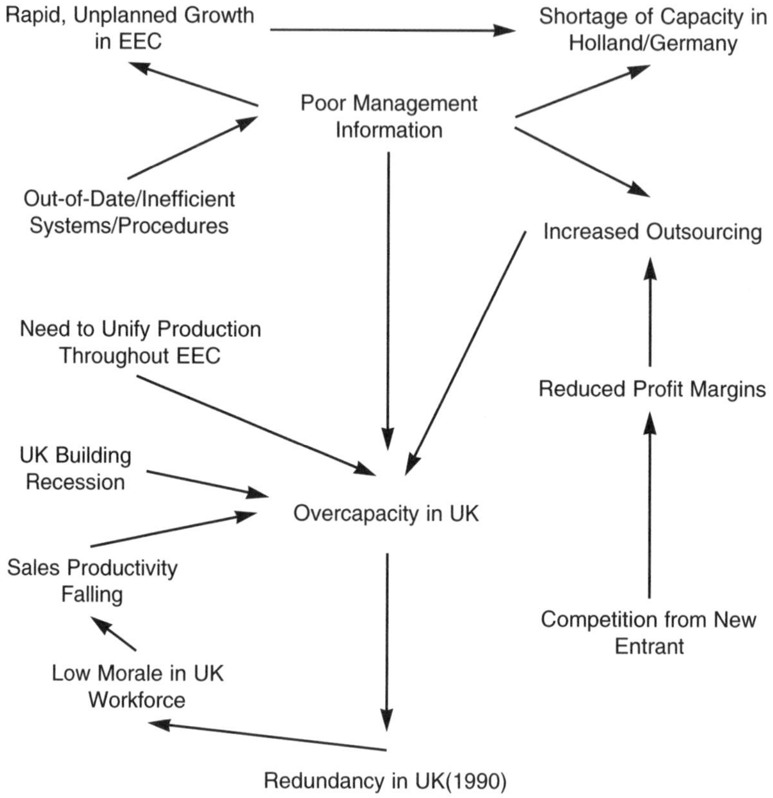

Figure 3

The example in Figure 3 is taken from a real-life situation, although the content has been slightly altered to maintain the anonymity of the business concerned. The theme of this example is used throughout the rest of the book to provide linkage and demonstrate the complete process. From the direction of the arrows and the clustering it is clear that there is a major problem with "Overcapacity in the UK" and "Poor Management Information". When I carried out initial interviews with the directors and senior managers, they all had different views as to what the problems were, how they had been caused and what should be done to cure them. However, when Figure 3 was presented at a meeting with all the interested parties present, after some heated discussion they unanimously agreed that the problems stemmed from overcapacity in the UK and poor management information.

This example could have ended in failure without the use of the diagram. At the point when I was first involved the consensus view within the company was that they should embark upon a Total Quality Management (TQM) programme in order to improve customer relations and thereby improve sales. Whilst this may have had some positive effect it would certainly not have solved the underlying problem of overcapacity in the UK or the lack of good quality management information.

Clearly in this study I had much more information available to me than is shown in the diagram. If I had recorded every cause and symptom that I had been told about I would have ended up with several charts, and all would have been very cluttered. I therefore had to reduce these to the key elements, and consequently some of the items actually represent many other items. However, the resulting diagram does contain all the major symptoms and causes. Having these present allowed a debate to occur concerning all contentious issues. Only when these were resolved could agreement be reached upon a strategy for solving the two key problems.

5. Problems with unaddressed "political" dimension

This was not one of the most frequent single causes of disaster in our study but was present as a contributory factor in many other cases of failure. Political manoeuvring in business is common, but in the UK the practice is mostly covert, so it is not the politics that causes the problem but the lack of its visibility.

There is no nice empirical way that you can deal with politics in a business, and consultants can easily end up as casualties if they try to solve political problems by themselves. Staying out of politics is the only safe course a consultant can follow. However, once it is identified as a potential cause of problems then the easiest way to get it resolved is to bring it out into the open. How this is achieved will depend on many factors and each instance will have to be dealt with as it arises.

6. Problems with many symptoms but few or no identifiable causes

This was a contributor to many failures but was the prime cause of around only ten per cent. The most common problem arose from symptoms identified as causes and treated as such. In other cases the correct cause was identified, but too much attention was paid to symptoms when attempting to resolve the problem. When this occurred, confusion developed as to which was the prime cause, and this diverted attention away from it.

In other instances a change programme was initiated because a number of symptoms had been identified, and it was believed that the solution lay in a particular proprietary solution. Very little attempt had been made to identify the precise cause(s) which gave rise to the symptoms. I was aware of several instances of this occurring with TQM projects and even more with IT projects.

The most troublesome group was one where, despite considerable effort on the part of those involved, a precise cause had not been identified, but lots of seemingly unrelated symptoms existed which needed resolution. Those of us at the Ecotech were puzzled by these. We used many techniques including approaches such as cluster analysis and multi-cause diagrams in attempting to identify the causes, but these did not yield the results we sought. However, someone (I believe it was Geoff Elliot) came across an idea known as drawing rich pictures. This involves getting several people to draw a cartoon-like picture of how they see the problem. A sample of such a drawing is to be found in Figure 4.

An Example of a Rich Picture in Schematic Form

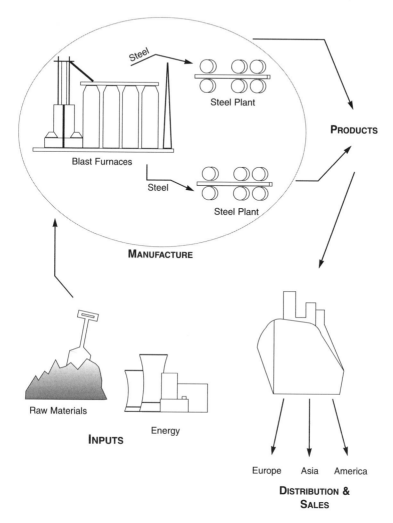

Figure 4

Here we can see an example of a rich picture intended to show the process of production from raw material input through to delivery of finished products, including the function of sales and distribution. There is nothing particularly exciting about this drawing except that it is a very simple explanation of what this steel company makes and how these processes link together. The attraction of pictures of this sort is their inherent simplicity. A good example from real life is the map of the London

Underground system. It bears virtually no resemblance to the actual position of the lines but it does provide an excellent means for people to navigate themselves around the system, which was the originator's intention.

However, when we use this technique in real-life situations we may be amazed by the results that can be achieved. Figure 5 is an example of where it had previously proved very difficult to get to the underlying causes of many problems.

An example of a Rich Picture from XYZ Company

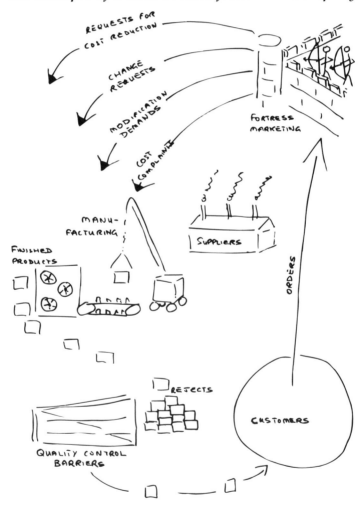

Figure 5

It is an excellent example of a rich picture. However, in this instance it is full of detail and in fact is far from simple, unlike the example in Figure 4. This picture enabled the originator, in association with two of the Ecotech team, to identify the real cause of many of the problems that had beset his department. It took the department manager about half an hour to draw it, and about an hour of further questioning for the problem to be fully identified.

7. Problems without ownership
All too often the cases we looked at had to some extent confused the issue of problem cause with that of problem solution. "Ownership" is an expression used to cover two separate but similar situations in this category and has nothing to do with ownership of the cause of the problem.

The first is relatively simple to understand and to solve. Ownership implies that the person who has ownership of a problem also has some responsibility for delivering the solution to the problem. Failure involves situations where there is no clear "owner" of the problem or where such a person has relatively little power in the organisation in general to effect change. It is worth noting that there was some evidence to suggest that this problem tends to afflict the modern "flatter" organisations more than the old steep pyramid structures that have many layers. This may be because many of the newer organisations are still learning about empowerment and other attributes of these more modern organisational methods. However, "ownership" remains an issue that has to be dealt with.

A sub-group of this type of problem could perhaps be better labelled "leave it up to the committee". Whilst committees form a useful purpose in the functioning of many projects, it is not wise to leave the overall management of projects to a committee. We are all no doubt aware of the joke about what happened when God delegated the task of designing a racehorse to a design committee and the result was a camel. However, this largely sums up the problems that some projects run into whilst attempting to define a problem area and to come up with a satisfactory solution. The consequence can often mean ending up with their very own camel!

In the course of our research we were aware of many successful projects where the main management task was left to a committee, but all of these reported to a powerful "champion" who was clearly recognised by all involved as the "owner" of the project.

The second aspect of ownership covers situations where a problem may map across and affect different constituent parts of a company. This can involve situations where the problem is seen as being owned by one part of the company but much of the change work that is necessary is being imposed on another. This type of problem has some attributes similar to the others in the "boundary problems" and "politics" groups. The problems that occur in these cases are often multi-faceted but always the problem comes back to ownership.

The simple rules for avoiding difficulties in these sorts of situations are to make certain that the successful resolution of a problem is seen as vital to the business overall. This should be ratified at a high enough level in the company to ensure that no individual is willing to get in the way of the project's success.

A Model for Defining the Well-formed Problem

Towards the end of my association with the Ecotech study I started to consider the possibility of producing a model or process that could assist in avoiding the pitfalls connected with badly-formed problems. From the information that had been distilled from failed projects and other later information that I had obtained from the USA, it seemed obvious to me that many of the elements of such a model, or at the very minimum the basis for the construction of a checklist, already existed. All that was really required was to pull together the existing elements in a manner that would be easy to understand and to identify any remaining gaps that needed to be filled. The outcome from this exercise was the model that we are now about to review.

Before I go on to describe the model I would like to regress slightly to the period when Bandler and Grinder were exploring the construction and content of the Meta-model as applied to therapy. A factor that is nowadays often overlooked concerns the Meta-model and the intent behind it. The original intention was not to design a tool to obtain the true meaning of the client's language and words but to provide a model that would positively identify a "Well-formed Outcome" for that person. It was in obtaining this that the real "therapeutic magic" occurred. Many clients were "fixed" just by use of the Meta-model alone simply because, perhaps after many previously failed attempts, they at last really understood what they wanted – a simple case of being able to identify a purpose in life or perhaps just making the trees stand out from the wood, or, in NLP terms, establishing a "Well-formed Outcome".

Perhaps because I was aware of Bandler and Grinder's approach to problem resolution in therapy, I too chose to look at the questions that needed to be asked in order to obtain excellent results with problem definition in business. Initially my list varied dependent upon the type of problems that I believed needed better definition. Thus if I was looking at an IT problem I had a slightly different list than if I was looking at an organisational problem. However, over time this list has now been refined to a list of eleven "universal" questions. Figure 6 provides this list.

The list is not exclusive, as these are not the only questions that can be asked. Often many supplementary questions are asked in order to further clarify the problem. However, they form the key questions that need to be answered satisfactorily in order to arrive at a Well-formed Problem. It is worth coupling these questions with Meta-model questions in order to obtain "clean language" and to remove any ambiguities. It is also perfectly all right to ask *why* questions in this scenario. Sometimes a *why* question will produce an indication of how a problem may be solved. Similarly, a question such as, "Why has this problem not been solved in the past?" may reveal a bear trap that you were not aware of.

Just obtaining a set of answers to these questions will not necessarily guarantee that you will arrive at a successful identification of the problem or problems. Answers come in many different forms like most things in life. The key here is quality. High-quality answers are those that are given by individuals after due consideration, and those that they will be prepared to stand by at a later date. Low-quality answers are those that are not thought through and about which people change their mind as regularly as they change their clothes.

Defining the Well-formed Problem

1. What's wrong?

2. How long have we had this problem?

3. What has caused and/or contributed to this problem?

4. How does having this problem limit us?

5. What will happen if the problem remains?

6. What was/is the worst example of this problem?

7. How have we tried to solve this problem previously?

8. Who else is affected by this problem?

9. Who are the problem owners?

10. Is the problem too large to solve as a whole?

11. Are we solving the right problem?

Figure 6

However, obtaining acceptance of a common set of answers from all those involved in the problem is a major step towards success, though it is certainly not unusual to obtain conflicting answers to the questions from different people in an organisation. Often the reason that a problem has not been resolved is that different people have divergent ideas about how a problem may be solved. It is of paramount importance that issues of this nature are identified and dealt with satisfactorily at an early stage. Otherwise it is almost certain that the resulting project will fail.

Once you have positive identification of the problem, you can then start thinking about an appropriate solution. Defining a solution to a known problem is the stage when most people seem to want to contribute. They nearly always do this by stating what they think will work best. However, often there are many potential methods that could solve the problem, and choosing the right one is the real test. Once again there are many opportunities to get this wrong, and this leads us back to item 2 in Figure 1: adopting an inappropriate change mechanism.

Chapter Seven

Preparation In Advance Of Choosing A Change Mechanism

At first sight, choosing an appropriate change mechanism does not seem to present too much of a challenge once the problem has been positively identified. However, as we have seen in Figure 1, there are many other causes or contributors to project failure and most of these have their roots in or around this stage of the project life-cycle. It is therefore vitally important to give due consideration to these, and some other factors, before moving on to the task of selecting a solution or possibly a series of solutions.

Decisions, decisions!

One of the most frequently occurring causes of project failure associated with choosing a solution can be attributed to poor or precipitate decision-making. In my view decision-making is an art and not a precise science. Over the past thirty or so years I have come across senior executives who are brilliant decision-makers and others who are not so good. I have also come across executives who are prepared to make instant decisions based on little more than the seat of their pants, and others again who perpetually "sit on the fence" and will make a decision only as a last resort. Some of the best decision-makers I have met cannot explain how they go about making their decisions. When pressed on the subject they often mention luck as playing an important part. Others will mention some inner sense of knowing what is the right thing to do. However, not all of us are blessed in these ways, and this has led me to believe that the only meaningful way of making an effective decision is to take as much of the guess-work out of the process as possible.

This book is not intended to teach the art of good decision-making. Instead I will concentrate upon the causes of bad decisions specifically as applied to Change Management. There are myriad books, training courses and even software packages available to assist those who wish to obtain a better understanding of the process of effective decision-making. IT offers a number of software packages that can help, ranging from complex Decision Support Systems to simple Decision Trees. All of these will assist in sifting the data and making the options more visible. IT can also assist in many instances by modelling a proposed solution in order to gain a better understanding of the problems that may be involved or to provide a demonstration of what the solution will be like when installed. However, when all is said and done, the actual process of making a decision comes down to personal choice, be it the choice of a Board of directors or that of just one individual.

A significant number of failures associated with decision-making occur as a result of rushing the actual process of making the decision whilst not being equipped with all the facts. This is perhaps best summed up by the phrase, "the fox is in the hen-house", or "being in headless-chicken mode", which in certain circumstances can be adopted by senior executives when suddenly confronted with a metaphoric "fox". Unfortunately, as yet I have still to come up with a panacea for corporate panic attacks of this nature. Joking apart, this is a very serious problem, and, when it occurs, one that is difficult to contain and control.

The psychology of this is complex, but has a great deal to do with the mental domains of "certainty" and "uncertainty". Usually panic becomes the modus operandi only when the problem has been positively identified and has attained the status of "certainty". Executives can live for quite a long time with the knowledge that something is wrong within their business without doing very much about it. This situation is tolerated simply because they are "uncertain" as to what is wrong and even more "uncertain" as to how to fix it. They may even have hoped that the problem would just "go away". However, having employed professionals (that's us) to look at the problems and having now been presented with the facts (certainty), panic sets in. Imagine that a Board of management is presented with a statement such as, "The reason that you are losing customers is because the quality of your goods has fallen and still is falling and, by the way, if the trend indicated by the current sales figures continues, you will make a loss next year instead of the profit that you have already announced to the press". For a moment put yourself in that Management's position. Wouldn't you be inclined to think, "This is a time for action"? Only, for "action" read "panic".

Managements have a nasty knack of panicking when suddenly confronted with hard facts which indicate that their business has developed a severe and damaging problem and particularly so if they believe it is rapidly going to turn their "bottom-line figure" an ugly shade of red. This is when the fear factor creeps in, as mentioned in Chapter One.

Once fear is driving Management, they become surprisingly open to suggestions as to how their particular problem can be solved. This is the opportunity for the "snake oil" vendors of the various packaged solutions to move in to extol the virtues of their particular version of the Emperor's New Clothes. Sometimes stopping this happening can be difficult, particularly when the vendor is a management consultancy of considerable stature.

Case Study

I can remember one particular instance when this happened to my group where we had identified the problem as "the Company being too distanced from its customers' needs". Our proposed remedy was to completely overhaul the organisation and the methods employed by the Sales and Marketing functions and to shake up the Research and Development departments so that they were more aware of what the marketplace demanded. The Marketing Director did not agree with our findings and with the permission of his co-directors invited one of the largest firms of management consultants to give my team's work "the once-over".

Shortly afterwards I was advised that the Company had been persuaded by the management consultants that their salvation lay in implementing TQM, not the proposal that we had made. As it was abundantly clear that we could not possibly retrieve the situation, we thanked them for the work that they had passed our way and wished them well in their venture with TQM, whilst at the same time pointing out some of the risks involved. Lastly, we told them that we looked forward to working with them in the future and that, if they ran into any problems, to please give us a call.

Around two years later I came across the Group Finance Director at a formal function. He informed me that all was not well with the business. TQM had been partially successful at solving the underlying problems that my group had identified, but it seemed it had also created as many problems as it had solved. Added to this was the loss to the competition of several key members of the R & D team who had cited the TQM project as their reason for leaving. This and other matters attributed to the TQM project had led to an enormous altercation among the directors which resulted in the Marketing Director resigning. The consultants who were responsible for implementation had assured him that the problems that had been encountered were only teething problems. Eventually, they claimed, everything would function perfectly, but this in their view was still at least two years away.

The Finance Director had serious doubts about their promises and was worried about the Group's future profitability and some major adverse shifts in the corporate culture which he also attributed to "the manner in which TQM was being implemented by the consultants". He was also concerned that implementation of TQM appeared to be responsible for creating a whole load of new problems in the manufacturing side of the business which was delaying the introduction of a vital new product line. He asked me to visit him at his office to discuss matters in more depth.

After several meetings with the FD and the CEO I was asked to carry out a review of the TQM project. This was undertaken in a matter of six weeks. A report on "the state of the progress in solving the original problems" together with my recommendations was produced and subsequently accepted. The report recommended that much of the TQM work should be retained, but where it had been applied incorrectly it should be removed, and the original and underlying problems identified by my team should be addressed as a matter of urgency. My team, in association with the directors and staff from the client company, then spent six months undoing the damage caused by applying TQM to the wrong problem. Simultaneously, other members of my staff implemented the original changes that we had put forward with respect to the Marketing, Sales and the R & D departments.

It would be wrong to say that TQM had not brought benefits to this particular company, because it had. The Company had refocused on the importance of its customers which had been long overdue. It had set in train a programme to continuously improve customer relations and the quality of its products and services, all of which were to prove highly beneficial to the business in the years ahead. However, on the other side of the equation it had failed to address the underlying causes that lay at the heart of their problem. It had also created (mainly through insensitivity and poor project management) a significant and unwanted shift in the corporate culture. This had led to a major HR problem in the manufacturing side of the business which was wreaking havoc with the very thing it was supposed to cure: customer confidence. I must admit I had great difficulty stifling the words "I told you so", but we all need learning experiences, do we not?

Panic is also often the driving influence behind managements' attempts to force-fit a solution to the problem. At a surface level this may appear to have much in common with the case study above. However, in the case study the instigators of the problem were the management consultants, not the client company's management. The driver behind this behaviour seems to be the need "to be seen to be doing something" about the problem with a "now" or even "yesterday" component. Unfortunately, when the two are combined the original phrase becomes interpreted as "being seen to be doing anything now that seems remotely right". Consequently the right solution gets chosen only by chance and not by the process of rational appraisal.

There are a number of ways in which situations like these can be ameliorated and, with skill, avoided altogether; primarily, and perhaps most obviously, not to create the panic in the first place. This can be achieved by gently priming key management players who may reasonably be judged to be less susceptible to panic. Softening of the overall costs and financial implications with a few generalisations and "maybes" thrown in for good measure can take the heat out of the situation quite effectively in the short term. Concentration on the positive aspects of solving the problem rather than the negative ones also helps a great deal. Overall stressing the need for a measured response to the problem and the production of a rigid but realistic timetable to produce a solution also work well. Managed adeptly, this should leave you in charge of the task of assessing the correct solution.

Human Factors

In my experience, the people involved in a project always matter more than the technicalities of the project itself. No matter how clever the technology is, if you cannot get the people to buy into the project goals, then the project will almost certainly fail. Often the human factors are the most difficult to manage effectively. Changing people's ways of working and indeed their ideas about working practices takes time and effort. Throughout the period of change, staff morale must be maintained and/or improved. In order for a project to be deemed successful, human factors must be carefully assessed, and an effective strategy for change developed. This should always be supported with a dedicated set of Critical Success Factors (CSFs), always remembering that there really is nothing more critical within a project than the proficient management of human factors.

In situations where employees are required to change values and beliefs, sufficient time must be allowed for the process of change to occur. Rarely does such a change happen quickly in a few days or weeks. More often, change takes place over months or years and is a complex process to understand and to manage. Unfortunately, morale is rarely improved just because the senior management think that the change happens to be a good idea. Employee morale can at the best of times be fragile but when change is in the air it can become very unpredictable unless positive action is taken to support it. Uncertainty is perhaps the most effective destroyer of morale. Thus the starting point of any action-plan to maintain or improve morale must be set well in advance of the commencement of the project itself. By creating an environment in which staff attitude is seen to be given due consideration when a potential change is under consideration, staff morale usually improves. Maintaining this throughout the project's life-cycle requires commitment and constant monitoring.

It is interesting to observe that in studying successful projects good leadership and high staff morale are nearly always present. This connection between leadership and morale is a well established factor and one that must not be ignored. It is worth noting that provided good, strong leadership is given, even when things are not going as planned, staff morale will often still remain high or even improve. Several examples from history spring to mind:

Henry V at Agincourt with his men outnumbered ten to one; Winston Churchill after Dunkirk and facing invasion; General MacArthur in the war in the Pacific against the Japanese, and in Korea a few years later. All these people were able to raise morale at a time when their armies or even their countries were facing defeat. Some may attribute this to the charisma of the individuals concerned, but it is their words and deeds that are remembered.

One of the underlying principles of psychology which is associated with the process of change is concerned with our "state of mind". Briefly it states that if we are in a "negative state of mind" we are going to be more resistant to new ideas than when we are in a "positive state of mind". Therefore, ensuring that staff are in a positive state of mind in advance of the introduction of new ideas is a vital prerequisite if success is to be achieved. Similarly, the power of presupposition has already been mentioned as an important driver of attitudes in change scenarios. It is therefore essential that success is constantly expressed in the form of a preconception and reinforced appropriately as the only possible outcome to the project by the project management team.

For those who have difficulty in persuading others of the importance of positive states of mind I offer the following exercise which I learned some years ago from John McWhirter, the well-known originator of a new and incredibly powerful psychological technique known as Developmental Behavioural Modelling®. All that is required is a chair with an upright back and a volunteer to sit on it.

Step One: Ask the volunteer to sit on the chair, whilst you stand behind the chair with your hands on their shoulders. Exert a steady but not too heavy pressure on their shoulders with your hand.

Ask them to close their eyes and imagine some really negative event, for instance losing their job, losing a lot of money or perhaps just feeling depressed.

When they have accessed such a situation fully in their mind by seeing, hearing and feeling it, ask them to stand up. It is unlikely that they will be able to do so, and even if they do it will be with great effort.

Step Two: Remove your hands from their shoulders and ask them to stand up, turn around a couple of times and, whilst they are doing so, to forget the previous negative thoughts and to reacquaint themselves with the room they are in and the general surroundings. When they are happy with this ask them to sit on the chair again.

Step Three: Again place you hands on the subject's shoulders, exerting the same level of downward pressure and then ask them to recall some very pleasant experience, perhaps getting married, being given good examination results or winning at something, in fact anything that makes them feel really happy.

When they have fully accessed this state, again ask them to stand up. It is highly likely they will rise as though you were exerting no downward pressure at all.

The major learning experience that is established by this simple exercise is that physiology is affected in a powerful way by our state of mind. Negative thinking reduces our physical power measurably, and positive thinking has the ability to empower us. However, just as the mind has control over our bodies, it does not end there; the mind also has the ability to restrict or empower us mentally as well. This is a major factor in changing the beliefs and attitudes of those people involved in any change programme.

It is vital therefore that a "can do" environment or culture (to borrow an American phrase) is developed well before the project starts. In the instances where I have looked at projects which have failed through "a bridge too far" problems I have often felt that, had the project team started out with, or been able to maintain, a "can do" attitude, the project might, with a little luck, have succeeded. Similarly, I have seen other projects that I would have rated as having little chance of success in the early stages of the life-cycle, battling through against all odds to become winners in the end. All of these have contained the vital element of a very strong team spirit along with a burning desire to overcome their problems despite any obstacles placed in their path. Plainly there is a clear message here that a strong culture is a key element which must be cultivated throughout a project's life if success is to be attained.

People often become de-motivated when things start to deviate from the plan or simply go wrong. Once this occurs de-motivation can spread like a plague through the whole organisation and bring the project down. However, if there is a strong culture which is committed to success, often such problems are dismissed as "just another challenge to be overcome" rather than "a road block to further progress".

In circumstances where change requires staff to modify attitudes and beliefs, it is not unusual to find them agreeing to change just to ensure that they will keep their jobs. When this occurs, full commitment on the part of the staff is often absent, and there is a real danger that over time they will slip back into their old ways of working. This is not uncommon where a business has enjoyed considerable success in the past. Staff often believe that it is because of, not in spite of, the way they do things that success has been achieved. They may fail to realise that the success the business enjoyed came from things like new products or services, a wide-open market with no competitors or any number of other factors which they do not fully comprehend. The belief that their existing mode of working has contributed to the business's success may also have been reinforced in the past by awards or accolades handed down by Senior Management. In such situations staff will often quote these as reasons for not changing.

When change covers a whole business, care must be taken to involve everyone in the process. It is vitally important to address staff at a level which is appropriate to their understanding of the situation. Clearly communications made to senior managers are unlikely to be appropriate to shop floor workers and vice versa. Considerable care and attention must be given to these matters in order that everyone should feel directly involved and understand why the change is necessary.

The ultimate goal must be to leave each employee feeling that the change is absolutely necessary, vital to the future growth (development, survival, etc.) of the business and that everyone has a part to play in it. This should be the case even when the change will result in a reduction in the staff headcount or produce other results which employees may not welcome. Announcing a strategy for dealing with redundancy, relocation or other similar matters should be a key part of any communication about a proposed Change Management programme. If there are staff councils or trade unions or other forms of employee representation present, then it is vital to involve them in the change programme as early as possible. Do not wait until the grapevine is already humming with misinformation because by then it is far too late. Tackling a thorny problem, such as redundancy, head-on is usually a far more successful strategy with fewer risks attached.

It is vital to remember that all communication is open to interpretation by the recipient. Thus if ambiguous statements are made they are not always likely to be interpreted in a beneficial manner. Over my working life I have had experience of literally dozens of Change Management situations where careless or poorly thought-through statements have been made by senior managers which have resulted in near mayhem breaking out among the workforce. The cost in time, money and employee confidence resulting from these "unfortunate incidents" has been enormous. In some instances the whole project has had to be abandoned or put on indefinite hold pending restoration of employee relations to a more amicable level.

Bringing about changes of belief is rarely easy and requires a considerable amount of skill. Few managers possess these skills. Therefore if radical changes are required a first priority must be to ensure that the people who will be expected to bring about these changes have sufficient training to enable them to complete their task effectively. In my experience the greatest source of resistance to change has come from the very people who will bear the brunt of such re-education programmes, the middle managers. It is often this group that feels, rightly or wrongly, that it has the most to lose from change. Winning the battle for the hearts and minds of these individuals is a prerequisite in any change scenario. Fail to convince this group and the project is as good as doomed before it really gets under way.

In all change projects it is vital therefore that employees' attitudes towards the change are constantly checked as the project proceeds. Staff feedback sessions which encourage two-way communication fulfil a useful function in providing information in addition to a normal project-management reporting system. A further check on real progress can be obtained through facilitating feedback using anonymous comment slips or suggestion boxes. In fact anything which encourages open dialogue is likely to prove helpful in avoiding problems. Incorporating these methods in a Change Management project provides the necessary assurance that change really is occurring at all levels and is not just a tick on a project progress chart.

One of the best ways of achieving success is to establish a series of short-term goals and to reward success when these goals are achieved. If goals are missed or there are signs that they are not likely to be met, concentrate on improvement and not fault-finding activities. Additional and visible rewards for staff who have made special contributions to the achievement of a goal also provide an incentive for others to contribute more. Ultimately, changing behaviours which are in reality the sum of people's attitudes and beliefs requires judicious use of the proverbial carrot and/or stick.

Many of the most recent innovations in management thinking such as TQM, Business Process Re-engineering and Right Sizing/Restructuring implicitly require employees to change attitudes, beliefs and values. Of the failures associated with these subject areas reviewed by the Ecotech study, the majority were seen as having run into significant problems in dealing with human factors. In most cases the cause was seen as not placing sufficient effort into winning over employees to the need for change or not allowing sufficient time for the concepts associated with the change to be fully accepted.

The clear message that emerged from this group and which applies to all other Change Management projects is, to paraphrase Tony Blair, the UK Prime Minister, "communication, communication, communication" and "education, education, education". Communication must be two-way and encourage feedback if it is to be effective. Therefore CSFs should be established to ensure that this occurs effectively and is not just composed of a series of "motherhood and apple-pie statements". Similarly, training initiatives should have their own CSFs which are capable of measuring not only progress towards learning new techniques but also measuring the commitment of the employees to the programme of change as well.

Case Study

All too often I have come across change programmes where human factors have been neglected and where the Management were left wondering why their particular change project went wrong. Among these was a thriving software house employing around six hundred people. The directors had grown the business from virtually nothing to a point where on paper they were all millionaires. The only real assets that the business had were the employees it had attracted to work for it. However, when the Executive decided to implement a major structural change to the business which it saw as necessary to facilitate further growth, it chose to restrict consultation to just a few selected senior managers. The Executive's attitude was that the staff would not really be affected, no one was going to lose their job, and in fact more jobs would be created. Therefore, there was no need to consult them as it would only distract them from their work.

About six months after the implementation of the change the business was in serious trouble. Many of the more valuable members of staff (who had not been consulted) left, often taking with them some of the more promising junior staff members as well. Nearly all the projects the Company was working on for clients had fallen behind and some were now in breach of their contractual terms. Recruitment was at an all-time low following adverse press comments. New business was not being won, also attributable to adverse press comment, and morale within the workforce was also at an all-time low. The bank was taking an increasing interest in the size of the Company's overdraft and pressing for a significant reduction – all for the sake of what amounts to little more than common sense and the foresight to recognise that, in this day and age, staff simply do not and will not put up with being treated like cattle. The outcome for the owners/directors was not good as within a year they were forced to sell the business to a large conglomerate for a knockdown figure, leaving the directors with virtually nothing.

Finally, I have written much about changing beliefs, attitudes and behaviours but I have not specifically mentioned using any of the NLP techniques associated with changing these important factors. Incorporated in the text above are what may be regarded as "best practice" techniques garnered from a number of fields of psychology including Behavioural Modification. Unlike the example I gave of the physiological effect of mental states there is as far as I am aware no consistently effective way of changing group attitudes and beliefs other than by the conventional use of the carrot and stick. Clearly the carrot will take many forms and should take full cognisance of the available "psychological" techniques such as developing a strong change culture.

There have been many attempts at producing a "magic" solution to this problem and many claims made as to their efficacy, but none has yet provided a sufficiently high success rate to merit mention here. Therefore, attempting to change the belief systems of every individual involved in the project is unrealistic. Almost inevitably, and regardless of what methods of persuasion are used, some individuals will remain unconvinced. Sometimes it is necessary to retain them on the project on account of the particular skills they possess; sometimes there just isn't the opportunity to do anything about them. Close management of these individuals is therefore important to the success of the project. Often, once the project shows early signs of success, they will be won over. It is important, therefore, to keep emphasising the progress that is being made and encouraging them to be seen as part of a successful team.

In Chapter Nine, under Logical Level Alignment, I have provided an explanation of the structure of our belief systems and how they affect our identity and pervade organisations as well. Robert Dilts wrote an excellent book entitled *Changing Belief Systems With NLP* (1984) which largely deals with changing beliefs at an individual level. It also provides a very clear description of the processes involved in belief change and as such is a valuable resource for anyone involved in Change Management.

The Critical Success Factors (CSFs) of a Change Management Project

These have been mentioned previously as playing a vital role in all aspects of any Change Management project, but in failed projects they are often absent or badly formed.

CSFs are the data or markers by which a Change Management project will be judged as a success or a failure. The emphasis is placed on the words "critical" and "success". For this reason it is vital that everyone involved in the project should be aware of their existence and make a commitment to achieving them. If full commitment to the CSFs is not obtained, then the project will almost certainly founder.

CSFs, or rather the lack of them, were seen as a significant cause or contributor to the failure of many of the subjects in the Ecotech study. In most instances failure was caused because the projects lacked a clear focus or did not have the full commitment of those involved in the implementation of the Change Programme. CSFs provide focus and force out the methods that will be needed to be deployed in order for a project to succeed. Once CSFs are established they also provide a powerful restriction on the possible choices of a solution.

Ideally, they should be defined immediately the problem has been defined and, at the latest, well before the process of selecting a problem solution commences. Carried out properly, and in this order, CSFs can in themselves form a barrier against panicky decision-making. Their existence can also provide a safeguard against outside agencies wishing to sell an inappropriate Change Management solution. In an earlier case study on page 105, had I been able to obtain full commitment from all the Board members as to the CSFs of the project, I believe it would have been very unlikely that they would have considered implementing TQM.

In order to be effective, CSFs must take the form of tangible entities, markers or activities which are either quantifiable or measurable. They are normally specified as measures of achievement that can be evaluated in time, money, goals to be reached, benchmarks or other events or activities that need to be realised for a project to be deemed successful. Examples could be, "Reduce inventory by £10m by 30th June" or, "New computer system to achieve minimum benchmark tests no later than 6th January" or, "Reduce the headcount in department X by ten by the end of the company year".

Often when identifying CSFs those associated with human factors are the last to be evaluated or are ignored altogether. This situation often arises where some form of high technology or new technology is being introduced. In these circumstances the main focus of management can become almost exclusively directed towards the technological issues involved rather than the people who will need to operate it or be affected by it. In projects that fail in these areas, quite perversely the staff rather than the technology are often apportioned most of the blame, despite the lack of adequate CSFs supporting the human factors.

In other situations in our study where technology was not a dominant factor, many of the failures attributed to HR problems had causes associated with inadequate training in one respect or another. This is a matter that does not seem to attract enough attention when a project is first being assessed, and often fails to be resolved later in the project life-cycle. It is therefore a wise precaution to include a CSF in all projects covering the requisite training needs.

It is worth checking each CSF for efficacy by applying the test of asking *when, where, how* and *with whom*? *When* should identify the period of the activity and its completion date. *Where* should identify the environment and location. *How* should point to the problem solution. *With whom* should identify all those who will be subject to the CSF as well as those who will be expected to deliver it.

It is important when defining a CSF that it is not going to be affected by factors outside the project boundaries. Examples of this could be factors concerned with the profit of a business or turnover. If these factors are used as a benchmark they need to be identified specifically, and the part that is expected to be played by them in the project also identified.

In large projects it is important to recognise that often there are sub-groups of CSFs within overall CSFs, and these also should be specified in detail. However, it is important when specifying CSFs to keep the focus on the word "critical" and not to get too deeply involved in trivia.

Generalisations have no place within CSFs. If they occur, they cannot be a "critical" element, so either revise them or remove them. Also identify any other Meta-model violations that occur within them. I have come across situations where there has been an attempt to include CSFs which, although laudable as a concept, are not practicable or achievable in reality. Allowing these to be included can be disastrous for a project. If they are allowed to remain they can eat up vast amounts of resources and demoralise the project team as they strive to achieve the impossible. They therefore must be confronted for what they are, and promptly removed.

Critical Success Factors have another important part to play once a project has "got under way". If new requirements are proposed during the project, they should be tested for relevance against the existing CSFs identified at the start. Quite often they will be found to have no relevance and should be considered as a diversion away from the existing project. Occasionally, however, new information does come to light which is relevant and gives rise to additional CSFs being identified. In these cases it is important to have a procedure in place to assess the overall effect and to gain acceptance at an appropriate level in the project/management hierarchy of their incorporation into the project.

Figure 7 lists the CSFs identified by the XYZ Company. These were arrived at after the directors had defined their Well-formed Problem as:

Having inadequate Management information available to:

a) ensure the effective day-to-day running of the Group's business;

b) confidently plan the Group's tactical and strategic direction.

Critical Success Factors of XYZ Company

1. Develop a "Pan-European Vision" which is accepted by all staff by end of current Company year.

2. Replace all the existing IT systems within 2 years with common hardware and software.

3. Achieve full integration of the new IT system across Europe within 3 years.

4. Develop standardised software packages for use outside Europe within 4 years.

5. Investigate what further advances can be made based upon the new system by completion of pilot project.

Figure 7

The arrival at this statement as being their Well-formed Problem resulted from several sessions with the directors involving all the methods outlined in Chapter Six. This had resulted in the separation of the problems associated with "Low productivity in the UK" from those of "Poor management information". Agreement was reached to manage these as two different, although associated, Change Management projects. What was perhaps a little surprising was how quickly these directors changed their minds as to what the key problems were. Several later stated that they had changed their minds when they were forced to consider all the questions posed in Figure 6, making comments along the lines of "Sorting the wood from the trees" or "Being too close to the coalface". At the start of the exercise most had expressed strong but divergent views as to what was wrong and even stronger views about an appropriate solution. Their original preferences are listed in Figure 8.

At first sight the actions listed in Figure 7 may not appear very daunting to anyone not involved directly with the business. However, the implications of these changes were considerable,

Main Board Members' Preferred Change Programmes of XYZ Company at the Start of the Investigation

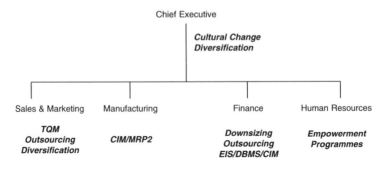

Figure 8

with each of the CSFs having subsidiary CSFs. At this point in the project the Company had six different and largely incompatible computer systems, ranging in age from one to six years. There was no common accounting, manufacturing or marketing system in use across the Group. Also, each country had largely been left to its own devices. This was not so much a matter of Management neglect but more a function of previous rapid growth outside the UK whilst in the same period the UK was entering a recession.

Previously I have briefly covered the importance of "Human Factors" but only touched on "Cultural Change" in passing. Often these two factors are inextricably linked so that a shift in beliefs by the staff in a business can cause the culture to change and vice versa. Both of these feature as significant causes of Change Management failures. The Executive of the XYZ Company were fully aware of this and took the view that, in order that the right "change culture" could be established, the first and most important step was to create a vision of the future that all staff would readily accept.

CSF number 1 was intended to cover these highly important matters specifically. It was also intended to cover, through subsidiary CSFs, many other aspects of failure previously identified in Figure 1. Creating a "Shared Vision" across a business is not an easy task for most people and requires the input of considerable amounts of skill and effort in order to be successful. It is a very important subject in its own right which could have been covered in this book but would have added several more chapters. For those who wish to obtain a better understanding of the subject I recommend an excellent book, using many NLP concepts, by Robert Dilts entitled *Visionary Leadership Skills* (1996).

The "Pan-European Vision" was not just a simple statement about some vague view of the future. It was a clear and precise series of statements about the need for change, the methods that would be employed to bring about change and the opportunities and benefits that these changes would bring to all staff employed in the Group. The document itself was produced in booklet form and a copy given to each member of staff within the Group. Shortly after receiving the document a series of meetings for staff (called staff forums) took place where Management explained all the facets of the strategy and sought further input from the employees.

The answer to the *when* question was clearly identified with a start date, dates associated with intermediate goals and an end date. The *where* question identified a pilot project starting in the UK and moving on to Holland, Germany and France followed by all other European countries. The *how* question described the concept of ironing out difficulties in the pilot project followed by implementation elsewhere. All staff would be kept informed of progress, and how this was to be done was described in detail. The *who* question stated that the pilot project would include staff from Holland and Germany with many staff from other countries taking part in training and other preparatory activities.

The choice of the term "Pan-European Vision" was made by the CEO and was a highly astute choice as at that time there was a lot of public discussion about the convergence of the various national markets within the European Union. Thus the importance of "convergence" within the XYZ Company was more acceptable to the people working in the business. In fact, little overt "selling" of the concept by the company was necessary as almost daily the press and television had something to say about the subject. Indeed the term Pan-European Vision was frequently used by politicians from many different countries within Europe. Thus the need to make small, subtle changes to culture were made at a national level with the Company apparently going along with the mood of the time.

Without doubt the second CSF was the most complex as it involved seventeen different phases in the complete project. These ranged from initial evaluation and selection of hardware and systems to the final stage of implementation. Every phase had a number of subsidiary CSFs attached to it, an example of which concerned the choice of an appropriate accounting package. The subsidiary CSF stated that the package chosen must have the ability to conform to the national requirements for taxation, accounting practice, etc., of each country where it was being installed.

Another subsidiary CSF of this project involved solving one of the symptoms associated with another problem previously identified as "Low Productivity in the UK". The symptom concerned lack of an automated linkage between Sales, Marketing and Manufacturing Systems in the UK and lack of a linkage to the two other factories in Europe. It is perhaps pertinent to note that both projects were proceeding in parallel, and considerable effort had been invested in project management to ensure that each stayed within its respective boundaries.

Complexity

Inevitably there are many Change Management projects which are extremely complex in nature and, except to the experts directly involved, very difficult to understand fully. Examples of these abound in areas which involve new technologies or new inventions. However, Information Technology perhaps stands out as the technology most familiar to those involved in managing complex change. There is virtually no business in the UK that has not at some time or other experienced difficulties with implementing an IT project. In the Ecotech study IT projects, or those associated with IT, accounted for by far the largest number of failures when measured by value alone.

Often consultants and employees involved in Change Management projects seem to assume that all senior executives possess the brain or thinking ability of rocket scientists, but this is rarely the case. Most senior executives are capable, well educated and able to deduce from incomplete information the pertinent facts necessary for the effective running of their business or some specialised part of it. However, they are not always able to comprehend complex arguments that fall outside their sphere of knowledge, and this is particularly true of IT.

IT not only involves a technology which is often not well understood but it often provides or facilitates whole new ways of organising a business and new methods of working for the staff as well. This is further compounded by the fact that IT as a technology continues to develop and evolve at what appears to outsiders to be an ever-increasing rate. So, as an executive in a business, even if you had a good handle on the subject of IT just a few years ago, the chances are that your knowledge is already out of date. Thus the scope for making the wrong choices and making poor choices is truly enormous.

This is particularly so when utilising leading-edge products from the IT industry. There is a well-known maxim about never rushing out to buy a brand new model of a car as new models always seem to have too many faults. It is said that a better strategy is to wait a year until all the wrinkles have been ironed out. Whether this is true of motor vehicles I am not sure, but I am convinced it applies to IT and software products in particular.

I always recommend to my clients that they talk to other users of the hardware or software before they themselves commit to purchasing it. Most IT vendors maintain lists of reference sites, and asking the existing users about their experiences, and particularly about any problems that they have encountered, can save a considerable amount of time and money. Learning from other people's experience is cheap by comparison with learning from your own mistakes, particularly with IT.

The original Ecotech study of the cause of Change Management failures (identified in the early part of Chapter Six) gives one of the nine causes as "a bridge too far". The majority of the cases involved the brave or foolhardy, depending upon your perspective, who made "leaps into the dark" with IT. Often this involved the development of new software applications which the vendors had promised would bring either major cost savings to the business or would gain for the client a significant advantage over its competitors. Another small but nevertheless significant group in this area was associated with Human Resource Development projects, and several of these involved attempts at "empowering the workforce" whilst simultaneously removing a layer or two of supervision.

It was interesting to note that a number of our study group had been sold the concept of gaining competitive advantage based upon one example from the USA. This involved a computerised seat-booking system developed for American Airlines. This project was in fact so effective in gaining advantage for the company over its competitors that it was successfully prosecuted under US anti-trust legislation for attempted monopolisation of the market. However, none of the UK clients had been told about the anti-trust action or the cost to American Airlines!

Complexity is not restricted to IT alone, as has already been mentioned. Occasionally, even minor changes in one part of the organisation of a business can involve extremely complex changes occurring in other parts of the organisation. Understanding all the ramifications of such changes is not easy but is vital during the project planning phase. When explaining this problem I often make an analogy to the human body where, if a doctor sets out to cure a malady in one organ by drugs or surgery, he can have a profound but accidental effect on other organs, which may lead to the patient's death. In all human organisations the same effects can occur. Therefore it is sensible to ensure that, whatever change is being proposed, any "knock-on" effects are beneficial. Item 7 of Figure 1 identifies this as a significant cause of Change Management failures.

Since the Ecotech study I have had the opportunity to investigate other failures concerned with complexity. Nearly all resulted from three causes: failure to break the overall project down into smaller, more understandable work packages; poor overall project management; and lack of communication with other parts of the business which were affected by the changes.

It is also worth appraising the term "complexity" for a moment. What is considered as a complex change by one business may be seen as relatively simple by another. It is all a matter of perspective and, to some extent, of past experience with similar problems.

I have found it helps considerably if the client is asked how complex they see the tasks lying ahead of them. The reason for this lies in simple psychology. If they see the tasks ahead of them as complex (presupposition: it is complex) then they are likely to need more help than if they see them as simple. My task then is to persuade them that by involving my team we can remove much of the complexity whilst simultaneously teaching them how to achieve the desired changes.

In the case of the XYZ Company they saw the task ahead of them as extremely complex and stated at an early stage that they needed my team to assist them through a number of the phases involved. Please note the term "assist", as they did not want us to undertake all the complex work without knowledge being transferred from my staff to theirs. This is an excellent strategy to pursue for both parties. It leaves the client with a good degree of independence from the consultants and it frees up the consultants to work on other projects without getting trapped into doing mundane tasks for the client.

The XYZ Company had broken the overall project down into several sub-projects with an overall Project Management Steering Group overseeing the whole. In order that the project was seen as a total commitment by the Company the CEO agreed to spend a minimum of one day per week on the project and in addition he took the chair at the weekly Project Management Steering Group meetings.

The CEO's commitment to the project by being seen to be taking an active role in its management was, as they say, "the cherry on the cake", as this ensured that total commitment was secured from all his subordinates.

Every Problem is Unique

"I know what your problem is. I finished fixing an identical problem in The Widget Company only last month. What you need is …" So said the management consultant to the client during the initial interview.

Obviously we all expect our "consultants" to have a track record of fixing problems "like ours", be they a brain surgeon or the local council's Rodent Control Consultant (rat-catcher). However, we also expect them to approach their task having taken into account the uniqueness of each individual situation. Unfortunately, this is often not the case with vendors of packaged solutions. Trying to replicate a solution from a different environment more often than not takes longer and is more expensive than devising a solution that fits your environment. This does not necessarily preclude the purchase of a packaged solution, provided that this is the right choice for the business and all the risks have been fully understood and quantified.

Establishing this concept as a fact in the client's mind early in the project life-cycle helps to stop them from rashly adopting someone else's "success" story. TQM was largely sold by consultants on the back of a limited number of case studies which sought to demonstrate the success achieved by these subject businesses. What they did not tell the clients was that many hundreds of other businesses who had tried to copy the success of the case study subjects had failed to replicate the same success.

It also helps to underscore the fact that every business is different even within the same industries and sectors of industries. Often it is these very differences that mark out a company as unique and which are the driving forces behind its success. So it makes sense to protect these differences and not destroy them.

Case Study

Several years ago I was invited to review the IT Strategy of a major UK conglomerate. The businesses that came under the control of the conglomerate were unusually diverse. Among these were a large building and construction business, a shipping company, a property investment business and an engineering business. None of these enterprises had very much in common in the nature of their businesses or in the manner in which they were managed or operated. However, for reasons that, despite my best endeavours, I never fully understood, the Group had decided that all the businesses should adopt a common IT strategy. This called for the adoption of common hardware and software across a range of core activities in all the various businesses. The strategy called for all software to be obtained "off the shelf" as packages with very minimal "in-house tailoring" required.

At the point at which I became involved there was considerable resistance within the various businesses to nearly all the proposed changes. Key to bringing about the changes that had been called for in the IT strategy was the adoption of a common approach to software development. Somewhere in Group Headquarters' IT function it had been decided that Information Engineering (IE) was the vehicle that would be used. This was initially intended to produce a common data model of the core activities applicable to all the various businesses. However, only one of the major businesses agreed with this approach, and the whole project had become impossibly bogged down in political shenanigans of all descriptions, ultimately escalating to Main Board level. I was asked by the Finance Director to find out what had gone wrong and also to give a view as to whether IE was the right approach for their business.

It was immediately obvious to me that what was being attempted was to force-fit on the other businesses in the group a solution already successfully adopted by the building and construction businesses. How anyone could come to believe that there was sufficient commonality between a construction business and one engaged in shipping or engineering to merit force-fitting an IT solution, God alone knows! Of course it could have been achieved if sufficient force had been applied, but at what cost to the operational effectiveness of the businesses concerned one can only guess!

On examining the IT strategy document I found an interesting comment claiming that in the areas of Accounting, Payroll and Personnel there was already over 90% commonality between the existing systems in use in all the companies and that they should therefore adopt a standardised approach to future systems. This, it was claimed, was good enough reason to make all the other administration systems common across the group. This of course ignored the critical facts that the 90% commonality reflected the very necessary requirements of the law regarding corporate matters, taxation and employee legislation and it was in the ten per cent of differences that the real importance lay. Ignore this and there was a significant risk that the businesses would founder.

After considerable amounts of oil were poured on troubled waters it was agreed that each of the companies in the group would, over time, convert to a selected standard package for Accounting, Payroll and Human Resource management. However, each company would make whatever changes they deemed necessary to the packages to suit their particular business needs. All other systems would be left to each company to specify, but as a token gesture to the corporate IT function all the businesses would use IE as the major data modelling tool.

It was interesting to note that in this case much emphasis had been placed upon "data modelling" but very little on human factors or the effects that commonality would force on the cultures of the existing businesses. Although I was not able to identify the champion of this cause I suspect the ideas really stemmed from some relatively lowly manager in the corporate IT function who happened to believe that IE would solve many bureaucratic problems for the group. The fact that he could have killed it stone dead undoubtedly never crossed his mind!

The Effects of Change upon the Organisation's Culture and Modus Operandi

Cultural aspects are frequently one of the most overlooked areas during the assessment of the effects of a planned change, and there are many reason why this happens. These represented the third most prevalent cause for Change Management failures in the Ecotech study. Unplanned or unforeseen changes to the culture of a business can have very profound effects upon the efficiency and operation of an organisation. When unplanned cultural change occurs, and it is deleterious to the business, it can require significant effort to repair the damage. Often in such circumstances attempts at recreating the original culture prove ineffective. All potential changes should therefore have as a key component the assessment of changes to the existing culture. When identified they must be carefully analysed and managed appropriately.

Before committing to any major change within an organisation there are a number of points that need to be considered in association with culture but which are often overlooked. Of critical importance is the effect that change will have upon the shape and purpose of the organisation and the people within it. Some of the questions already asked in defining the Well-formed Problem are intended to draw out any issues that are likely to arise in these areas and those that are associated with the problem. However, experience has shown that frequently not enough in-depth attention is given to these important factors when the focus moves towards the formulation of a solution. The consequence has often been that unforeseen, insurmountable problems arise during implementation which bring the project shuddering to a halt or, worse still, to complete collapse.

One of the first laws of physics relates to motion and it states that, "Every action has an equal and opposite reaction". In physics this is most often applied to matter but it equally relates to any form of motion. Change cannot take place without movement or motion, and this implies that when we change we *move away from* one state and while so doing we *move towards* another. Often we view such a change as occurring over a period of time, just as the metamorphosis of a caterpillar into a butterfly occurs over time.

The concept of "moving away from one state and moving towards another" has particular relevance in all Change Management situations as it implies simultaneous motion in two directions. This may be viewed as an equation where one side must balance the other in the same manner as with a set of scales. In a well-ordered change situation due consideration is given to both sides of the equation, ensuring that every aspect of the change is "weighed up" or assessed and called to account. This involves consideration of all those people and things that are going to be affected by the change.

In situations where the change is necessary to restore balance to a business or a part of a business by moving away from a situation we typically select what we wish to retain from the current state and take with us into the future, and leave behind those things which we want to discard. Normally these will be the things that are causing the imbalance to occur. However, we need to consider what other aspects or functions of the business are going to be affected by the process of change. The structure of the company may need to be changed or the attitudes/beliefs of the employees may need to be modified, or indeed the culture of the organisation itself may need to be changed.

The Meta-model questions can assist us significantly in establishing any potential causes of imbalance. The three key questions that must be asked are, "What do we want?", "How will we know when we have got it?" and "What will we *not have* in the future situation that we have now?"

The first question is likely to produce an answer such as, "To get rid of the problem", to which we reply, "How specifically?", and this should lead to a suggestion as to a possible solution based on the parameters provided by the already defined CSFs.

The second question should also provide an answer based upon the CSFs. If not, then the CSFs need to be revisited.

The third question is intended to reveal the things that we will not have in the future that result from making the change and do not form part of those things that we consciously wish to discard. Most often these are things associated with culture or other human factors that have not previously been considered, although almost anything can come up at this stage. Whatever is discovered by this question should be assessed, and, where necessary, new or modified CSFs should be created.

Similarly, when the driving influence is to move towards a new situation, there is a tendency to focus on only the new things we wish to obtain and ignore the things we are leaving behind or other items that inevitably will be changed. It is worth putting effort into identifying any other things which may occur as a result of achieving the change. Close examination will probably reveal that not all these things will be positive. Change always involves a price! So the same three questions asked about change that is driven from a desire to move away from have equal relevance in situations where the prime driving force is to move towards. Therefore these three questions must be answered satisfactorily.

Balance has been mentioned throughout this discussion of moving away from and moving towards. Balance is achieved only when a business or a unit within it is working harmoniously and effectively with the other parts of the business. Any non-evolutionary change is likely to bring about a period of instability whilst the transition from one state to another occurs. However, overall the intention of any Change Management project should have as one of its prime goals to effectively manage the uncertainties and imbalances that will occur during the period of transition. The overriding aim must always be to return to a "steady state" of balance by completion of the project.

Culture requiring change can be one of the most complex of all Change Management projects to undertake. In these situations such change must be planned and managed with the skill and deliberation akin to that possessed by a brain surgeon. I have often in the past likened changing an existing culture to tinkering with the soul or spirit of a person. Others have described changing culture in less ethereal terms but all agree that it is something not to be undertaken lightly.

Most people in business are familiar with terms such as "a marketing-led organisation" or "an R & D-driven business". These descriptions are in fact metaphors which describe the overall culture of an organisation and give some indication of the type of balance that exists within a business.

A company that is marketing led is quite simply one that is largely controlled by the needs and desires of the marketing function of the business, all other aspects and operations of the business fulfilling subservient roles to that of marketing. Thus the balance in such a company is tilted *towards* marketing and consequently *away from* the other functions within the business. There is nothing wrong with this, and there are many highly effective UK businesses which operate in just this manner. The Virgin Group is just one such business which belongs to this group of organisations. In the case of Virgin, maintenance of brand image is their most important function and every other activity in the various businesses that go to make up the group is largely subservient to this.

The purpose of mentioning this is to point out that often conglomerates such as the Virgin Group choose to operate in what may appear to others as an out-of-balance manner. However, this is the most effective way for Virgin to be operating and generating profit and growth. This out-of-balance is achieved and maintained to a large extent by means of the culture that surrounds a business, and any attempt to change or modify it would almost certainly be met with considerable resistance. Often the unit that has the extra weighting attached to it is seen by the other units within the business as warranting special attention. Maybe this is because the unit is responsible for wealth creation within the business or there is some other aspect that grants such credibility. So people working in such companies see themselves as "in balance".

Problems arise only when the out-of-balance is not planned, is resented by the other parts of the business, or does not deliver the value that the other units expect from it.

It is therefore most important to gain an understanding of the "culture" that exists in a business and to check out your understanding of this with a wide cross-section of the senior management prior to embarking on any Change Management project. During this process it is very well worthwhile establishing which parts of the culture are "sacrosanct" to these managers and which parts they expect will change. Armed with this information you can plan to avoid creating any unwelcome or unexpected changes to the culture.

The directors of the XYZ Company were asked to consult their managements and to produce a list of those things that they would be moving away from and those that they were moving towards as a result of implementing the "Pan-European Vision". They were then asked to evaluate the implications, and this gave rise to over one hundred requests to change various elements of the proposed implementation. One such example involved the UK Sales Division which flagged up a potential loss of flexibility in changing or modifying customers' orders as a result of the new system being imposed and the associated new ways of working. They felt that this could lose the Company valuable sales. This would of course exacerbate the low productivity problem in the UK. Consequently, the requirements of the UK Sales Division were incorporated into the design of the new systems.

Of the hundred or so proposed changes nearly half involved human factors that had not been previously considered and seven were concerned with potentially adverse effects on the culture of the unit involved. Eleven were new opportunities that had not been discovered earlier and possibly would not have been discovered at all without this exercise being carried out. The majority of the proposed changes were associated with things that would be lost by moving to the new systems.

Post implementation of the project, a survey found that most people involved felt that this exercise had been one of the most valuable. It had proved to be very effective in hunting out potential problems which would probably have otherwise surfaced only at a late stage in implementation. It thus saved a considerable waste of effort and resources. It was also seen as making a major contribution to the project's being completed on time.

The Effects of Change upon an Organisation's Relationships to Internal and External Forces

In this final section I shall consider the effect of balance as applied more globally to an organisation and the need to maintain a balance suitable to the needs of the organisation at this level. In the previous section consideration was given to maintaining balance within an organisation before, during and after a period of change. However, all change will affect other aspects of balance, and among these are the major forces that interact both internally and externally on and with the business. In the main they are the competitors, shareholders, customers, suppliers, workforce and the environment. Dr Michael E Porter describes the effects of these forces in his book *Competitive Advantage* (1985). However, whilst it is relatively easy to comprehend the interaction of these forces with an organisation at a conceptual level, they are very much more complex to understand at a functional level and particularly so where Change Management is involved.

At Cranfield we recognised that if a business had the ability to control and manipulate these forces as part of a Change Management programme this could afford the business opportunities for change that had not previously existed. However, how do you objectively measure or quantify the force applied by, say, the shareholders or any of the other major forces acting on a business, and in any case what form does this force take? If these questions can be answered, what other questions arise?

After a considerable amount of brain cell damage we stopped banging our heads against the wall and recognised that we were unlikely to be able to solve these problems in a way which would allow us to produce a "standard" model of these forces. Instead, we chose to take Dr Porter's concept, changed it a little and came up with a theory which described the balance between these forces in more subjective terms. We then turned this into a diagrammatic form and gave it the name the Business Forces Diagram for a Business in Balance (Figure 9).

Business Forces Diagram for a Business in Balance

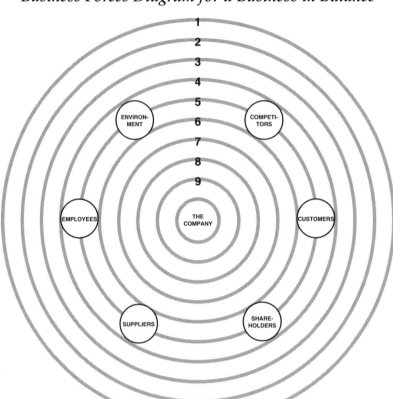

Figure 9

We gave each of the six forces a weighting, the sum total of which added up to 30. Thus if everything was in balance then each of the six forces would be exerting a weight of 5 units. We then drew ten rings around the entity that we called "the company" in a similar form to a target, with each ring representing a measure between one and ten, the innermost ring scoring 10 and the outermost scoring 1. Each of the forces was placed on the diagram with their relationship to one another being ignored. Figure 9 shows a business in balance with each element exerting equal force. However, Figure 10 shows a business that has become out of balance as a direct result of a failed TQM project. In this case the force exerted by "customers" has increased at the expense of weakening the forces of "suppliers" and "staff".

Business Forces Diagram for a Business out of Balance following a failed TQM Project

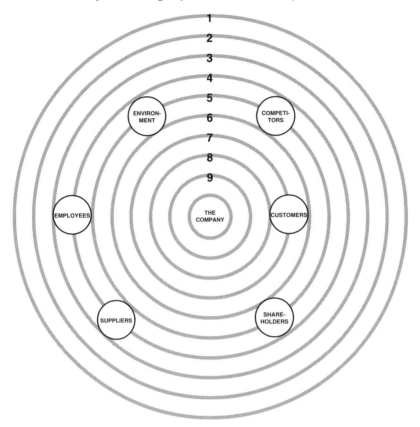

Figure 10

When we asked a number of students attending a Change Management seminar to produce a diagram of their business's current situation we were quite surprised at the results we obtained. Nearly all our students produced diagrams which were "out of balance". A minority stated that they thought this situation was perfectly all right, and normal for their type of business. However, a slightly larger group said that the diagram only demonstrated what they already knew to be wrong with their businesses. We asked these to then redraw the diagrams as though they had completed their planned change programme. All but one produced a diagram showing the businesses in balance. The exception's diagram was interesting as it showed the competition as scoring only three and the rest in equal balance. On investigating this further we discovered that the planned change was intended to gain very significant competitive advantage thus reducing the force generated on the company by its competitors.

I have found the production of these diagrams to be a valuable way of drawing out information that does not seem to freely come to hand by other means. In particular, senior executive staff when asked to complete these diagrams have often supplied considerable amounts of useful information about their expectations from a planned Change Management project in the course of providing an explanation of the differences between their diagrams. However, perhaps the most useful purpose of completing both "before" and "after" diagrams is to get senior executives thinking about the issues that lie beyond the project boundaries in the world outside their business.

These diagrams can also provide a "focal point" for discussion about change in general in a particular business particularly if, say, each member of a Board of directors is asked to complete a pair of before-and-after change diagrams and these are then compared one with another. Often there will be considerable inconsistency in the results. There are many reasons for this, not least of which is the closeness of each director to one or more of the entities involved. Obviously sales and marketing directors will have a much closer interface to "customers" and "competitors" than a finance director. Similarly, the finance director is likely to have a closer relationship with "shareholders" and "environment", etc.

This type of diagrammatic exercise is not limited to the forces listed above. Many forces exist within businesses, and it can often be a useful exercise to utilise the same technique in order to gain a better understanding of how various people see the interaction of forces between various parts of the business. All that is required is to change the names of the entities involved to: marketing, finance, manufacturing, R & D, or whatever else is appropriate. Some of the results obtained can be quite intriguing. I remember carrying out this exercise with a business that proudly proclaimed that it was a "market-led business". Whilst you could be led to believe this was true if you read all the advertising material that the business put out or if you chose to read the Chairman's Annual Report, the real power resided in the R & D Division, according to 80% of the senior executives.

Chapter Eight

Choosing The Problem Solution

It is easy to understand how the wrong change mechanism can be chosen if mistakes are made in the problem identification process. However, even when the problem is well known, fully researched and accepted, still many mistakes are made during the course of choosing an appropriate solution. This can initially be quite baffling, as one would think that there cannot be many "right" solutions to choose from, and that choosing the wrong one is almost an impossibility.

The causes of misjudgments in the choice of a solution are numerous. Some are associated with issues discussed in the previous chapter and others involve aspects such as the need to be creative in finding a "correct" solution and the need to think about the longer-term effects of the proposed change. Therefore it is appropriate first to give due consideration to these before moving on to the task of selecting a suitable solution to the main problem or problems identified in Chapter Six. As with the positive definition of the problem, I have developed a methodology to assist in the positive identification of a solution. To this model I have given the name "The Well-formed Solution".

Creative Solutions

Before delving into the definition of a Well-formed Solution I would first like to introduce the concept of creative problem-solving. In a world where change is constantly accelerating and new ideas appear almost daily, being creative in what we do is now valued more highly than repeating existing, albeit well-founded, solutions. Indeed, progress is made only by breaking out of existing boundaries, and the best way of achieving this is by being creative. A short while ago I came across a book called *Breakthrough Thinking: The Seven Principles of Creative Problem Solving* (Nadler and Hibino, 1997) which covers the subject area extremely well. The authors have clearly committed a huge amount of effort into thoroughly researching the subject of developing creative methods for problem-solving. Much of their work and my own seem to run closely in parallel and, where they diverge, complementary to each another. I have little doubt that I have borrowed and used a few of their ideas in the course of my own consultancy work and some may even have found their way into this book.

Breakthrough Thinking presents many new and interesting ideas about change processes and has some excellent suggestions regarding successful problem-solving. Figure 11 provides the major headings under which most of the authors' ideas fall. The items in this list are reasonably self-explanatory and should be easy to comprehend. All have originated from the real-life experiences of the authors and the people they have studied, whom they perceive as excellent at being creative in the problem-solving role.

The concepts and ideas expressed in Figure 11 are directed at the whole area of problem solution. Some of these can also solve, or assist in solving, many of the other problems identified in Figure 1 (Causes of UK Management Failures). However, a word of caution. Many of Nadler and Hibino's ideas are largely conceptual in nature and do not provide effective solutions in themselves. Therefore they are not capable on their own of providing all the answers required to guarantee the positive identification of the correct solution to any given problem. Neither are they capable of solving all the problems that we identified in the Ecotech study. This is probably because Nadler and Hibino were concentrating their efforts on the more "creative" approaches to problem-solving. However, if you need to be creative in your work, I strongly recommend that you read their book.

Factors Involved in Defining the Right Solution

In the Ecotech study many of the difficulties encountered in the problem definition phase could also be identified as occurring during the selection of the problem solution. Among the most frequent problems encountered were those concerning "politics", "ownership", "boundary problems" and a tendency to revert to attempting to cure symptoms rather than causes. It was also common to find our old friend "generalisation" getting involved with solutions even when a "Well-formed Problem" had been defined.

Successful Problem-solving

The Seven Principles of Successful Problem Solvers

1. Every problem is unique. Trying to replicate a solution from a different environment may take longer than devising a solution that fits your environment.

2. Focus on the purpose (i.e. *why* questions) of solving the problem to broaden the range of possible solutions. It will also help to answer the question: "Are we solving the right problem?"

3. Think ahead to the solution-after-next.

4. Think of the problem as existing in a larger system which will need to be considered if the solution is to be effective.

5. Limit the amount of information necessary to solve the problem. Avoid being trapped in the endless quest for perfect data.

6. Involve the people who will implement the solution and/or will be affected by the solution as early as possible. Otherwise success is unlikely.

7. There is no such thing as a solution. It is only a step in a never-ending journey of continuous improvement. So plan to improve the solution before it's implemented. Fix things before they become a problem. Set a plan to move forward to the solution-after-next.

Nadler and Hibino (1997)

Figure 11

Politics is nearly always a difficult nut to crack unless there is strong leadership from high up in an organisation which overtly discourages it. Human nature being what it is, it should not be surprising to find people jockeying for position in any "change scenario" because often this is where the corporate limelight so frequently falls. Being involved with the management of change brings with it the opportunity to stand out from the crowd and also the chance to "win your spurs". It therefore forms a magnet for aspiring high-flyers just like bees around a honeypot. But do watch out – bees sting when they feel threatened and consultants can appear to be a threat in these situations.

Politics can also be the cause of some managers declining to accept responsibilities for problems within their own departments and seeking to lay the blame on others. However, when it comes to solutions everyone seems to want to have their say or to get involved in some way or other. This creates a different type of problem, particularly when there are several potential solutions. Choice is a wonderful thing, but making the right choice is never easy, except with hindsight. Some of what follows will assist in dealing with this type of problem, but the best advice I can give for dealing with the politics associated with problem-solution is to address it head on. Recognise it for what it is, "power broking", "jockeying for position" or whatever, and bring it out into the open and make sure it is resolved quickly.

When we compared successful with unsuccessful change programmes in the Ecotech study, one of the main differences that we noted was that the successful projects nearly always had a powerful champion who acted as mentor to the project overall. The word "powerful" usually implied someone very senior in the organisation, but not always. Sometimes the champion was a person who had charisma or was seen as a person to be respected either for their abilities or their potential. Having a powerful champion alone did not guarantee success but it clearly helped when projects ran into difficulties. It also stopped any unhelpful politicking from developing.

Ownership is very important and can overlap onto the issues surrounding the political ones. Recognition that the problem owner is not always the person who is best suited to be responsible for the problem solution is absolutely vital. In fact, in many instances the problem solution cannot be provided by the problem owner as this person may not have the skills or ability required for the task. Consequently, it is often sub-contracted to others who do possess the necessary skills.

Good examples of these abound and range from all sorts of specialist activities with new technology to fairly simple tasks which may involve people with specialist knowledge. Information Technology stands out as perhaps one of the most popular of today's subject areas to be sub-contracted to other agencies. However, in all cases there must always be someone who will own the solution after the sub-contractors have gone. This person or these people should be involved through all stages of the process, including solution selection, if success is to be achieved.

Boundary problems most frequently occur when the problem or the solution stretches across organisational boundaries. Problems with selection can occur here when there are multiple choices available. Setting up a good "project management" team or working party which is genuinely representative of all interests can assist in avoiding some of the common pitfalls associated with boundaries.

Generalisations and nominalisation occur everywhere, and the simple answer is to keep checking for them particularly when they involve any form of "action plan" or "selection criteria" that may be drawn up to assist in the process of selection. Once they are identified they must be tackled and removed, otherwise ambiguity will quickly creep in.

One of the most common arguments that spring up within organisations concerns whether the solution should be a "bespoke, home-built product" or an "off-the-peg packaged solution" tailored to the needs of the business. There are many arguments for and against either approach. Similarly, with more complex changes, issues as to whether external consultants should be employed or own staff should carry out the management of the process can occur. There are no simple clean-cut answers to these questions as there are so many factors and variables involved in making a choice. Chief amongst these are normally cost, internal skills available and the resources needed to complete the task. Ultimately the right choice can be arrived at only by balancing all the risks, opportunities, constraints and variables with extreme care.

Thinking Beyond the Current Solution

Finally, adopting a strategy of always thinking ahead to the solution-after-next can save considerable amounts of time and money in the future regardless of the complexity of the project. What comes next, after this change is complete, is a very important matter to consider – and vitally so if IT or any other new technology is involved. What may be today's most brilliant idea may be tomorrow's millstone, particularly if it limits a business's options for change at some point in the future. Always bear in mind that the market leaders in any sector of business and commerce are usually the ones who have the greatest number of options available to them, thus providing them with immense competitive advantage.

There are many thousands of examples to draw on to demonstrate what can occur when managements do not think ahead. One that springs to mind involved the advent of robotics in production processes in the late 1970s and early 1980s. In this period many Western manufacturing companies were desperately seeking ways to become more competitive in the face of competition from the Far East, and many chose robots as their means of salvation.

Short term the robots worked really well, by cutting labour costs very significantly, improving quality and increasing productivity, even though the capital cost in investment was high. However, those who rushed to use robots during the early stages of their development found that in the longer term the robots that they had acquired had very limited functionality. They were excellent at doing the original job for which they had been acquired but could not cope with changes to production methods which were introduced just a few years later. This left these companies in somewhat of a Catch-22 situation. On the one hand, they were locked into using their existing robots because the cost of the original investment had still not been fully recouped, while, on the other, they were locked out of newer technologies which would provide even lower unit costs.

The IT arena is full of such examples. One of the phrases coined by the computer industry in the early 1970s was "lock-in". "Lock-in" in IT jargon occurred when any company reached the point where it had invested so much with a particular vendor in the form of hardware and/or software that it simply could not afford to change suppliers. From the vendor's position this was obviously highly desirable, and most worked exceedingly hard to achieve this, even to the extent that they would give away hardware and software to achieve this objective. Thus, what on the surface appeared to be a simple decision to purchase and install maybe a package such as a relational database could have enormous ramifications a year or so down the line if for some reason a change was deemed necessary. Even worse scenarios occurred when the software vendor later chose to develop the package in ways that did not suit the customers and discontinued maintenance of the original product. The choice for the customer was to change the business to suit the needs of the new software, stay with out-dated software or change to another supplier. None of these options were readily acceptable.

Testing for Efficacy of a Proposed Solution

When we considered all the causes of failure associated with the selection of a solution, we decided that what was needed was a more prescriptive approach that would provide a test for the "best solution" capable of being applied to any given problem or set of problems. It became apparent that often when we had defined a Well-formed Problem there was more than one candidate "solution". The model would need to be capable of dealing with this.

A further requirement of the model was that it would also have to be capable of producing the right results on a consistent basis and also that it should be capable of testing any particular proposed solution for its efficacy in resolving a specific problem. This last factor was of great importance as so many of our study subject failures were due to the wrong solution being chosen. This is a key factor which is also supported by Nadler and Hibino (Figure 11).

Early in 1993 I had taken the idea of the "Well-formed Outcome" as applied to therapy and applied the underlying concepts to my own model for the "Well-formed Problem". As in NLP terms I was now seeking a Well-formed Outcome, it seemed logical to revisit the Meta-model to see if this could again further my cause. My original intention had been to produce a model which would be capable of solving all the remaining causes of failure identified in Figure 1.

Early results with the model when applied to real life were encouraging but not good enough to recommend to others. I had a feeling that using the Meta-model in this way was rather too random in its application and what I needed was something more rigid and structured. My model also failed to provide answers to all the problems identified in Figure 1, although it was forcing out information previously not recovered by more conventional means. The one area in which it excelled was in proving the potential efficacy of a selected problem solution. So I concentrated on developing this aspect first and based much of the work upon the standard NLP concept of the Well-formed Outcome. Persistence eventually paid off and by the end of 1993 I had whittled down my key questions to the ten which are identified in Figure 12 for this Well-formed Solution.

The prime inputs for this model are the identified Well-formed Problem and the Critical Success Factors, plus at a subsidiary level all input resulting from the other items covered in Chapter Seven including culture, human factors, external influences, etc. In nearly all the cases that I have dealt with since developing this technique, a desired solution has been identified before reaching this stage. However, no matter how convinced I have been as to the correctness of the chosen solution, this model has always provided a very necessary final quality-control check on the efficacy of the solution.

In the few instances where a solution was not clearly identified before commencing this stage it was because either several problems had been identified and a pause had occurred whilst prioritisation took place, or one problem had been identified but several solutions had been possible. In the former case, after the process of prioritisation had been completed each element was subjected to testing by the model, resulting in the selection of a solution. In the latter case, when the model was applied to all the candidate solutions, one solution stood out from the rest as the most appropriate.

The Well-formed Solution

1. What, specifically, do we want from this solution?

2. Why do we want this solution?

3. How will we know when we have achieved it?

4. What, if anything, is stopping us achieving an effective solution?

5. Under what circumstances, when and with whom, do we want this?

6. When we have achieved this, what else will improve?

7. Will anything be put at risk by achieving this?

8. Which of the resources that we already have can be used to help achieve this?

9. What new resources must we acquire in order to achieve this?

10. What is the first step that we need to take now in order to achieve this?

Figure 12

As with the Well-formed Problem questions, this new model also requires support from supplementary questions in order to obtain results of a sufficiently high grade. In most instances the initial answer to many of the questions resulted in answers containing our old enemies "generalisation" and "nominalisation". These, once challenged, produced more specific answers which were acceptable.

Question 1, "What specifically do we want from this solution?", can produce some really interesting but sometimes unexpected answers. It seems to encourage people to explore their own personal requirements from the solution rather than expressing the "corporate line" or what they think would be expected of them, for instance, "I would prefer x, but everyone else wants y." In one or two instances this has led to the discovery of something of considerable value that was previously unknown about the problem or the proposed solution. However, ultimately I would be expecting an answer that would be a clear and concise statement about how the chosen solution would resolve the previously identified problem.

Question 2, "Why do we want this solution?", involves a little covert psychology as, in order to consider the merits of the chosen solution, comparisons need to be made to other possible solutions. Ultimately, this question should be answered with a strong statement such as, "Because this is the only right solution to our problem". If, instead, we get answers such as, "It is the only one we can afford," or, "Because the Finance Director says it's right," then something is wrong with the chosen solution and it is not likely to solve the problem!

Question 3, "How will we know when we have achieved the solution?", should produce an answer which directly relates to a CSF defined earlier in the process. If it does not, then the process of defining the CSFs has not been completed adequately and this must be addressed before proceeding further.

Question 4, "What, if anything, is stopping us from achieving this solution?", should produce an answer of "nothing" or some such equivalent expression. If it produces any other answer then the alarm bells should immediately start ringing and further investigation is required. However, do not be surprised to find subsidiary issues surfacing as a result of asking this question. These may prove to be just a diversion or they may have content that should not be ignored. The most common reservation expressed here has been concern about resources allocated to the project. This may relate to any aspect of resourcing, from the numbers and quality of the staff employed to the finances allocated to the project. Concerns of this nature need to be actively addressed, otherwise the solution, whilst being the correct choice, may be doomed to failure before it starts!

Question 5, "Under what circumstances, when and with whom, do we want this?", includes the "under what circumstances" part of the question to bring out any "environmental" issues which may have previously not been addressed. Supplementary questions can also be asked about effects upon the other forces acting on the business such as staff, suppliers, shareholders, etc. In large organisations the question can be useful in identifying other elements of the business that may be affected by the proposed change.

Question 6, "When we have achieved this solution, what else will improve?", is associated with the concepts of "moving away from" and "moving towards" discussed in Chapter Seven.

Question 7, "Will anything be put at risk by achieving this solution?", makes it possible, even at a late stage, for some really important issue to surface which could otherwise form a road block to further progress or even stop the project altogether. Often, initial answers to this question are vague, e.g. "Well, no, not really". Such answers should be challenged until the real concern has surfaced and been addressed. Supplementary questions such as, "Is there anything that we are doing now that we will not be doing after the change which will adversely affect the business?" are useful in forcing out items that have been forgotten.

Question 8, "Which of the resources that we already have can be used to help achieve this solution?", is a question intended to identify any hidden resources that have not been previously identified. I have often been surprised to find people coming forward with valuable suggestions at this stage which are of real practical value.

Question 9, "What new resources must we acquire in order to achieve this solution?", is of course virtually the inverse of the previous question and again often produces valuable information not previously identified. Common among these are skills that have to be acquired or developed but may have been overlooked in setting the CSFs associated with the training task. Occasionally it can involve the acquisition of new assets which may not have been identified with appropriate CSFs.

Question 10, "What is the first step that we need to take now in order to achieve this solution?", may appear to be the most obvious question to answer, provided that all the previous questions have been answered satisfactorily. However, the project still has to be initiated by someone, funding has to be approved, etc., and there will undoubtedly be many tasks associated with the commencement of the project that need to be completed. All these steps should be identified and planned for. A project that gets off to a faltering start requires a disproportionate amount of effort to get it up to speed, compared with a project that starts in a planned and controlled manner.

It is normal for iteration to occur through the process of obtaining satisfactory answers to all these questions. Quite often it will be necessary to loop back to change or revise such elements as CSFs or to revisit other items or issues that have been covered at an earlier stage. When this occurs it is important to ensure that this will not create a knock-on effect causing possible revisions to answers already obtained to earlier questions. If this does occur then these too must be taken into account.

When sound answers are obtained to all the questions there is a very high degree of certainty that the correct solution has been chosen. The project will have a strong foundation from the start and, provided it is given the necessary resources and is well managed throughout the remaining stages of the project life-cycle, success should follow.

The output from applying the tests provided by the Well-formed Solution model is intended as a powerful motivational force towards new thinking. Often when the model questions are applied they encourage people to consider other possibilities and this then leads them to changing their views about what might prove to be a "best fit" solution. This can be very useful when someone has become entrenched in their views and resistant to new thinking.

Occasionally the model will throw up a total "show-stopper" that kills any idea of using a particular solution. More often the model produces a long list of "difficulties" if the first chosen change programme were to be implemented. In these circumstances most executives will usually search for another solution with fewer "difficulties" rather than stay with their original choice. This is simply because the Change Management task will be perceived as easier to manage and consequently possess a lower potential risk of failure. However, this does not necessarily mean the right choice has been made just because fewer difficulties have been identified with one solution rather than another. The fact that a large number of difficulties has been identified is often just a further indicator of the overall size or complexity of the problem which will need to be overcome. Obviously, if there genuinely are too many difficulties present to deal with in one project, it makes perfectly good sense to break the tasks down into more manageable chunks or sub-projects until they do become manageable.

Often it is possible to identify the same "difficulties" occurring regardless of the choice of solution. Often these common difficulties can be easily identified as they often form "clusters" when the completed Well-formed Solution sheets have been analysed and collated. When this occurs it is a clear warning that the difficulty or difficulties must be resolved prior to attempting to implement any of the proposed solutions. Perhaps the most common of these "difficulties" involves finance for the project. Often businesses will attempt to "scope" a Change Management programme in terms of time, money and resources required long before it knows all the facts needed to come to firm conclusions about what is needed. These constraints then provide a straitjacket to what can be expended on the project often in association with a fixed timescale. This is not a very sensible thing to do as almost always the budgets are set too low and the time allowed to effectively complete the project life-cycle far too short.

In some perverse manner, setting financial limits at a low level early in the project life-cycle is nearly always an attempt to stop over-runs on budgets at a later stage. Of course there has to be a limit to what can be expended, and a pragmatic approach coupled to accurate costing is a vital part of any Change Management project. In some instances projects have to be scaled down to fit the finances available but this should be done only when all the facts are available and carried out in a well-researched and controlled manner.

Similarly, setting over-optimistic and inflexible time constraints too early in the project life-cycle can also contribute to the creation of major problems. Again, sometimes these cannot be avoided as the time scale may be a critical factor in the whole process. Should this be the case, it is wise to carry out a full risk-management assessment which is accepted by all concerned prior to full commitment being made.

This completes all the phases of a Change Management project up to the point of project initiation. There are many project management techniques available to support the effective management and control of projects through the remaining phases of their life-cycle. Selection of the right one will depend upon many factors including the nature of the project itself and its size and complexity. Although this book is not intended to delve into the subject of project management, many of the tests applied to the selection of a problem solution can also be applied to the selection of an appropriate Change Management control tool.

In the case of the XYZ Company the model questions were used to test the validity of the chosen solution. This was achieved in individual meetings with each of the Main Board Directors and other senior staff. These meetings produced a large amount of detailed information which I collated into a concise report and presented to the CEO. Overall, the result was a positive endorsement of the proposed solution, which was to embark on a complete and radical overhaul of all of the company's business systems. This was intended to encompass the restructuring of many of the existing business units within the group as well as the supporting IT systems and the rest of the supporting infrastructure. However, in the course of establishing this solution, a number of other issues arose which also needed to be resolved. Some of the more complex of these are dealt with in Chapter Nine where I deal with conflict resolution.

Among the many uncontentious examples was one concerning the original decision to split the overall task into two separate projects, one dealing with the problem of "poor management information" and the other with "low productivity in the UK". In the former it had been found that the major cause of the problem was chronic incompatibilities in the existing IT systems and an almost total lack of common data standards across the group. Much of the focus on solving this problem, it was agreed, would be placed on overhauling the group's IT systems and the establishment of common data standards. In the latter project it had been identified that there was the need to solve problems associated with information-flows as a key CSF. This would normally be a classic recipe for creating boundary problems. However, in this case the problem of ownership had been recognised at an early stage, and it was decided by the mutual agreement of all those concerned to sub-contract responsibility for solving this to the "poor management information" project. However, it was not until a later meeting with the Group Manufacturing Director to discuss the Well-formed Solution that he noticed that no CSF had been identified for this activity in the "poor management information" project.

This in itself presented no great problem but it did require that a definition of the CSF should be agreed with the "low productivity in the UK" project and its formal inclusion within this project. This was clearly a case of something "falling between the cracks" and being subsequently revealed by the model questions. However, this is not the prime purpose of the model and it should not be relied upon to perform this function.

As mentioned earlier, the process of obtaining answers to the model questions also caused a number of conflicting views to surface between the different parts of the group. Some of these were "political" in nature and could have presaged some sort of impending "turf war" if not controlled quickly. I felt this matter to be of sufficient concern that I recommended that the CEO chair a meeting to resolve this and a few other problematic issues. The techniques involved in this process are discussed in detail in Chapter Nine.

After some weeks, with all outstanding issues resolved at a meeting of the Board, the project was "signed off" by the Main Board members, and the really hard work commenced in initiating the project. Three years later the group had an up-to-date, fully integrated Management Information system in place which was able to provide the type and quality of information that the CEO had only dreamt about when the project first started. The project itself had formed a catalyst for the rejuvenation of the group as a whole, which in turn had resulted in the restructuring of many of the business units. Turnover and profit had risen significantly as had market share in the UK. Staff morale was estimated as being higher than at any time in the previous twenty years, and this was reflected in high levels of productivity which were the envy of their competitors.

Not all the credit for these factors should be attributed to the project as, whilst it was in progress, the UK emerged from recession, providing some of the stimulus for growth. Clearly a major factor in the project's success was the strong leadership and management provided from the very top of the Company. Without this the project could have easily stalled or failed altogether. However, recently I have canvassed opinion from several of the senior executives who were involved. All are convinced that the strong platform upon which the project was initially founded was the major contributor to success.

The example of the XYZ Company was no different in many respects from other Change Management projects that I have been associated with, except in the chosen solution. From the above it may not be totally clear as to how the Company arrived at the decision to solve its immediate problems by overhauling its business and information systems. In fact, it was the lack of modern integrated systems that was holding the company back. Every other candidate solution to the Company's problems required a solid foundation of good, reliable and integrated information flows if these solutions were to be effective. Without the supporting infrastructure provided by fully functioning IT systems they would almost certainly have been doomed to failure. In all cases when these competing solutions were tested against the criteria expounded in this chapter, everything pointed to the need for high quality IT systems. At an early stage in this process the majority of the directors agreed that this was the only viable solution. They also recognised that the "low productivity in the UK" problem was exacerbated by the considerable incompatibilities between the Marketing and Manufacturing IT systems.

Summary

The XYZ Company is not unique in its experiences. Many businesses have faced similar problems and, using the Change Management techniques detailed in this book, have also had highly successful outcomes to their projects.

When presenting the case study represented by the XYZ Company I am occasionally challenged by a member of my audience who claims that the techniques involved are like "taking a sledgehammer to crack a nut". This is not a view I share, nor is it the view of a number of senior executive officers who contributed much of the content of the case study through their joint personal experiences. All too often in business "quick fixes" are applied to a perceived problem, and it is realised only afterwards that the fix chosen fixed only the symptoms and not the underlying cause.

None of the developments discussed in the last few chapters would have been possible if other people had not made mistakes. All the methodology in this section of the book is based upon the learning that others have experienced in getting their Change Management programmes wrong.

My own experience suggests that we can learn much from observing excellence in others and that we learn even more by observing others not doing so well. These are factors that are often overlooked in this age when it has become fashionable to attempt to replicate others' success by simply copying rather than by the more traditional methods of careful evaluation and establishing what will not work.

Most human behaviour is based upon a mixture of copying and trial and error. This can be seen in the progress that a small child makes in first learning to stand up and then learning to walk. Most of the copying takes place by the child observing the behaviours of its parents and other humans. However, no child has ever learned to walk by observation alone because standing up and walking can be learned only experientially. He or she can find out about the art of balancing only by trial and error.

As far as I am aware nothing changes in this process throughout the rest of our lives. First we observe, then, after a process of evaluation (usually based upon our past experience represented by our internal maps of reality), we attempt to repeat the process. We then evaluate the result by comparing our achievement against our desired outcome, continually modifying our behaviour until we are content with the result we obtain or we give up and do something else.

It should also be remembered that copying brings with it many problems of its own creation. When we copy there is always a danger that we will not copy only the desirable elements but we may also unwittingly copy some unwanted traits as well. I am not aware of any technique that can with any degree of certainty avoid this happening. Personal experience is always involved, and this again brings us back to trial and error.

The techniques detailed in this book should therefore be looked upon as being made up of a number of models based upon trial and error rather than copying. They have been designed to weed out the many errors made by businesses and set them on a tried and tested path to success in Change Management.

Over the last ten or so years I have started the vast majority of my presentations with the following quotation:

> *The reasonable man adapts himself to the world: the unreasonable man persists in trying to adapt the world to himself. Therefore, all progress depends on the unreasonable man.*
>
> *George Bernard Shaw (1903)*

It is noticeable that those who are deemed to be most successful in the art of Change Management are not those to whom the term "reasonable" would readily be ascribed. In fact, many successful Change Managers are among the most difficult people to understand, as they persist in constantly checking and testing the boundaries of normality. Thus, perhaps, George Bernard Shaw's little homily contains more than an essence of truth. There can be no doubt that all the members of the Ecotech study group would comfortably wear the cap of the unreasonable man.

Chapter Nine

Resolving Conflict
And
Aligning Attitudes
And
Beliefs

The previous two chapters of this book have concentrated on the methodologies for positive identification of the problem or problems and the process of evaluating possible solutions. To a large extent the issues of resolving internal conflict have not been fully addressed, nor have the methods involved in aligning attitudes in support of a common cause. Mention has been made of "politics", "human factors" and other issues which do give rise to conflict in organisations, and suggestions have been offered both for their avoidance in the first instance and for controlling them in the event of their arising during a project. However, conflict is rarely far away in any Change Management project simply because few people (including many senior executives) really like making changes other than those of the slow, evolutionary type. Therefore a discussion of these issues, plus some pertinent pointers towards controlling them successfully, would seem appropriate at this point.

There is a considerable amount of evidence available to support the hypothesis that in general the more radical the proposed changes within an organisation the more likely it is that there will be resistance to them. Most people, be they senior executive or manual worker, are wary of change in any form, as it inevitably creates some degree of uncertainty. When people become sufficiently uncertain about their status or their future prospects within an organisation there is an increasing likelihood that they will either seek alternative employment or become uncooperative or, in the worst instances, disruptive. Thus during all Change Management projects, avoiding creating unnecessary uncertainty must feature high on the list of the Change Manager's priorities. Having a mechanism available to monitor levels of uncertainty and disaffection throughout the project life-cycle can assist in identifying them and provide an opportunity to address them before they become a major disruptive influence.

It is worth recognising that uncertainty affects all employees. However, whereas more junior staff will often express their concerns collectively through a Trade Union or other representative body, more senior staff can present the greatest threat to any Change Management project. This is largely because of their status and their ability to use their personal power to create obstructions and diversions. Occasionally they can also create disaffection in their staff towards the change agents, and, if there is a high level of loyalty present in the staff towards their leader, this can generate a major road-block to progress.

Although resistance to change, sabotage and other disruptive behaviours were not mentioned as prime causes of failure in the Change Management projects analysed in the Ecotech study, there was considerable evidence to suggest that these factors were present in many of the failures examined. Conversely there was little evidence of this occurring in successful projects, although occasionally mention was made of the extra efforts that had needed to be committed to limit the development of such behaviours.

This chapter is about these vital factors and recounts the various stages where conflict was identified and dealt with in the example of the XYZ Company. Figure 8 (Main Board Members' Preferred Change Programmes) displays the preferred solution(s) championed by each of the Main Board members of the XYZ Company. These had been identified at a Board meeting held two months prior to the commencement of my team's involvement with the Company.

All the directors at that time were fully aware that the Company had a number of serious problems which needed urgent attention and most of these are identified in Figure 3 (The Multiple Cause

Diagram). However, each director held separate views as to the causes of the problems and consequently came to different conclusions as to what needed to be done to correct them. Whilst some directors had proposed using more than one change mechanism, the important factor here is that there was an almost complete lack of consensus about the most suitable solution. In fact the only things they all agreed about were that the Company urgently needed to improve profitability and regenerate growth across the whole of the group.

After my team had become involved and we had produced the results from conducting the Well-formed Problem exercise, most of the directors dropped their original suggestions and assisted in a search for an appropriate solution. However, two directors still wanted to implement their own proposed solutions and dug in their heels over the issue. This is not untypical of such situations and particularly so where there are many potential causes or more than one possible solution. One significant cause may be when individuals believe that if they do not succeed in getting their own way their credibility may somehow be damaged.

My original intention when formulating the Well-formed Solution model was to construct it in such a way that it would take the guesswork out of situations like this and also hopefully be capable of deducing the "only" right solution. However, it was never likely to work effectively because human beings frequently make their choices based upon personal preference and not upon a systematic approach, never mind a logical one. Personal preferences should never be ignored or cast aside as irrelevant, as they often represent the stored knowledge of an individual built up over many years. Sometimes the information possessed by such individuals is extremely valuable and, if lost, irreplaceable. To demonstrate this I will quote a story from Steve Andreas:

> *There is an old story of a boiler-maker who was hired to fix a huge steamship boiler system that was not working well. After listening to the engineer's description of the problems and asking a few questions, he went to the boiler room. He looked at the maze of pipes, listened to the thump of the boiler and the hiss of escaping steam for a few minutes, and felt some pipes with his hands. Then he hummed*

softly to himself, reached into his overalls and took out a small hammer, and tapped a bright red valve, once. Immediately the entire system began working perfectly, and the boiler-maker went home.

When the steamship owner received a bill for $1,000 he complained that the boiler-maker had only been in the engine room for fifteen minutes, and requested an itemised bill. This is what the boiler-maker sent him:

For tapping with hammer:	$ .50
For knowing where to tap:	$999.50
Total	$1,000.00

Bandler and Grinder (1979)

In my business career I have unfortunately come across many instances where a business has fired someone loosely equivalent to the boiler-maker because they believed the person concerned was an anachronism in the "new organisation". Then subsequently the business was forced to spend large amounts of money trying to replicate his skills or hire a replacement.

There is another powerful reason for not overruling personal preference. This involves avoiding the cause of many failures highlighted earlier as item 5 of Figure 1: "Not developing a **genuine** 'shared vision' by all those involved in the change process". Human nature being what it is, if a person is overruled about their views as to the appropriateness of a particular solution, they are not likely to willingly accept someone else's "vision" of how things should be changed. Conflict in these circumstances is not uncommon and, when it occurs, poses a serious risk. This is particularly so if the conflict is not resolved rapidly, as it can then have a knock-on effect and create problems infinitely larger than the original causal problem. Similarly, unresolved problems can, in time, lead to acute polarisation over the issues involved, which makes them even more difficult to resolve.

In the case of the XYZ Company the only person who could have forced through his proposed solutions was the Chief Executive.

However, he would have needed to adopt an autocratic or dicta-torial stance in order to achieve his goal, and this was not his nor-mal way of managing the business; his style was that of a team leader. Had he attempted to be autocratic he would almost cer-tainly have caused a great deal of alienation among his co-direc-tors and destroyed the already fragile "team spirit" that existed on the Board. Whilst he was prepared if all else failed to dictate a solution, if a consensus could not be obtained at this stage, his preference was to spend more time and effort on trying to obtain agreement with the majority.

During the Problem Definition phase the CEO had recognised that there was already a major difference of opinion beginning to develop between the Marketing and Manufacturing Directors individually, and among the rest of the Board as a whole, as to the appropriate way forward. These two directors had both already shown some degree of resentment at my team's involvement in identifying the underlying problems and had been reluctant to co-operate fully with the study. Both directors claimed that they knew all the answers and that they did not need outside help on these matters. They were also pushing very hard for their own preferred solutions and had involved their staff in actively cam-paigning for their implementation.

The CEO was extremely worried by these events and was con-cerned that the Marketing Director might resign if he was not able to obtain agreement to the implementation of TQM. Whilst he did not feel that the Manufacturing Director would resign over the non-implementation of MRPII he felt he had the potential to be highly disruptive. At this stage the CEO was already con-vinced that no progress was going to be made by the group as a whole if it was not able to update its information systems as a first priority. He also saw this as such a major exercise that it would inevitably absorb significant amounts of management effort over the next two years, leaving barely enough resources for the business to continue being run effectively. He was there-fore not prepared to countenance starting any other projects before the new IT systems were fully bedded in.

After seeking my advice on these very important issues he decid-ed to shift the emphasis from discussion about localised issues to more global matters. This gave rise to what became known as the "Pan-European Vision". The further development of this theme and its wider promulgation eventually led to its becoming the Number One CSF. The CEO had come to this conclusion as a result of reviewing the overall situation and setting a number of parameters upon which he wished to build his vision of the future.

First he felt he had to find a method for binding together all the members of the Board around a common purpose and heading off a potential battle between the two rebellious directors. This comes back to developing a "common vision" on which everyone can willingly agree. In situations where conflict already exists or is likely to break out, it pays to establish a common denominator upon which all parties are certain to concur. At the highest level, agreement can be reached on a phrase such as "the survival of the business" or some other generalised expression of a similar nature. In practice, no matter how dire the situation, a lower-level statement can usually be established which is more focused and about which consensus can be obtained. With this in mind the CEO set out to develop a high-level vision of a fully integrated business working in harmony across the whole of the EU. This he felt sure would not give rise to any objections in principal, and he gave it the name "The Pan-European Vision".

The process of moving up from lower levels of detail to higher levels is referred to in NLP jargon as "chunking up". The opposite process of moving from a higher level to a lower one is known as "chunking down". The latter is particularly useful when dealing with large or complex problems by reducing them to their component parts. This is often reinforced by the old joke, "How do you eat an elephant?" Reply, "One bite at a time".

To return to the XYZ Company, initially the "Vision", as it became known, was simply a series of statements of intent rather than a precise action plan. At the highest level a new mission statement was developed which expressed a commitment to be judged "best in class" by the customers, shareholders and employees within three years. This was supported by statements concerning a need for retraining at all levels within the Company and the setting of targets for performance in all aspects of the business. Up to this point there were no dissenters on the Board, and the concept was quickly accepted as the basis for the future strategic development of the group.

By this stage the Well-formed Problems had been defined, and agreement had been reached on the Critical Success Factors listed in Figure 7. However, this formed only part of the "Vision" and was considered by both the Marketing and Manufacturing Directors as purely an enabling exercise before they could implement their own proposed "changes". With this in mind the CEO felt that considerable effort needed to be placed on ranking all the subsidiary problems in order of importance and establishing a timetable to resolve them, thus leaving no doubt as to his intentions or what he considered should be the order of priorities for several years into the future.

Finally, he felt that serious consideration should always be given to thinking ahead to the "solution-after-next" in order to avoid creating potential road-blocks to future progress (item 3, Figure 11). His insistence on this approach was extremely valuable in overcoming many of the arguments being put forward by the Marketing and Manufacturing Directors for early implementation of their proposals. However, he assured both directors that he viewed the issues of quality and productivity as having a high priority, and they were added to the list of problems requiring resolution.

In all situations like this the task is not to force the key decision-makers to change their minds but to open up their minds to other possibilities or to view the problems from a different perspective. Some of the questions contained in the Well-formed Solution model are designed to assist in this respect by querying the validity of unsound arguments and forcing consideration of wider issues.

NLP Techniques which Assist in Resolving Conflict and Increasing Understanding

There are several techniques derived from NLP that are specifically aimed at assisting us in these important areas. However, in order for the following techniques to work really well, the development and maintenance of a high degree of rapport with the person or persons involved will be required throughout the process. Meta-model questions will also be required in order to challenge generalisations, nominalisations and other linguistic violations that will almost certainly arise.

Reframing

Although one of the seminal works on NLP has the title *Reframing*, this technique was in widespread use in many psychotherapeutic settings well before NLP was invented. There are many different variations of reframing currently in use, and some of these have different names such as "redefining" or "relabelling". However, they all have the same basic principle at their core and similar methods of application.

The purpose of reframing is to enable a client to view something from a different standpoint and by so doing to change their original attitude to something. This is perhaps best demonstrated by quoting an example involving Leslie Cameron-Bandler (a brilliant therapist and the first wife of Richard Bandler) who was working with a woman who suffered from obsessive-compulsive disorder. In her case she was continually cleaning the house even down to dusting all the light bulbs at least once a day. Her family, husband and three children, coped with this reasonably well except in regard to her constant attempts to care for the carpet. She spent much of her time trying to get other members of the family not to walk on it, because they left footprints – not mud or dirt, just dents in the pile.

Whenever the woman saw a dent in the pile of the carpet she would rush off and get the vacuum cleaner and immediately clean the carpet vigorously. As a consequence she was vacuuming the carpet many times a day and this gave rise to some fearful rows. Leslie asked the woman about her behaviour and discovered that she never felt the need to clean other people's carpets. She also discovered that when the family rented a house for a holiday she behaved quite normally and showed no great desire to clean the carpet.

Leslie considered all the information that she had obtained and asked the woman to close her eyes and imagine that she could see the carpet with not a single mark anywhere. The woman obeyed and sat with her eyes closed with a beaming smile on her face. Then Leslie said, "… and realise fully that that means you are totally alone, and that the people you care for and love are nowhere around". The woman's expression shifted radically, and she felt terrible! Then Leslie said, "Now, put a few footprints there and look at those footprints and know that the people you care most about in the world are nearby." Instantly the woman felt fine again, and her problem with dents in the carpet disappeared from that moment on!

Leslie had realised that much of this woman's unwanted behaviour in regard to the carpet was connected to her beliefs about possession or ownership. She also recognised that the woman would be most likely to value her other possession, "family", as of more value than a carpet without dents in the pile. By encouraging the woman to recognise that a permanently dent-free carpet was mutually exclusive of the presence of her family, she was forced to choose between the two alternatives. She chose her family.

This is an example of reframing in a therapeutic setting. In the above example it is important to recognise that the stimulus in the world (dents in the carpet) does not change; only the meaning of it is changed or reframed. The rules of reframing stay virtually the same when applied to the business world or to any other area for that matter. The objective is to obtain a different response to a given stimulus, not to change, delete or alter the stimulus.

The simplest method for offering a change to a given stimulus is to ask questions. Questions such as, "How would it be if you did x instead of y?" or "What would have to change to allow you to do things differently?" are powerful levers towards creating new frames of reference and therefore new ways of thinking.

A slightly different way of thinking about framing is to recognise that, without a frame, you have no meaning. Therefore, meaning is wholly dependent upon the frame it is put in. Consequently, changing the frame will nearly always change the meaning in some way.

Taking this concept slightly further, NLP defines a number of key frames that are termed "As If" frames. In the business setting there are four "As If" frames that work consistently well in many different situations. These are:

Time Switching: Ask the person you are working with, or indeed a whole group of people, to pretend that they are at some period in the future, say, six months. Then ask them to look back and ask themselves, "What steps did I take to resolve this particular problem?"

Person Switching: Ask the question, "If you could become any other person, who would you become, and how would he/she solve this problem?"

Information Switching: Ask the question, "Let's suppose that you had all the information you needed, then what do you suppose would happen?"

Function Switching: Ask the question, "Just pretend that you could change any part of the situation, what would happen then?"

The "As If" frame provides a valuable tool when dealing with people who are resistant to change. Pretending does not usually create anything like as threatening an environment as when we face real change. Consequently, as much of the threat is removed by pretending, people's minds become open to new opportunities and choices and less concerned about possible threats or their own perceived weaknesses.

There is a famous story told about Tom Watson, the founder of IBM. One of his employees made a mistake which caused the company to loose $10 million. Having admitted to being responsible the employee said to Watson, "I suppose I have no choice but to resign before you fire me." Watson looked him straight in the eye and said, "Are you kidding? We just spent ten million dollars giving you an education". This is an excellent example of reframing. In two short sentences Watson had shifted the frame from "blaming" to that of "empowering" and in the process probably created his most loyal employee.

Logical Level Alignment

"Chunking down" and "chunking up" are useful to obtain a better understanding of something by either viewing it in its component form or on a more global scale, seeing the big picture. However, there are other useful ways of thinking, and within NLP one of these is known by the term "Logical Levels". In fact a better term would be "Neuro-logical Levels" because it has more to do with the way in which our thinking processes function than anything else. The concepts that lie behind this technique were originally developed in the 1950s and 60s by various individuals including Koestler (1964), and Hall and Fagin (1956). The latter two played a major role in the development of systems theory. However, it was left to Gregory Bateson (1968) to develop these concepts into a form that provided them with both a structure and meaning. Bateson had a considerable influence upon the early development of NLP, and subsequently a number of Bateson's ideas, including those on Logical Levels, were taken up and further refined by Robert Dilts (1980).

It is worth mentioning that there are many other similar techniques which could be applied, most of which have been derived from psychotherapeutic applications. All these techniques are concerned with ensuring that communication and understanding are occurring at an appropriate level within a given hierarchy and that the resulting communication is of the highest quality. Perhaps the closest comparison to Logical Levels which has been in widespread use for some time within the business world is Transactional Analysis (TA). This subject was originally pioneered as a psychotherapeutic tool by Dr Eric Berne in Northern California (the birthplace of NLP) in the 1950s. However, Berne is perhaps best known to the general public for his very accessible work, *The Games People Play* (1964). This book when first published became an overnight bestseller and remained so for nearly a decade after its first launch. To this day it can still be found on bookstands around the world in many different languages.

In TA the conceptual communications hierarchy is divided into three main categories: Parent, Adult and Child. We are all aware that conversations between an adult and a child are different from those between an adult and an adult and a parent and a parent. However, the communication aspects of TA in the main focuses on what is known as crossed communications, or communications between people which are not appropriate. It is also a methodology for recognition of malformed communication and a means for correction.

So whilst it is okay for a parent to communicate with a four-year-old child in a parent to child manner, if the same words, intonation, inflection and body language were used by the parent with another parent, the most likely response would be something like, "Don't treat me like a child". In this instance it is highly unlikely that the first parent would get the results that they were seeking. However, if they changed their style of communication to that of adult to adult or parent to parent then the probability of success would be much higher. Unfortunately we all make mistakes on a regular basis with the way we communicate, in the business world as well as in every other aspect of our lives. People more often resent being "talked down to" than anything else, although there are many occasions in business as well as in the rest of our lives where it may be appropriate to "talk down". The only question is: are we talking down from a position of parent to adult or parent to child or adult to child? It is almost a certainty that only one of the three possibilities will be appropriate.

Therefore the highest quality of communication is only likely to occur at a level which is appropriate to the needs of the participants. In the past, when businesses operated within the classic steep pyramid structure with many layers of management, one of the most significant causes of industrial strife was miscommunication between workers and their unions and the management that controlled them. All too frequently the workers were treated more like children than adults by managers who thought they "knew better" and adopted the role of parents. In many instances the workers began to react like children and withdrew their labour (sulked) whilst the management behaved more and more like frustrated parents and issued more and more threats on an escalating scale. Finally, when both sides had had enough of playing this silly game they came together and both sides started talking like adults. Only then could order be restored.

Perhaps the biggest gift that TA gave us is the realisation that we all have the ability to communicate on different levels according to how we perceive the person with whom we are communicating. TA has also made us aware that we are all very good at choosing the wrong communication levels some of the time. The Logical Levels notion has many similarities to TA in that it addresses the same issues but in a more detailed manner.

Logical Levels encompass a large and fascinating area, and several books have been devoted almost exclusively to the exploration of the subject. Other newer developments have also resulted from the further exploration of the subject in conjunction with other techniques. However, it is not my intention to delve too deeply into the subject but simply to make use of some of the concepts contained within it which I have found useful in resolving conflict associated with change within organisations.

At its simplest, the theory of Logical Levels defines a number of levels of human understanding which influence our thinking and therefore also influence our behaviour towards the world around us. Gregory Bateson noticed that, in the processes of learning, change and communication, natural hierarchies exist. Bateson asserted that the function of each of the levels within the hierarchy was to organise the next level below. He noticed that the rules for changing something on one level were different from those for changing something at a lower level. He also noticed that changing something on a lower level could, but would not necessarily, affect the upper levels. However, changing something on an upper level would always require change on the lower levels in order to support the higher-level change. Bateson noted that it was often confusion of the Logical Levels that was the cause of problems involving change in groups of individuals and that this confusion also lay at the root of many communications problems between individuals. He also noted that extrapolating the methods for change from a higher level to a lower one was nearly always a recipe for creating major problems.

Many schematic diagrams exist which are intended to demonstrate the concepts of Logical Levels including those in this book, and most of these originate from the work of Robert Dilts (1996). Figure 13 provides a basic diagram demonstrating the typical structure of the Logical Levels which exist within an individual working in a business setting.

At the highest level defined in Figure 13 is the term "Universe". This is intended to encompass everything that exists, including us. More or less at the middle level we find "Identity", and this may be seen as the core of our individual personality or the level at which we operate in the world about us. The lowest level is "Environment", which represents the external influences that act upon us and our businesses. These act as external constraints over the choices we make and are factors over which we have very little influence or control. These include the laws of the country, government, geography, weather and other such factors that have a direct bearing on us as individuals. We each interact with the "Environment" through our "Behaviour". In a business setting these can be seen as extending to other factors over which we have little control, such as our customers or our suppliers. Ranged between these points are a number of other positions.

The levels that exist above "Identity" are those which form a component of a larger entity, whilst those below "Identity" are the composite parts that contribute to making us the people we are. Therefore our "Identity" is largely defined by our "Beliefs" about the world around us. Our "Beliefs" are in turn influenced by our personal "Capabilities", and these are in turn influenced by our "Behaviour" which in turn is generated by the "Environment" in which we operate. Moving up the levels takes us first to "Department" or "Division", although this can be interpreted as the lowest level at which we exist in an organisation. Next is the "Organisation" itself, and then there are higher levels that we can determine if we wish. For example I have chosen "Planet", but it could be expressed as "Country", "Market Segment" or some other level of significance as appropriate.

Logical Levels

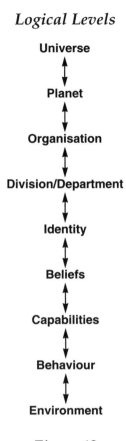

Universe

↕

Planet

↕

Organisation

↕

Division/Department

↕

Identity

↕

Beliefs

↕

Capabilities

↕

Behaviour

↕

Environment

Figure 13

There is of course an inverse to the previous paragraph in that if we have a change at the "Environment" level it may require a change in "Behaviour", which in turn may require a change in "Capabilities" which in turn may require a change in "Beliefs" and so on. However, what we cannot have is a leap up the levels in the form of a change at the "Environment" level requiring a change in "Identity" without first making the necessary changes in the lower levels of "Beliefs", "Capabilities" and "Behaviour". Making the mistake of attempting to leapfrog up or down levels is a significant and common cause of strife in Change Management projects.

Organisations operate in a similar manner, and no two organisations share the same identity, although they may have some attributes which are similar if they are operating in the same or a similar environment. However, the more "different" organisations are, the more they will not have in common, e.g. a steel-maker and a stockbroker. Even so, both organisations will have many things in common because of the needs of the law, government controls, etc. Structurally they will also have to run accounting systems, HR functions, IT, etc., which will have only superficial differences. In fact the amount of difference between organisations is often more to do with the culture and skills employed in the business than with the methods used to manage and control it. Thus the hierarchy of Logical Levels of nearly all businesses tends to be very similar regardless of the nature of the business, the market it operates in, and its mission. However, the content of this hierarchy will almost certainly be unique.

When we take a high-level view of a business we are in fact looking at a system. The system will be composed of many "hard" entities such as assets, computer systems, management structures, etc. Also alongside and directly coupled to the hard entities are soft entities (culture, skills and capabilities) which facilitate the operation of the hard entities. These soft entities most often map closely onto the elements within Logical Levels. The high level or corporate system will have embedded within it other subsystems, each of which may in turn have other subsystems, and so on, within a hierarchy. In an industrial organisation such as the XYZ Company one would expect to find a number of different operating divisions such as Sales, Manufacturing, Finance, R & D, Administration and HR, which would be operating specialised subsystems made up of hard and soft entities directly associated with their method of working but communicating with the systems above and below them in the systems hierarchy. Clearly there will be some commonality between each subsystem to allow each to interact with others, but in most cases they will largely be composed of unique modules.

Figure 14 is a typical example of a simple matrix of Logical Levels for a basic low-level subsystem. In this example "Identity" is supported by three "Beliefs" or "Values", and these are in turn supported by five "Capabilities", and so on. Other matrices may have as many as a dozen or more key "Beliefs/Values" and consequently more "Capabilities", etc. It follows therefore that each level of process involves progressively more of the system. Thus a change in identity would involve a much more pervasive change (and, consequently, more risk) than a change at a lower level, for instance one involving a change in "Behaviour".

Logical Levels Diagram

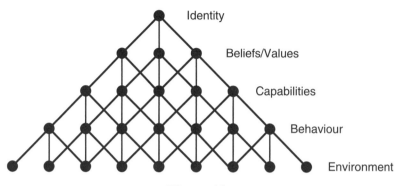

Figure 14

In a business setting, "Identity" will nearly always be the Mission or Purpose of the system or subsystem. This identity will be expressed in the form of core values which in turn are connected to the key capabilities of the unit. The "Values" and "Capabilities" determine the types of "Behaviours" and actions undertaken by the subsystem within the "Environment" in which the subsystem is operating.

When large matrices are encountered it is wise to break them down into smaller component parts, otherwise it becomes difficult to understand them readily. Situations where this would not be advisable would be where artificial boundaries would be created or where the structure of such elements departed from the existing organisational structure.

When using this mapping technique the most common cause of problems has been assessing or developing an understanding of the level known as "Beliefs" and "Values". Quite why this should be I have never managed to ascertain. My best guess is that most British people live in a culture where overt discussion about one's beliefs and values is something that is not encouraged and, when it does occur, often causes embarrassment. This is perhaps because beliefs are emotionally-held views which are not necessarily based upon fact, and discussion of emotional issues is not usually encouraged in the workplace. However, businesses are themselves largely based upon beliefs. The first and most basic belief has to be that the business will be a success, as without this belief it will almost certainly fail!

Other beliefs exist overtly within all levels of a business: beliefs about service levels, reaching sales or production targets and many other measures of success associated with the core functions of the business. There will almost certainly be many covert beliefs some of which can have a powerful effect upon the success of the business. These are often beliefs that are not expressed openly because they represent views which are contrary to those held by the management. Often these exist because the "official" management belief is not supported by the necessary "Capabilities" or "Competencies" (as they are sometimes called) from the level below. If capability or competence levels are inadequate, it is very hard to persuade people to be committed to the associated belief.

Some beliefs may be out of date or inappropriate and these usually are either a misfit with "Identity" on the level above or occasionally they show up as not being supported from below by "Capabilities", "Behaviour" or "Environment".

Overlapping Subsystems

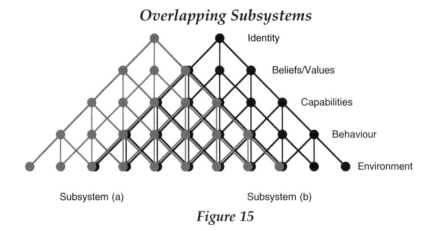

Identity

Beliefs/Values

Capabilities

Behaviour

Environment

Subsystem (a)   Subsystem (b)

Figure 15

Figure 15 shows how two separate subsystems overlap in some areas and share a number of common "Capabilities", "Behaviours" and "Environments". Note that both subsystems do not share common "Beliefs" and "Values" and thus do not share the same "Identity". Such a diagram could apply to a great proportion of subsystems within many business. In fact it is very difficult to imagine any business that did not have overlaps within its subsystems. If it did not, it would be a very fragmented business indeed.

The most significant point about overlap is that, when change is required in one of the subsystems, such a change may not be appropriate for the other associated subsystem. It is fairly obvious that a change of "Identity" due to change of mission occurring in Subsystem (a) would have considerable potential for the creation of problems for Subsystem (b). However, this need not be the case if both subsystems possessed common "Capabilities", "Behaviours" and "Environments" prior to the change taking place, as nothing would be lost by Subsystem (b) after the change had occurred. Nevertheless, there would still be potential for the creation of a significant gap between structures (sometimes referred to as "underlap") if a change of this nature were to take place.

In all change scenarios there is potential for creating misalignment of the Logical Levels. It is therefore vital to remember that the levels of process within an organisation correspond closely to the levels of perception of those involved in the change. Unfortunately, I have come across many examples of misalignments caused by attempting to fit a new "Capability" to an operational unit without giving due consideration as to whether it will fit with the "Beliefs/Values" and "Identity" of the unit involved. Figure 16 demonstrates what this would look like schematically.

New Capability which does not fit in with the existing Organisational Identity

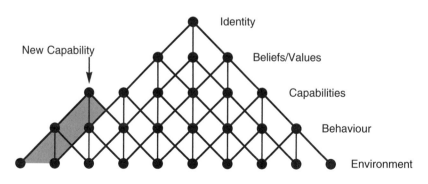

Figure 16

Obviously there are many occasions when just such a change is absolutely vital, and in these situations due regard must be given to what else needs to change and how the resulting changes to "Beliefs/Values" and "Identity" will be engineered effectively. Good examples of these types of change occur when new methods of working are introduced or new products are added to the product range. However, they can also occur when organisational structures are re-organised and a group of skills is moved from one unit to another. Clearly an inverse situation can occur if a "Capability" is moved to another unit leaving unsupported "Beliefs" or "Values" in the original unit.

A major part of the problem created by the Marketing and Manufacturing Directors in the XYZ Company falls into this category. Both directors were trying to force the adoption of new ways of working (TQM and MRPII) which were radically different from the existing methods. Therefore their proposals, when assessed through Logical Levels, looked very much like Figure 16. Had they been able to obtain acceptance of their proposals the result would ultimately have brought about a major clash between the existing "Values" and "Beliefs". Eventually, this might have led to the development of rival identities which would not fit with the direction to which the CEO was already committed in his "Pan-European Vision". The resulting situation would have looked something like Figure 17.

An Identity Conflict
An Identity Conflict may occur when New Capabilities and Values lead to a type of Identity that fails to match the Present Identity.

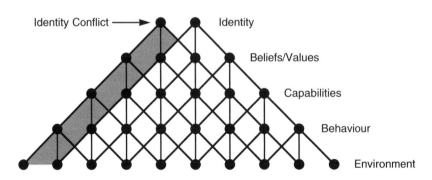

Figure 17

Another use of Logical Level diagrams is to trace through the Critical Path for a given activity. The reason for doing this may well be to prove that there is a clear linkage between all the Logical Levels or to look more closely at other functions closely associated with the Critical Path. Carrying out this type of exercise can be very valuable when planning change, as often multiple paths or points of tension show up clearly. Effective change-strategy formulation and path-finding involve assessing the interaction and alignment of all the various elements within the network. Often such an assessment will reveal gaps in the Critical Path or multiple or redundant paths that may have resulted from muddled thinking.

This was precisely the situation in the early stages of the development of the "Pan-European Vision" by the XYZ Company. Whilst it was realised that a major change of this nature would involve considerable shifts in the culture of all the associated business units, little attention was given to how this was to be achieved. Before the "Pan-European Vision" was mooted the structure of the group as a whole was a classic pyramid, with virtually all control on strategic matters held in the top two layers of the structure. All the major policy-making units were located in or close to the UK headquarters of the group, including Research and Development, Marketing, Manufacturing and Finance. The operational units outside the UK had little scope to make their own decisions, other than at a tactical level. There was, however, active two-way communication between group headquarters and the subsidiary businesses on most major issues involving policy.

The CEO was aware that flattening the pyramid through the removal of several layers of management and simultaneously devolving much of the decision-making away from the centre would inevitably cause a major upheaval. At a minimum it would require the re-engineering of many of the information flows and other vital aspects of the business. He was also aware that it could cause significant and undesirable shifts in the "Identity" of the business as a whole or in component parts of the business. Quite how he intended to manage this I have never been sure. But I am convinced that when he set out on this course of action he did not have half the answers to the problems that would be created, because at that stage he was not aware of what they were. All he had was a vision of how he felt the group as a whole should operate to be able to achieve its maximum potential in terms of future growth and profitability. Whilst I am sure he had thought through the changes that would be required to the hard systems, I am confident that he had not considered the shifts that would occur in the Logical Levels within the new structure and the associated implications.

This is a very typical situation that occurs when any organisation devolves power, whether at a high level as with the XYZ Company or down at departmental level. Often considerable effort is expended upon the construction or re-construction of data flows, reporting paths and the rejigging of the existing hard systems. But little effort is devoted to mapping the Logical Levels of the soft systems within the businesses and correcting any problems that may arise. Consequently, when the great day arrives and the new organisation structure is inaugurated, all hell breaks loose!

When I had first broached this subject with the CEO he looked at me rather quizzically but when I explained the subject in more detail and drew a couple of Logical Level structures applicable to the business he rapidly warmed to the idea. The Logical Level mapping technique was then utilised to review changes in the soft systems as part of the overall Change Management process. However, after about a year of the business using Logical Levels, they were also being used to plan and create changes in such elements as "Identity" and to work through the necessary changes in the levels above and below. Suddenly the Company had moved away from using Logical Level mapping as a defensive tool to using it pro-actively to plan and bring about desired change.

This is only a very brief introduction to the concept of Logical Levels and how they apply to business. For those seeking a more detailed explanation I would recommend reading Robert Dilts' book *Visionary Leadership Skills*. The figures used to demonstrate Logical Levels above are adapted/reproduced by permission of Meta Publications.

Perceptual Positions

Several times in this chapter, and earlier, I have hinted at a technique for gaining increased understanding of a problem. Often I have referred to this as viewing matters from a different perspective. In NLP jargon this is known as accessing different Perceptual Positions.

Recognising that as human beings we view the world from a number of different points of reference offers tremendous potential for enhancing our communications with others. However, perhaps its greatest value lies in allowing us to gain a better understanding of other people's views.

NLP describes four basic but different positions from which we perceive a particular experience or point of view. "First Position", sometimes referred to as "Self", involves experiencing something through our own eyes, *associated* in a first-person point of view. In this position we look at the world from our own viewpoint and take no account of anyone else's position.

The "Second Position", sometimes referred to as "Other", involves experiencing something as though we were viewing it whilst standing in another person's shoes, i.e. in a manner *dissociated* from "First Position". Standing in this position we take into consideration how a communication or event would look, feel and sound from another person's point of view. In this position we are looking out from the other person's body, thus looking at ourselves through their eyes.

In this position we can take account of what we look like, and sound like, and assess what feelings we get, from the other person's point of view. We can also develop empathy for the other person's point of view simply by gaining an understanding of how they might feel about our conversation and behaviour. Standing in this position therefore represents a powerful aid in any conflict situation.

"Third Position", or "Observer", involves standing back and perceiving the relationship between ourselves and others from an observer's perspective. From this position we are able to observe ourselves in first position and the other person in second position.

The advantage of this position is that it offers us the opportunity to almost completely detach ourselves from the detail of the conversation between positions one and two and take an objective view of the total situation.

To enter this position, imagine that you are out of your body and off to one side of the conversation between you and the other person. Some people find it easier to look down from above. It really does not matter where you make the observation from.

"Fourth Position" or "Meta Position" was first defined by Robert Dilts (1997) in his book *Visionary Leadership Skills*. He defined this position as the collective form of "We", or to put it another way, an overview position of the system as a whole. This provides us with the widest and largest level perspective which is of practical use in a business setting. Others have gone on to describe yet further possible positions right out to include "God position", the "Universe", etc. However, I have yet to find a practical use for such a high-level abstraction in Change Management – but on the other hand I have never carried out a consultancy for a religious order or a group of astro-physicists!

To take Fourth Position, step aside and adopt the overview perspective of the whole system so that you can consider what would contribute to the best interests of the system. In most cases this will be at a level of Company or Group but can come down to levels such as Division or Department when appropriate.

It was in this position that the CEO of the XYZ Company came up with his concept of "The Pan-European Vision". He achieved this by asking such questions as, "If we consider our common goals for the group, what do we need?"

Whether we realise it or not, we shift between all these perceptual positions as we live our lives. Most of us spend the majority of our time in First Position, however, and only occasionally access the other positions. For the majority of people the process of moving from one position to another is carried out subconsciously. However, having a conscious knowledge of this valuable process allows us to improve our ability to understand more about human interaction, and this in turn facilitates improved communication.

The four positions are demonstrated pictorially in Figure 18. In many instances it helps if the First, Second and Third Positions are viewed spatially as in the diagram. By placing three pieces of paper on the floor, in a triangular form and about four feet apart you can actually move between each of the positions and look at the other positions. This helps considerably to understand how "Perceptual Positions" work.

Perceptual Positions

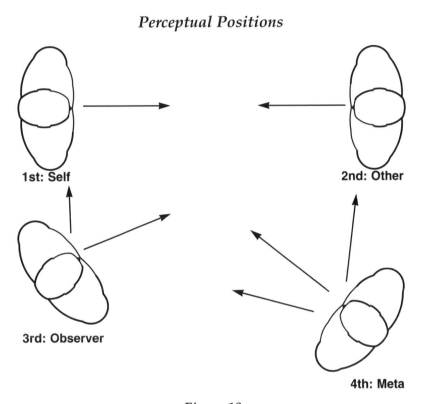

1st: Self

2nd: Other

3rd: Observer

4th: Meta

Figure 18

To further gain an understanding of this technique it is worth carrying out the follow short experiment with yourself:

Recall the last major argument you had with someone. Initially remember this event from the First Position and remember what you saw, heard and felt. Do you still feel the negative emotions that you experienced then?

Now, imagine yourself in Second Position, the position of the person you were arguing with. You can imagine stepping into the other person's shoes or just drifting out of your body into theirs if this makes the transition from one position to the other easier. Look through their eyes at yourself. Notice how you looked during the heat of the argument. What tone of voice did you use? How do you feel as you look at yourself and hear your tone of voice?

Now move to the Third Position as the observer of the argument. Perhaps move off to one side where you can see yourself and the person you are arguing with. How do you view the argument from this position? Notice your reactions and feelings.

Compare the feelings, and notice how they differ when experienced from the three different positions. Has your perception of the argument changed now that you are able to view things from these other positions? Would you have responded differently to the argument had you been in possession of this extra information?

Once you have mastered this technique with yourself you are ready to move on to using it with other people in such situations as conflict resolution, mediation, influencing others and for your own increased personal flexibility.

Aligning Attitudes or Obtaining Consensus

This is a further development of the Perceptual Positions technique and is designed to explore problems more deeply, and hopefully resolve them. It involves each person taking part and occupying in turn the positions of "Self", "Other" and occasionally "Observer". It can perhaps best be seen in the form of an exploration exercise involving a minimum of three people. The purpose is to allow each individual to explore each of the three different Perceptual Positions whilst tackling the same problem.

Having carried out this exercise a number of times with different organisations and at different levels within organisations I know it can work extremely well. However, employing this technique should be seen as a high risk strategy particularly if the participants are known to have already taken a polarised position. Emotions can often run high and get out of hand if care is not taken to control the interplay rigorously.

Do explore the subject with each individual first and carefully note their reactions. It should not be undertaken if any of the participants show any sign of reluctance to take part.

This technique was used to resolve the growing enmity that was developing between the Marketing and Manufacturing Directors of the XYZ Company during the selection of an appropriate change mechanism for the Company. Difficulties in the relationship between these two directors had been in existence long before major change was proposed. Several attempts had been made to resolve the problems, but neither director had been prepared to discuss the issues openly.

When this exercise was set up, the CEO had suggested to me that it would be beneficial if he did not take part. This was because he felt that if it did not succeed, or, as our American cousins say, "if push became shove", he might have had no alternative but to seek the resignation of one or other of the protagonists. Instead he chose to nominate the Finance Director (who was also the deputy CEO) to take part in attempting to resolve the conflict.

I had in my possession a considerable amount of material that I had collected in the form of worksheets and notes from a number of meetings which I had had with both directors. Of this information, the worksheets associated with the Well-formed Problem and the Well-formed Solution models were the most valuable. These pointed to issues involving the problems in the UK rather than the more global ones involving the rest of the European operation. Both directors had variously accused each other of either creating the UK problem or contributing to it, although hard facts to support their respective claims were rather thin on the ground (see Figure 5 – a rich picture drawn by the manufacturing director). Prior to attempting to resolve this matter I sought input from the CEO and some of the other directors to check out various points of detail.

Armed with this information, and after a short discussion with the CEO and the Finance Director, we agreed we would invite both directors to a meeting to discuss the "low productivity in the UK" problem. This was a deliberate set-up. The CEO issued the call to the meeting leaving the clear impression that these issues must be resolved and, to ensure success, he would take the chair. However, he had agreed with me that he would absent himself at the last minute on some other important business, leaving the Finance Director (who had been pre-warned) to take the chair.

The meeting was set up in the boardroom, which had a large area at one end to enable presentations to take place. This area of around four metres by six metres was cleared, and three large pieces of card were placed on the floor marked SELF, OTHER and OBSERVER as in Figure 18.

The absence of the CEO was explained by the Finance Director, who went on to explain that the CEO expected this meeting to resolve all outstanding issues between the two directors connected to the change programme. He then left me to explain the techniques that I intended to employ. Both of these directors were already aware of the concepts involved as I had used the Perceptual Positions techniques with each of them at an earlier stage.

The first round involved the Manufacturing Director standing in the circle marked "Self", the Marketing Director standing in the circle marked "Other" and the Finance Director standing in the circle marked "Observer".

The Manufacturing Director was invited to begin by stating his reasons for choosing MRPII and how it would solve the problem of "overcapacity in the UK". He was aided by reference to the Well-formed Solution worksheet that I had completed during my interview with him.

The Marketing Director then asked the Manufacturing Director a number of questions about how MRPII would help with the problems that he perceived existed in Manufacturing. In the course of this interchange a number of statements were made that had not been made by either party prior to this meeting. The most significant of these involved late delivery, inadequate attention to detail, inflexibility, and a number of points concerning quality. The Finance Director finished by making a number of comments from his position as Observer.

Both directors were then asked to exchange positions and to imagine they had quite literally exchanged roles. Again a number of questions were asked by both parties: the same issues arose, only the methods of dealing with them were different. The Finance Director commented on this and added further observations suggesting that both directors were in fact dealing with only the symptoms and not with the real underlying problems. It also seemed clear that both of them were spending most of the time trying to score points off one another regardless of the roles they were playing.

The above is but a brief résumé of the whole process, but going into detailed content would be of little value. At this point about an hour had elapsed, and a break was called by the Finance Director.

On reconvening, the same process was followed, this time with the Marketing Director in the "Self" position and the Manufacturing Director occupying the "Other" position, but now the subject under discussion was TQM. This session was conducted in a very similar manner to the first, although the Finance Director was forced to intervene on several occasions as matters became quite heated. What was surprising was that again many new issues bubbled to the surface which had not been mentioned before. Chief among these were: major changes required to orders when the product was already in the process of being manufactured causing large levels of scrap and increased costs; excessively short lead-times being quoted by salesmen to the clients causing jobs to be rushed; and large numbers of orders being taken requiring non-standard modification often associated with poor specification.

Again another hour had elapsed, and at this stage I called for a short adjournment in order to discuss matters privately with the Finance Director. He, knowing both directors very well, was clearly alarmed at some of the statements that had been made and seriously wondered if it was at all possible to arrive at a meeting of minds. However, when we returned to the boardroom I presented my logical level diagram of both MRPII and TQM (Figure 16) which showed that neither could possibly be made to fit within the current Change Programme without creating more risks than possible benefits.

I pointed out that there were clearly a number of major issues existing between Marketing and Manufacturing that had nothing really to do with either MRPII or TQM and that these needed to be resolved immediately. The Finance Director made a number of suggestions which he believed would help, but which received little positive response from either of the other two directors until he mentioned worsening trading conditions and new competitors entering the UK market. Only then did the Marketing Director reluctantly admit that this was a factor. He suggested that, whilst he knew only too well what conditions were like in the UK market, he had failed to convince the rest of the Board that this was a major problem. The Finance Director disagreed and pointed out that these factors had been identified and charted as contributing to many of the problems identified at the start of the project (Figure 3).

There then followed a heated debate about what could be done to stimulate sales and hold on to market share. By this time I was sure that we had hit upon the real cause of all the problems between the two warring directors, and the Finance Director concurred. It was also now clear to me why they were backing different approaches to their problem and that these were in fact purely defensive.

At this stage it is normal to rotate the roles again with each of the protagonists taking the role of "Observer", in turn whilst the Finance Director would have occupied the position of "Other". However, both the Finance Director and I felt that we had recovered sufficient information at this stage, and continuing might have proved counter-productive if matters became heated still further. However, in many situations it has been only when this third phase of the exercise has been completed that the real causes of conflict have become apparent.

Two years later when I reviewed what had occurred I was able to see the whole picture, which was very close to the position the Finance Director and I had agreed at the time. The story went as follows:

The industry in which the XYZ Company was operating had gone into a period of recession about three years prior to the commencement of the project. At about the same time foreign competitors had entered the market offering similar products at lower cost. The XYZ Company had responded by reducing its prices and at the same time attempting to increase the quality of its products. In order to achieve this some of the manufacturing work had been out-sourced to specialist businesses, whilst within Manufacturing, costs were closely examined and, where possible, cut to the bone. In fact, all concerned felt that Manufacturing had responded extremely well and had achieved its targets. Unfortunately this strategy worked for only a short while, as the competition responded by largely matching the XYZ Company in terms of price and, shortly afterwards, quality.

This pressurised the sales force into seeking other means to secure business. Foreign competition was not good at supplying non-standard products, so this was one area where the XYZ Company's sales force could start to concentrate. The only problem was that these specialised products were being sold at the same price as standard products. Often this was being achieved by placing orders initially for standard products and then subsequently requesting Manufacturing to modify them during the production process. The competition was also not good at dealing with very short lead-times, and the XYZ Company's sales force had capitalised upon this aspect as well.

Both of these selling strategies created considerable strains upon the manufacturing process. Manufacturing's response to this was to attempt to move away from traditional Batch Processing towards Just-In-Time (JIT) manufacturing, and to do this they felt they needed MRPII. This they thought would give them control over the ever-decreasing lead-times demanded by Marketing and would also facilitate late changes in product specification.

Marketing, on the other hand, were sure that by imposing TQM they would get better quality products with fewer defects and at the same time expose deficiencies within the manufacturing process.

After the meeting in the boardroom later that day the Finance Director and I reported back to the CEO with our findings. We were not surprised to find that both the Marketing and

Manufacturing Directors had requested an urgent meeting with the CEO to discuss the issues that had arisen. The CEO listened to what we had to say and suggested that I left whilst he called the Manufacturing and Marketing Directors to his office. Later I was called back to see him. He thanked me for my help and informed me that the two warring directors had agreed to set up a joint working party to solve the problems that had been identified. He had also apparently advised them that he saw merit in both JIT and TQM and these should be investigated further but not implemented until after the new structure and reporting systems were in place and bedded down.

Aligning Perceptual Positions is a very powerful technique and must be seen for what it is: a full confrontational approach. Normally anyone who has worked through the Perceptual Positions on their own will rapidly realise the risks involved with carrying out the exercise face-to-face with the person they are at odds with. It is also interesting to note that it is a technique that works well with bullies who like to feel that they can "manage" the process. This, of course, they cannot do if the "Observer" ensures that the all the rules of the game are adhered to, i.e. people get to speak only when asked to or when it is their turn.

Part Four

Understanding
The
Function
Of
Time
In
Planning Change

Overview

Time is a function that acts on our lives continuously from the moment we are conceived until the moment we die. It is most often seen as an inflexible, rule-based system and something we have no control over. There are, and are always likely to be, twenty-four hours in a day, seven days in a week and fifty-two weeks in a year. The watches we wear on our wrists are there constantly to remind us of the progress of time.

A very large proportion of the judgments we make about how we run and manage our businesses are driven in part or totally by the function of time. Company years are probably the most obvious of these functions. Company Law and Fiscal Laws dictate that once a year all of us, be we a one-man business or the largest company in the world, must account for the profit or loss we have accumulated during the year. Many of our day-to-day judgments are based on the pace or speed at which things get done, and managing time is an important part of any manager's life.

So at one level, time is an inflexible – but major – controlling influence on business overall. However, there are many other dimensions of time that do not have such rigid rules. In fact often we use the term "time" in a more metaphorical sense when we consider such things as the past and the future. Indeed the further out in time that we try to project our thinking the less relevant time itself seems to become. The same applies as we consider the past. The events of yesterday are still no doubt clear in our minds. We have a rough idea what happened during our day and in what order things occurred, and we may also remember at what time they took place. However, if we go back a few days earlier, our perception of what happened and when will be less clear and not quite so reliable.

Just as our minds can play tricks with our perception of time in respect to the past, they can also play tricks with events occurring in real time. A good example of this involves our judgment of speed when we are a passenger in, or are driving, a car. If we make a journey on a motorway and travel at an average speed of, say, 70 miles per hour for, say, one hour, when we leave the motorway and enter a minor road with a speed-limit of 30 miles an hour our perception of speed is changed. Suddenly 30 miles an hour can feel as though we could get out of the car and walk faster! This is called, in NLP terms, time distortion.

This section of the book brings together a number of ideas from NLP and other sources concerning this softer, less rigid, aspect of time. In particular, one of these concepts involving our ability to "warp time" can be turned into a very powerful tool for use in Change Management processes and in the development of strategic plans.

Chapter Ten

Using Time Functions In Strategic Applications

Time exercises one of the most powerful influences on our lives in general, and is a major driving force in business in particular. Virtually all business activities are controlled by cycles which are in turn driven either by the calendar or by the clock. Annual accounts, quarterly reviews, monthly reporting, working hours, annual holidays, hourly/weekly/monthly/annual pay rates, etc., are all grist to the mill of time.

Our ability to plan for the future or even to review the past is facilitated by our capacity to integrate time into our maps of reality. In fact, time has such a powerful effect upon our understanding of the world which surrounds us that, if time were deleted as a function from our internal maps, our ability to reason would instantly become chaotic. Think about it for a moment and, without referring to any outside source such as diaries, calendars, etc., ask yourself, "How do I know for certain that it is not tomorrow or yesterday, now?" Then, when you have a satisfactory answer to that question, store it away until the next time a Public Holiday occurs on a Monday. How many times then on the first day back after the holiday will you think it is Monday when you are in fact at work on a Tuesday, or, when it is the Thursday after that Public Holiday, will you think you still have two more working days until Saturday? So our perception of time in certain circumstances can become unreliable or warped. Whilst time has rigid rules governing its function, from the earth circling the sun regulating the length of the day, to the watch on our wrist ticking away the seconds, our mind is quite capable of playing tricks with us when dealing with this phenomenon of time.

To demonstrate this further, think of the effects that jet-lag can have on people, and you will realise how, by distorting our view of time simply by travelling a few thousand miles in a modern jet airliner, a large percentage of the population can become zombies! Sleep deprivation can have a similar effect. For the moment, however, just be aware how easy it is, by tinkering with our internal clock, to upset our equilibrium without even trying.

Some of the stranger effects of time, such as jet-lag, are considered by us as normal, even though we may not fully understand the reasons for how or why they occur. Whilst jet-lag affects some people to a greater extent than others, no one disputes its existence. It is not something that we have direct control over. We cannot choose to have, or not to have, jet-lag: it happens outside our conscious control. However, it is interesting to note that, if a skilled hypnotherapist makes contact with our unconscious mind, simply by suggestion alone, he/she is often able to provide instant relief from the effects of jet-lag.

There are many more functions of time which exist at a subconscious level and which have even more powerful effects upon our lives, some even involving our very ability to survive. However, in this chapter I want to concentrate on just one function of time that exists at both a conscious and an unconscious level and which constitutes a highly valuable but under-utilised resource in facilitating strategic thinking. This involves our ability to have a spatial awareness of time and to move backwards and forwards through time in our minds, just like a time-traveller.

All of us have some comprehension of time being a continuum, with the past being in one place and the future in another. This comes across most strongly in our use of language where a phrase such as "putting the past *behind* us" tends to imply that that is the right place for the past to be – somewhere behind us. Similarly, "I am looking *forward* to meeting you" implies that this future event lies somewhere out in front of us. So, whether or not we have thought consciously about time as a spatial entity before, our subconscious mind has no problem in understanding the concept.

Is this phenomenon just coincidental, or is there a reason for it? The psychological community agrees that it most certainly has a purpose, but not all the factors surrounding this phenomenon are known, and research into the field continues. Current thinking on the subject suggests that the brain has evolved primarily to use the visual sub-modality of size and location to store our representation of time. As location is in fact an analogue sub-modality of the visual modality, it permits the brain to store and access events sequentially. The other major modalities (auditory and kinaesthetic) whilst contributing to our memories of the past, do not seem to possess the same capability as the visual modality for storing information in a sequential manner.

Recent research has demonstrated that some people who have been born without the gift of sight and who normally have a dominant auditory modality still resort to using the visual modality to recall information from the past or to think about the future. This tends to suggest that we are born with this skill; it is not a learned behaviour, although it is almost certainly enhanced during our early years of life.

Whilst our ability to conceptualise time is primarily visual, it does not mean that the visual modality alone is capable of triggering memories of the past. The sound of a special piece of music or some particular aroma can send our minds racing back to some past event instantly. However, our ability to differentiate between past, current and future events is controlled by our ability to categorise them by use of the visual modality. Thus, a particular piece of music, whilst triggering memories associated with the non-visual modalities, will also trigger some form of visual image, although we may not be fully aware of this at a conscious level.

There are many expressions within our language system that also support the fact that all of us store our representation of events in the visual part of our mind. One such expression is "the mind's eye", which suggests that our mind has its own ability to see beyond that of normal sight.

How we store our spatial concept of time is a very personal matter, and there is no "right" or "wrong" way to store this information. However, most of us seem to fit a model which places the past behind us or to our left, whilst the future is in front of us or somewhere out to our right. The present is usually represented as being slightly in front of, or slightly to the left of, or occasionally right inside, our head. This model is a close fit with the way in which we metaphorically describe time in our language systems.

In order to gain a better understanding of how all this fits together it is worth carrying out a short experiment to establish where you store your images of the past, present and future:

Sit down somewhere where you are not likely to be disturbed and close your eyes. Think of something which has pleasant memories for you at a time way back in the past. It could perhaps be a birthday when you were a child or some other similar occasion. For a moment notice all that was going on at that time, including the sights, sounds and feelings. You will no doubt have a picture that you are seeing, although your eyes are shut. Note where this event is located spatially. Remember that there is no right or wrong way to experience this.

Open your eyes when the memories of that past event have faded. Close them again and remember another happy event which occurred some years later. It could be something like your last day at school or perhaps another birthday that has particular meaning for you. Notice again all the elements that go to make up that memory and where this is located in your mind.

Open your eyes and, when these memories have faded, close them and remember a happy event in your very recent past – perhaps your last holiday or some special event in your life such as receiving a pay-rise or a promotion. Notice all the elements that go to make up that memory and where this appears on the big screen in your mind.

Open your eyes and look around you, and then close your eyes again. Now think about getting out of bed this morning. Notice where these sights and sounds are situated in your mind's eye now.

Again open your eyes and look around for a moment. Now close them and think about some future pleasant event. This could be going on holiday or some social event that you are looking forward to. Notice where the pictures associated with this are located in your mind.

Now for the last time open your eyes, look around and, when you are ready, close them. This time think way out into the future, some years ahead. Perhaps you could think about retirement from work or some other major event in your life way out in the future. Notice where your thoughts and the associated pictures, etc., are located. Now open your eyes.

You may have noticed differences in the way that you have stored your memories of the past. If you recall these pictures again you may notice differences in the sub-modalities. For instance some or all of the pictures may be in black and white or in colour. Some may be three-dimensional or just flat and two-dimensional. Some or all of the pictures may be panoramic whilst others may have a frame around them. Often people find that the further back in time they go the less bright the images appear or the less distinct they may be, until the earliest memories appear slightly out of focus or almost washed out. Similar effects can occur with images of the future as well.

Wherever and however you have located all these events from the past, present and future in that part of your brain which is often called your "mind's eye" is fine. If you now draw an imaginary line linking up these events as you see them in your mind, you will have constructed something called a personal "Time-line". You may find that your Time-line is straight, curved or some other shape. It may run from left to right, or behind to in front, or it could even be up and down or any combination of these, or maybe even some other representation. Whatever form it takes is perfectly alright, as each person has his/her own way of representing their personal Time-line.

If you have been unable to carry out the exercise above to elicit your own Time-line, don't worry, as this often happens when someone first attempts to access this type of information. For some people, just asking them to point in the direction of the past and the future will identify their Time-line. However, you may not come into this category and will need to carry out the exercise a number of times before you are able to get a clear result.

The good news is that, whilst it is useful to be able to know your own Time-line, it is not vital in the context of the rest of this chapter. Realisation that we have an innate ability to represent time spatially and mainly unconsciously is the important factor that is relevant here.

The exercise of establishing our own Time-line involves what is often termed right-brain activity, and it appears that most of our understanding about time emanates from the right hemisphere of our brain. It is now well known that it is the right brain that is responsible for our creativity, and consequently our ability to think strategically. Of course our ability to think strategically must involve time, likewise our ability to think of events as forming a continuum across or through time. It is in situations where creative and strategic thinking are required that the use of the Time-line can often produce remarkable results.

For the purposes of the rest of this chapter we shall assume that all Time-lines form a straight line and are limited in length by the space available within the place in which we are situated. So if we stand in the middle of the room, we can imagine that our Time-line starts somewhere on the floor within the room immediately behind us and that the future lies somewhere on the floor immediately in front of us as in Figure 19. Therefore, logically, by standing in the middle of the room we must be standing in the "now" or "present" position.

Time-line

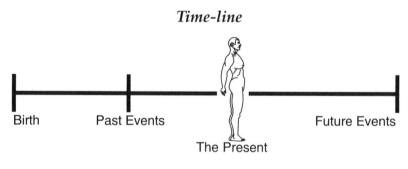

Figure 19

If we now turn around and face the "past" we can look back to some point on the Time-line which could represent our last birthday, or we could go all the way back to our conception, birth or perhaps one of our earliest memories. Some people are able to view many different events in their past as they look at that part of their Time-line. It sometimes helps if we close our eyes for a moment and imagine an event from the past which has particular meaning and, when we have a clear view of that in our mind, we can open our eyes and position that event at the appropriate point on the Time-line.

Once a line to the past has been established, we can turn around and face the opposite direction which represents the future. The process is then repeated, but this time we can imagine some event that is going to occur several months into the future, perhaps a holiday, a social event or some other event that has particular meaning. When this event has been clearly established in the mind we can place that event in the appropriate place on the part of the Time-line which represents the future.

Now for the really interesting part of the exercise. Remember where the past and future events are on your Time-line. If it helps, place a marker of some sort (a couple of pieces of paper will do) on the two special events, one in the past and one in the future, that you have just been considering. Now, whilst standing in the "present" position, look back towards the past event and ask yourself, "What do I know now that would have been useful to me in that past event?" Think about the things that you would have done if you had had this information, and the things that you would not have done or would have done differently. We all have things that, with what is called "twenty-twenty hindsight", we would wish to change. Consider these things for a moment and recognise them as opportunities to learn something new, either about yourself or about the world about you.

Now go to that past event on your Time-line and, whilst standing in this position, look forward towards the future, to the point where you were previously standing in the "now" position. Imagine you are fully back in that past time and remember some of the sights, sounds and feelings that you had at that time. When you feel fully integrated into that past experience look forward to the future, represented by your marker for "now", and ask yourself, "Am I happy with this view of my future? Is there anything that I would wish to change?" When you have examined these things fully, you can ask yourself, "What messages would I like to take with me to the future?" When you are happy with the answers that you obtain, move forward to the "now" position. Turn around and face the "past" and for a moment take full cognisance of what you have learned from this experience. You may find that you remember something from the past that you had forgotten and which is of value to you now, or in fact you may discover many other things that are of use to you now and could be of use to you in the future.

Now turn around 180 degrees and face the "future" part of your Time-line. Look at the point where you have placed your piece of paper representing the "future" event that you chose to consider. Allow yourself to become fully focused on this event and then ask yourself, "What resources do I need now in order to make that future event really successful or better in some way?" You can also ask yourself other questions of a similar nature which you may believe are useful. Make a mental note of anything that comes to mind.

Next move forward on your Time-line into the "future" and stop at the marker you placed on the floor at the beginning of the exercise. Allow yourself to integrate completely with that future event. Be aware of all the sights, sounds and feelings that you are aware of here. When you feel comfortable with this, turn around 180 degrees and face the "present". Now you can ask yourself a whole series of questions which may help you with planning that "future" event such as, "What resources will I need to acquire to make this future event a success?" Note particularly anything that will require you to obtain or learn something new. Then you can ask yourself, "What do I *not* want now that I currently have in the 'present'?" Again note anything that comes to mind as a result of asking this question. As we go through life we collect a whole pile of what is metaphorically termed "unwanted baggage", and this can be a good opportunity to look towards the present and decide to discard those things that you do not need in the future. There may even be things in this domain which, if not discarded, could hold you back from achieving your full potential. Think about these things for a moment.

Now remember the mental notes that you made when you were standing in the "present" and looking towards the "future". Allow yourself to mull these over and consider how being in the "future" may be changed by some of your "present" thinking about these matters.

Allow all these things to integrate into your thinking and now move back to the "present" and turn 90 degrees and face out from your Time-line with the "past" on your left and the "future" on your right. Close your eyes and be aware of those thoughts that come from the past and the future, and allow these to integrate in your mind for a few moments.

So what has all this to do with the world of business and Change Management specifically? It can prove of considerable assistance when planning for the future. The real magic comes from the need to use both the right and left hemispheres of the brain in order to carry out the exercise effectively. Historically, most tactical and strategic planning has been a purely logical function with a major orientation towards the financial aspects of the planning process. Such thinking involves mainly the left brain, and not the right brain. Therefore, if we want to be creative in our planning of our corporate futures we have to adopt processes that satisfy the needs of the right brain, and walking Time-lines fits these needs to a tee.

Unfortunately, reading about Time-lines and actually seeing the process working in practice is separated by a considerable gulf in most people's understanding. This is because, whilst the process itself can be described fairly accurately, the actual experience can lead to so many variations. Some people become slightly bemused or focused on their own internal thoughts and appear a little distanced from the world about them; some find difficulty in expressing verbally what they experience; others become more emotional. The emotional aspect can be the most difficult for consultants and executives to cope with, simply because in the Western business world the accepted norm (whether right or wrong) is not to show any sign of emotion, almost regardless of the situation. Involving the right brain in processes of this nature is almost always going to open up other pathways in the brain, e.g. the emotional aspects, but this is the price we pay for creativity. The connection between imagination, creativity and emotions has long been established. Indeed, Albert Einstein noticed these connections in his own thinking process whilst he was being creative. He also noted that whilst he was in a creative state he was totally incapable of recording his thoughts in words, signs or symbols. It was only later, after he had moved out of the creative state, that he could talk about what he had been thinking or indeed attempt to write down his thoughts (Hadamard, 1945).

So, as you experimented with finding and walking your Time-line you may well have experienced some emotional feelings, or felt slightly different whilst doing it. Whatever you felt is fine, because Time-lines are a very personal thing, and feelings you may experience whilst exploring are neither right nor wrong. A tip I picked up when I was first introduced to the subject was not to attempt to cut off the emotional aspect, as emotions are in themselves very significant driving forces for creating new thinking – and indeed for generating new behaviours. If you encounter problems with people who disengage from the process for fear of displaying their emotions, use the quotation above concerning Einstein and explain the connection between emotion and creativity. Also point out that the most creative people are often those whom the rest of the world often describe as "temperamental" simply because they are so closely in touch with their emotions.

Walking the Corporate Time-line

It may appear to be a big jump from establishing and exploring your own Time-line to thinking in terms of a whole enterprise. However, there is really no great difference in respect to time between a business and a human being: both have a life running from conception to their eventual demise. The method of conception may be a little different, but like human beings, all businesses have a starting point. This may stem from one individual's bright idea, a merger, a management buyout or other such event. Similarly "death" can result from bankruptcy or liquidation, being taken over and swallowed by a larger organisation or simply just closing down.

Nearly every business that I have worked with in the last twenty years has had problems in deciding its future destiny, and few have actually been very good at it. Most have been reasonably efficient at tactical planning over horizons of up to two years. But when it comes to longer-term strategic issues, looking beyond the two-year horizon, there are remarkably few who seem to have been consistently successful at either planning, setting goals or achieving those goals. The reasons for this are many, but perhaps the most significant has been the swing away from strategic thinking in the late 1970s towards what is now called "short-termism", an approach strongly espoused by Margaret Thatcher and Ronald Reagan.

This movement of focus towards short-term planning caused the dismantling of many strategic planning functions in government as well as in commerce and industry. Only in the mid to late 1990s have we seen the resurgence of interest in long-term planning. However, because long-term planning was out of favour for nearly two decades, business lost many of the skills required to allow it to think and plan strategically. This has been further compounded because training people to be strategic thinkers also went out of fashion in parallel with this lack of emphasis on the subject.

To some extent Time-lining can fill this gap in expertise by tapping into the already existing knowledge of the people involved in the business. However, perhaps its greatest value is in the validation of a proposed strategy. Whilst the focus here is on longer-term planning, it is worth noting that Time-lining will work on the shorter-term horizons just as well.

As everyone has their own unique and very personal Time-line, it is important to respect this and not interfere with the personal aspects of it during a corporate Time-lining exercise. However, part of each person's Time-line will encompass the period of their employment by the business, and this can be of great use during the exercise. Clearly, walking any Time-line is a personal experience and, whilst on occasions I have worked with individuals alone, most commonly I have worked with small groups of up to eight people. I have found that even eight people can be too many, as the process of walking the Time-line can take up to an hour with some individuals.

This leaves the problem of how to productively occupy the time of the other members of the group whilst the exercise is in train. One approach is to have more than one physical Time-line and have other people assisting in the process. Another approach is to have the rest of the group actively involved in another exercise such as drawing a "rich picture" of the current situation or even perhaps of what they see as the future situation, say, in three years' time. A rich picture can be a really useful prompt when people come to actually walking the Time-line. Sharing the content of rich pictures with other members of the group can also stimulate new thinking and sometimes assist in the resolution of old problems.

When working with a group it is important to protect the personal and private aspects of the life of each individual involved.

Walking the Time-line should therefore be carried out with each person in private. When everyone in the group has walked the Time-line, they should be encouraged to fully share their experiences with the rest of the group, but again any personal aspects that may have surfaced should, of course, remain confidential.

Physically constructing a Time-line for the business is the first step in the process. Obviously, the first requirement is a room large enough to accommodate the process of walking the Time-line. I have found that a room with a clear, straight space of around 6 to 7 metres in length by about 2 metres wide is ideal. I would not attempt to do any Time-line work in a space of less than 5 metres by 2 metres. Having more space is fine, but if a large space is available, set some sensible boundaries and limit the length of the Time-line to a maximum of 15 metres.

To assist the process, it helps if a straight line is drawn or laid out on the floor. The line itself can take any form that works for you and the group you intend to work with. I have used string, packing tape and I have even drawn (with permission) a white chalk line on a dark blue carpet on one occasion. Nowadays I have a ball of white linen tape which I use. Anchor your string or tape at both ends so that it will be held in place and not move.

The next task is to access the history of the business. It helps if you obtain some advice on this from the people you will be working with. All businesses have a history which many are justly proud of, but occasionally you will come across some part of the history which it may not be a good idea to raise with a particular audience. It therefore pays to check this out beforehand. What you should be looking for are the birth of the business and other major events or milestones in its history.

I once worked with a company that was very successful but which really did not have any major events in its past apart from relocating to larger premises. So I used the growth of the business in terms of turnover as the key milestones. Other functions of growth such as headcount, share of the market, launch of new products or services, etc., can also be used if these are appropriate. However, whatever is chosen must be relevant to all those involved in the exercise.

Once the milestones or major events have been established, pick the most significant four or five which are reasonably spaced out in time between the birth of the business and the current time. Using card or a sheet of white paper, write down the names of these event such as "Company first registered – 1975", "First Widget launched – 1982", "Super Widget launched – 1990", "Achieved ISO 9002 – 1996". Also make three larger cards with the words PAST, PRESENT, and FUTURE written on them. I have found that it helps if these three cards are of a different colour to the "history" cards. The ones I use are yellow with words in black whilst the historic events are on plain white paper.

Place the "past" and "future" cards at opposite ends of the Time-line and in the middle place the "present" card.

Now with all the practical preparation out of the way, everything is set for the first person to walk the corporate Time-line. However, before you do this you need to consider why you want to do this and what your expectations for the exercise are or the, in NLP-speak, "Outcomes".

The question, "Why do we want to do this?", should now be addressed to the group that you are working with. As it is likely to be rare for Time-line walking to be employed, and then as only a "last resort", you need to ensure that the group recognises that this is the situation. Normally, I have succeeded in eliciting a number of reasons from the group and have these written up on a sheet of flipchart paper which occupies a prominent position. Often, many of the responses suggest that the group or the business itself is facing a crisis or has arrived at some sort of impasse and does not quite know what to do next, or is in some other way in a "stuck state".

Having established the problem that needs resolution, you then need to establish the criteria for a successful solution or outcome. What we are seeking here is not the solution itself but what judgments would have to be made by the group as a whole to accept a solution. A good crib in this situation is to use the content of Figure 12, The Well-formed Solution, and to remember the Meta-model challenges of *when, where, how* and *with whom* in assessing the validity of the chosen outcome. Again this should be recorded on something like a sheet of flipchart paper and placed in a position where it is constantly in view.

The next task is to tell the group about the process itself. I have found that using a simple explanation of how we represent time works consistently well. However, whilst the introduction to this chapter explains that Time-lines are very personal in nature and may take many different forms, I tell my groups that Time-lines can normally be seen as starting somewhere behind us and extending out in front of us into the future. I further reinforce my statement by saying that much of this is encapsulated in the language we use such as "putting the past behind us" and "seeing into the future".

Occasionally, I have come across people who have some experience of Time-lines and in these circumstances I usually state that there are other representations of Time-lines but the most common is the one described and this is the one we will work with today. Allowing the introduction of other representations of Time-lines I have found is usually counter-productive and leads only to confusion. However, if someone is really insistent that their Time-line is different, accept what they say but tell them, for the sake of this exercise today, to please just imagine that their Time-line is a straight line such as the one drawn on the floor. This usually solves the problem.

It is at this point that the Time-line that has previously been prepared is brought into play. Point out to the group where the past, the present and the future are on the Time-line. Then invite them to place the prepared cards with the milestones of the business's history on them on the past area of the Time-line. Once this is done, ask for the first volunteer to explore the corporate Time-line whilst the rest of the group go off to do something else.

Explain to your subject what you want them to do before they walk on to the Time-line. When you have answered any questions that may arise, ask them to go and stand on the Time-line in the "present" position facing in the direction of the past events. Ask your subject to consider all the milestones that are laid out on the Time-line and particularly the relevance of these events to them personally. When they are ready, ask your subject to close their eyes and to remember the day when they first joined the business. When they have a clear picture in their mind of this, ask them to open their eyes and to walk down the Time-line and stop at the point on the Time-line that this would represent. When they stop at the point that they have selected ask them to turn around and face the "present" position on the Time-line and then to close their eyes for a moment. Now ask your subject to imagine that they have gone back in time to this, their first day in the business. Ask your subject to remember what it was like to be a newcomer to the business, to see the people they were meeting for the first time and what their surroundings were like.

Look closely at their face and notice any changes that occur. Perhaps they will nod their head slightly, frown, change their posture or give some other clue as to their association with the memories from the past. Suggest that perhaps they can recall the sights, sounds and smells of the place they were in, and what hopes they had then for their own future. Ask your subject to imagine that they are fully back in that past time, bringing back into memory all that they are aware of at that time. When you feel that they have become integrated into that past experience, ask them to open their eyes and focus on the future, which to them at this stage is represented by the present marker. Ask your subject, "Are you happy with this view of the present time? Is there anything there that you would wish to change?" If the answer is yes, tell them to remember what these things are as they may be useful later. Then ask them, "Are there any other messages which you would like to take with you from the past back into the present?" Tell them to again make a mental note of these things. If they are standing at a point on the Time-line where there are markers between them and the "present" position ask them to move towards the "present" position but to stop at each of the markers and for a moment or two to remember the events surrounding each of the milestones represented by each marker.

Once they have reached the penultimate marker and finished exploring the events surrounding this occasion, tell them, when they are ready, to move forward into the present. Once they are in this position allow them a moment or two to reintegrate with the present and, when they are ready, ask them to turn around and face the past. Once they have turned around, say to your subject,

"Give yourself a few moments to take full cognisance of what you have learned from experiencing the past, and consider all the events that have occurred since you joined the business." Prompt them by asking them to remember anything that they think would be useful for the future which maybe they have forgotten about up to now.

When you are satisfied that they have completed this part of the task, ask your subject to turn sideways and face away from the Time-line for a moment. Ask them to loosen-up a little by shaking or rubbing their hands and arms. This is known in NLP jargon as "breaking state" and is intended to assist in bringing the subject back to the here and now, with both the conscious and unconscious mind fully integrated into current events. Once you are sure that they are fully back in the present, ask them about their experiences and record any aspects that the subject believes to be important.

The next stage is the most important part and involves looking into the future. Ask the subject to look again at the two separate sheets of flipchart paper that identify the reasons why this exercise is being carried out and the criteria that have been established by the group for an acceptable outcome.

When the subject has had sufficient time to remind themselves of these factors, ask them to turn to face the "future" part of the Time-line. Allow the subject a little time to reorientate themselves and then ask them to see a significant event some relatively short time in the future on the Time-line.

It is most effective if this is kept to within one year. Therefore an event such as the ending of the current company year, the launch of a new product or service or some other major milestone of particular relevance to the subject is ideal. It is likely to be even more effective if linked directly or indirectly to something that has been written on the flipcharts.

Once the subject has chosen the future event, ask your subject to close their eyes and to imagine what that event is likely to be. Next ask them to open their eyes and then to move to the relevant position on the corporate Time-line. Now ask them to integrate fully into that experience by seeing, hearing and feeling what is going on and even perhaps smelling or tasting the event. Once they have integrated into the situation, ask them if there is anything of relevance that they want to tell you. Questions such as, "Is there anything missing, or could this experience be improved in any way?" are useful to prompt responses from the subject. If the experience is not a good one or they are not happy with the situation, ask them to clarify what has gone wrong and how the situation could be improved. When you are satisfied that everything of importance has been retrieved, thank them for their co-operation. Ask them to keep in their mind all that they have discovered, but now to turn around and face the "present" marker.

In this position ask the subject if they feel that there is anything that they have left behind from the "present" or "past" that they are happy to leave behind. When you are satisfied that you have obtained as much information as possible, ask if there is anything missing from the "present" or "past" that they regret leaving behind or which would be useful in this situation now. As a final check it is worth asking the subject to change some of the major sub-modalities such as increasing the brightness of the picture or heightening the colour or increasing the sound or feeling associated with this event. Test to see if any of these will change the situation for better or worse. If significant changes are experienced, it is worth asking more questions to establish what may be the underlying causes of the changes.

When all useful material has been recovered from this event, ask them to now turn around and again look towards the future and to pick the next significant event in terms of time in the future which forms part of the events established on the flipcharts. Again allow the subject time to integrate into the event by doing all the things that they did for the previous event. When they are happy with this ask them to open their eyes and to move forward to the point on the Time-line where this is represented. Repeat the previous processes and make notes of the responses that the subject makes.

When this is completed, continue to the next event from the flipcharts and so on until either these have been explored or the person concerned wishes to end the exercise.

As a last part of the exercise, have the subject go back to the "present" and turn around and look towards the future. Ask the subject to contemplate all that they have explored whilst on the corporate Time-line for a few moments. You can assist by mentioning items that have been noted down whilst they were engaged in the exercise. Ask if they now feel different about the future and what this specifically means to them and the business in which they work. Note everything that they mention as being of importance plus any observations of your own.

Finally, ask the subject if they would like to walk the "future" part of the Time-line again, this time using some event from their own agenda which has not been listed on the flipcharts. Ask them if they would like you to assist or if they would prefer to walk the Time-line on their own. Do not make notes unless asked to do so. I have found that many clients seem to want to carry out this part of the exercise and having done so appear to be satisfied.

At the end of the exercise ask the subject what they wish to share with the rest of the group and what, if anything, they do not wish to reveal. Remember that whilst you are acting in this role, as well as being an instructor you are also a confidant, and under no circumstances should you break any confidences.

Once everyone has had their turn at walking the corporate Time-line get the group back together to discuss what has occurred. I have found that the best way of initiating this phase is to seek feedback on the exercise but not on the content. Once this is complete refer back to the flipcharts and allow the group to comment on how they now see things have progressed. The original objective of the exercise was to satisfy a chosen "outcome" and to seek how this could be achieved. You may well find that the exercise has caused many other "hares" to start running which will also need to be addressed.

In most instances I have found that by this stage the group has largely taken control of "content" and I have just been left in charge of the "process". This is good, because there will almost certainly be a plethora of new ideas to be addressed. Consequently, proceeding may well become a little chaotic. Your job now is to stay in charge without interfering in the free flow of ideas. If, on the other hand, things become a little dead, start to use some of the notes that you have made and draw the participants into discussing the points raised.

It is not unusual for a session of this nature to end without a clear objective or series of objectives being agreed. In fact, nowadays I suggest to my clients that they may feel as though they are suffering from indigestion following a large meal of new information and may well wish to go away and digest what they have discovered. Some do and some don't, but those who don't usually request help in formalising what they have discovered before they leave.

I am often asked how I manage to obtain co-operation from senior executives in "walking" their own or their business's Time-line. Many consultants seem to think that this is a rather strange activity to ask senior executives to undertake. This, however, has not been my experience. Perhaps it is because when people really are committed to solving problems either for themselves or their businesses they seem to be prepared to try almost anything in order to find the right solution – even if it does involve walking up and down a room and allowing their imagination to run riot!

When I first used this technique in a fairly prescriptive manner in the late 1980s I did occasionally come across a few individuals who questioned its validity. However, once I began to introduce the concept as an interesting experiment in human understanding, I never thereafter encountered a serious dissenter.

In all circumstances it helps if you already have a satisfied client base from which to draw examples. Nowadays I always tell prospective candidates that the techniques that I am using have been applied with great success by the Board members of one of the UK's largest financial institutions. Using this technique alone, they were able to plan the transformation required to change the overall direction of the business and evaluate most of the implications that these changes would involve. It also helps to know that at least 15% of the executives of the other top 100 UK companies have had some experience of taking part in similar exercises. So it is not quite as "off the wall" or "freaky" as some people might believe, although for fairly obvious reasons, few people seem to want to discuss their experiences publicly.

Case Study

Looking back over my career as a management consultant I have no hesitation in stating that the most challenging assignment that I ever undertook was for one of the UK's largest financial institutions. The organisation concerned approached me seeking assistance in establishing a long-term strategic plan for the business. I must admit when they first knocked on my door I was both flattered and somewhat surprised at their choosing me and my team. However, apparently I had been chosen on the recommendation of another enterprise that we had worked with shortly before, and the financiers were also aware that I had spent part of my business career in a strategic planning role within a Top 100 Company.

The enterprise concerned had, it transpired, already spent nearly a year and a large amount of money on the development of its own "Long-Term Corporate Strategy" (LTCS) and at the inception of the project had announced this to the press. Unfortunately the Main Board had not felt comfortable with the outcome of the internal planning process and subsequently had the plans vetted by one of the world's best-known management consultancies. However, the Main Board were far from satisfied by the efforts of the consultants and were in a considerable quandary as to how to proceed. Worse still, time was no longer on the Board's side as they were rapidly approaching the point where the Chairman would have to commit to writing his overview of the past year and his assessment of future prospects for inclusion in the Annual Report to shareholders. He desperately wanted to be able to announce that the business had developed a new strategy and to provide a clear indication of the new direction in which the business would now be heading.

Against this background my associates and I were expected to come up with a solution in the space of a little less than four weeks. We agreed that we would first review the work already carried out, which we estimated would take about ten days. This was to be followed by a meeting lasting two days (a Saturday and Sunday) with all the key members of the Board (eight people) to thrash out "the way ahead", as it was now being called.

Our first task was to gain an understanding of what had already gone before. The strategy document mainly took the form of a report amounting to around 700 pages of detailed financial tables with supporting narrative. The management overview alone ran to 30 pages, and it was here that we discovered that the core of the strategy was centred around a "Ten-Point Plan". On detailed examination we were amazed to find that of the ten strategies identified, seven outlined plans which could be described as "moving away from" situations with no specific indication as to where they were "moving towards". Two others were "moving towards" situations with no indication as to where they were "moving away from". Only one strategy consisted of a balanced "moving away from" coupled to a "moving towards" situation. Clearly, implementation of such strategies could not be successfully accomplished, and it remains a mystery as to how the management consultants had failed to realise this.

From the detail provided by the client my team rapidly came to the conclusion that the current state of the existing business was poor. This was summed up by one team member who described it as "very tired" and by another as "having lost its way". Clearly there was an urgent need for a great deal of creative thinking if the business was to have a long-term future and not fall prey to the many predators active at that time. However, we also felt that the much-needed creativity would need to come from the Main Board members rather than from ourselves if they were going to accept ownership of the resulting ideas.

With this in mind we set about constructing our own view of the problems facing the business that required to be addressed by the strategy. This was largely centred around a situation analysis which we based upon the financial information given to us, plus other information drawn from the LTCS. This provided us with a very good understanding of the current strengths and weaknesses of the organisation as a whole and formed an excellent foundation upon which to build further.

We then added to this the apparent threats and opportunities that would need to be addressed in the next five years. In drawing this up we again leant very heavily upon the market research contained in the LTCS document. This contained much useful information about the projected future of the industry in general and the specific segments of the market in which the business was operating.

On to all this we attempted to map the existing Ten-Point Plan. This resulted in many key issues showing up that had not been addressed, together with others that, although partially recognised by the client, had not been dealt with satisfactorily. Many of the outstanding issues were difficult to define in terms of the area that they covered and where their boundaries lay. There were also several "problems" identified in association with some of the issues that seemed to be just symptoms of some deeper underlying problems but with no clear indication of what these might be. Other outstanding issues had potentially a multitude of possible solutions, all of which were right to varying degrees, but by inference also wrong to some extent.

All this information was collated, summarised and listed in a preliminary report amounting to six A4 pages. This was then sent a week before the workshop to each of the Board Members together with an outline of the programme that we would be following.

The workshop began on the Saturday morning with a review of the report that we had prepared along with feedback from the Board members. This was rapidly followed by a debate concerning the many deficiencies contained within the LTCS and particularly the fact that many of the Ten Points within it lacked either "moving away from" or "moving towards" components. The rest of the morning and much of the afternoon was taken up by working through many of the processes described in this book such as the Well-formed Problem and the Well-formed Solution. This proved an extremely fruitful exercise and caused many of the Ten Points to be reassessed and reformulated with several being dropped altogether and new ones added in their place. However, what was still obviously lacking was "creativity", and the final part of the first day was used to explain the concepts of Time-lines and to allow each participant to discover their own Time-line and explore this individually.

On reconvening over a working breakfast early on the Sunday morning a review of the previous day's events was carried out and further feedback from the group was obtained. It was clear that the group felt happy with the progress that was being made although several participants thought that our methods were a little strange albeit apparently highly effective. We then introduced the group to the concept of a Time-line for their organisation. This had already been laid out on the floor in an adjacent room with the key events from the past already marked on it. We invited the group to examine this and make any overall corrections to it that they thought fit and, when they were happy with it, to return to us in the lecture room.

We then asked for the first volunteer who would like to experiment with walking the corporate Time-line. Whilst the first person carried out his exploration the rest of the group became involved in resolving the issues that had arisen from the previous work. As each person completed walking the corporate Time-line we asked them to keep their own discoveries to themselves for the time being as we intended to have a complete group session to discuss these immediately after the lunch break.

When we started this part of the process I was a little concerned that we had not allowed sufficient time for each participant to "walk" the corporate Time-line. However, I need not have worried as most of the participants spent around twenty minutes carrying out the exercise. Several of them came up with some interesting new ideas but perhaps the most significant factor was that all stated that they now saw their problems in a different light or had gained a different view as to what now needed to be done. At this point I felt that the exercise had not produced the results that I was seeking, i.e. lots of really creative ideas. We had recorded the output from each of the individual sessions for use if required at a later stage.

The group as a whole, when not walking the Time-line, made significant progress on their task. However, it was interesting to note that each member appeared to be more motivated after walking the Time-line than before.

Over lunch, discussions continued about some of the key issues that still remained unresolved, and it became obvious that concern was mounting over one particular problem that seemed to have no acceptable solution. Once the group reconvened we reviewed progress and were able to gain consensus on methods to resolve several outstanding sticky problems. We then set about considering the output from each individual who had walked the corporate Time-line. As several individuals had seemed a little reticent to divulge their more creative ideas we had decided not to attribute any of the ideas unless the person concerned was happy for us to do so.

Among the unattributed and more "creative" ideas was a suggestion that the Board should actively seek a benign purchaser for the business and sell on the best terms that they could achieve. The owner of the idea had gone on to state that lying at the root of all the problems was the fact that everyone present believed that the business needed to grow by over 50% in the next two or three years if it was to survive in the longer term. He had gone on to say that a major part of the group strategy was directly connected to the early acquisition of one of the group's smaller competitors, and this was further supported by the identification of two potential targets. However, such an acquisition would of necessity require a very large injection of new funds, and it was recognised that the group was unlikely to be able to raise all the cash required through a rights issue of stock to its existing shareholders alone or through the issue of bonds.

Having announced this, both I and my team were a little surprised to find it met with a complete silence, although it seemed to have elicited many sideways glances between the members of the group. Added to this an air of tension or unease seemed to fall on proceedings which seemed to stifle any constructive debate. Shortly afterwards, whilst discussing the next topic, the Chairman asked if we could stop for a short time-out whilst he had a private discussion with the rest of the Board. We left the room. After about twenty minutes I was called back. The Chairman told me that the Board was very satisfied with the progress that had been made so far, but they had now reached a point where they wished to discuss a number of points between themselves in private. About an hour later the whole of my team was summoned back and informed that they had made very considerable progress due almost entirely to the work that we had put in and the innovative way we had conducted the process. He also told us that he could not discuss what they had decided with us at this stage but would keep us informed of progress.

Over the next three months I had a number of discussions with the Chairman and other members of the Board, during which time it became clear that major changes were afoot, but I had only the vaguest inkling of what the outcome might be. Late one afternoon I received a telephone call from the Finance Director to say that the scene was now set and to expect a major announcement the next day. The following morning the Chairman announced to the Stock Exchange that a takeover of the business had been agreed, and that it was to become part of a significantly larger organisation. He went on to say that he and his Board felt that the takeover was in the best interests of the customers, the shareholders and the employees.

Shortly afterwards I had a meeting with the Chairman during which he informed me that he was highly appreciative of the work that we had done for him. He picked out "that little Time-line trick" as being particularly useful and went on to say that he felt that the value of that exercise alone was worth ten times the fee that we had charged for the whole consultancy. When I asked him why, he explained that nearly all the members of the Board had, by walking the corporate Time-line, been forced to consider many future options that they had not previously been prepared to consider. However, deep down most had felt that the only really viable long-term solution lay in becoming part of a larger organisation rather than by attempting to grow by taking over a smaller business. Herein lay the reason for the apparent lack of creativity that we had experienced with the participants whilst they walked the corporate Time-line. The logic behind this is incredibly simple. How can you possibly be creative about a future that you really don't believe can possibly exist for you or your business?

When I introduced this case study I mentioned that it was the most challenging assignment that I had ever undertaken. This was not because it was different from other assignments but rather that the size and complexity of the task were coupled to an extremely stringent time constraint. Looking back on this assignment now with the benefit of nearly a decade of hindsight, there is little that I would change in terms of the techniques that we used or how we applied them. However, I would not wish to undertake such an exercise again without having significantly more time available during all phases of the project.

All the techniques described in this chapter have been used extensively with a variety of different businesses and organisations. Sometimes these have been used at Board level and sometimes with small units much lower down within a business. Although the method of application may have varied slightly dependent upon the group involved, nothing changed in the basic techniques employed.

The main purpose of using these techniques has always been to generate creative thinking in a specific subject area, but there have been many other useful spin-offs besides. Chief amongst these has been the facilitation, or building, of team-working within the group involved. The process can often also assist in identifying those within a group who may be running their own covert agenda, as it is extremely difficult to hide such things when walking a Time-line.

Part Five

Understanding
Modelling
and
Modelling NLP-style

Chapter Eleven

Modelling

In the past I have noticed that the very mention of the words "modelling" or "models" has sent wise men scurrying for the hills and lesser mortals often adopting a blank or vacant stare. For some peculiar reason these two words seem to conjure up for many people thoughts of either the black arts, magic or mysticism and for others some incredibly complex mathematical formula that is way beyond the ability of their brain to even contemplate! However, neither perception is valid, so perhaps a bit of gentle debunking would be appropriate before we proceed further.

Many of the methods and techniques demonstrated in this book are, by construct, behavioural models. A common example of a behavioural model is a typical job description. This is the description of how a particular task in an organisation is to be carried out along with other factors pertinent to the effective execution of the task. It is likely that there will be a linkage between the job description and the "person specification" which is yet another model by which potential candidates can be judged as to their suitability to carry out the stated job. The job description, or at least its title, will also appear on some form of organisation chart, which is yet another model, in this case mapping out the hierarchy of the organisation. And so it goes on throughout an enterprise: lots of interlinking models which describe how the business functions, with usually no mention of the words "modelling" or "models".

The technique of constructing and using models provides change agents and managers with methods for demonstrating and testing potential changes. The days of gauging the wind with a wet finger have long gone, and with it the "suck it and see" brigade have been forever consigned to the elephants' graveyard. Now far greater rigour is demanded in all aspects of business from the evaluation of tentative ideas and concepts concerning a potential change programme through to the process of conducting a post-

delivery performance assessment. Models of various types provide a large portion of the tools that are required to plan, control
and to validate these types of procedures. Sometimes it is not obvious that models or modelling techniques form a key part of many
of the other tools that we use, for example the tools that we use to
map and support the task of project management. Similarly it is
easy to forget that we find the task of constructing a budget much
harder without the help provided by our computers and the ubiq-
uitous spreadsheet.

Models help us to take a significant amount of the risk out of
developing Change Management programmes by allowing us first
to test our assumptions and then to examine and compare other
potential options. However, a note of caution here. Models can
also unfortunately mislead and, to the uninitiated, blind them
with science. So it is a wise precaution to never, ever take the
results from someone else's spreadsheet at face value unless you
can be absolutely certain that you can trust that person implicitly.
Otherwise you run the risk of being conned! Far better to ask for a
copy of the spreadsheet and then examine it on your own computer. That way you can examine all the mathematics and validate
the internal dependencies that go to make up the calculations.
Unfortunately over the years I have seen far too many spread-
sheets that have provided seemingly highly plausible solutions
which in the fullness of time have turned out to be seriously
flawed. Models are exceptionally useful tools, but until refined
and worked on will almost without exception contain an inherent
blind spot.

Closely allied to modelling is simulation, and sometimes it is difficult to recognise the differences between the two. Some of my
peers have suggested that simulation is just a more dynamic form
of modelling or even a model put into motion. Some industries are
almost totally dependent upon simulation to prove their designs
and ultimately their products. The aeronautics industry is a typical example, as no new aircraft gets off the ground without being
subject to many computer-aided models, many of which simulate
the aircraft in all stages of flight. Bridge builders and large portions of the engineering and construction industries also make use
of computer-aided simulation. From a Change Management perspective my personal preference is to regard simulation more as

an experimental approach designed to replicate a given situation in order to prove a concept. A good example of this would be the setting up of a pilot project and the study of the results of the pilot before commitment is given to proceed with a more major project. Whilst this approach might be expensive on time, it could save a fortune particularly when any form of new technology is involved.

Modelling in the last fifty or so years has become integral to many business activities and will play an ever more important role in building successful businesses in the 21st century. Therefore any wise change agent is advised to ensure that they stay cognisant with the available modelling techniques and particularly those designed to assist in testing and managing change.

Having explained what I mean by the term modelling, let me now focus on the non-mathematical models associated with human behaviour.

Behavioural Modelling

Behavioural modelling lies at the very core of human behaviour, as I mentioned earlier in the summary at the end of Chapter Eight. It is the mechanism that we utilise from birth or even perhaps before birth to learn how to be a human being. This may sound a grandiose statement, but the fact remains that it is through copying, mimicking and simulating other people's behaviour that we obtain most of our knowledge about how to cope with everything in the world about us.

The study of human behaviour has captivated academics and philosophers for thousands of years, although Behavioural Modelling (BM) as a distinct subject or discipline has existed only since the beginning of the 20th century. It was principally the domain of sociologists who were interested in gaining a better understanding of how human beings interacted and the behaviours that their subjects exhibited in life in general. However, already in the mid 19th century some industrialists were attempting to understand how their best employees performed their tasks in order to transfer their skills to other workers or to create machines to undertake those tasks. By the start of the First World War, industry and commerce were starting to put into practice many of the techniques developed through the study of BM in order to further increase the productivity of their workforces. So substantial were the gains achieved through using BM techniques that some historians now claim that Britain could not have won that war without them.

After World War One, BM largely became known in industry by the name "work study", and this term is very descriptive of what BM was mainly concerned with for nearly two decades. Business seems to have "rediscovered" the wider applications of behavioural modelling in the middle of the 20th century. This rediscovery coincided with the period when popular psychology first entered the public domain in the USA. It was also the time when management science first began to blossom, engendered to a greater or lesser extent by the publication of books such as *The Practice of Management* (Drucker, 1954) and the birth of Organisation and Methods (O & M) departments within the major businesses of the western world.

By the 1960s, BM was being used to gain an understanding of how people undertook specific tasks from a psychological rather than simply a physical standpoint. There were a number of applications of this new technology which were spurred on by the introduction of the computer and the need to increase productivity in the office as well as on the factory floor. Indeed the science of ergonomics, systems theory and systems analysis were vehicles intended to map and simplify the task of understanding how humans carried out their tasks both from a "thinking" as well as a "doing" perspective.

Over the years these technologies have themselves become mechanised, and techniques such as systems analysis have grown into extremely complex systems in their own right. Systems design and analysis of the 1960s were largely mapped with flow charts and recorded via the medium of pen and paper. Now in the 21st century, and after several developmental stages, it has become known as Business Process Engineering (BPE), often requiring the power of the computer to process its complex structures.

Beyond the design of systems, businesses in this day and age are full of models representing various parts of the business or a particular business activity. For example, all businesses require budgets, and these can be seen as a model or representation of intention to achieve certain financial targets such as cash flow, profit or turnover over a given period of time.

Occasionally, we see examples of modelling at much higher levels where the activities of one business are transferred to another. A good example of this approach is contained in the book, *In Search of Excellence: Lessons From America's Best Run Companies* (Peters and Waterman, 1982), where a number of businesses are put forward as exemplars or models of good practice to copy, or, in my book, where the causes of failure are studied in order to avoid repetition of failure.

BM is usually used to observe, analyse and map the behaviours of a particular individual who demonstrates high levels of performance, the intention being to transfer that behaviour or skill to others in the workforce. Occasionally, behaviours found in one group of people are modelled and transferred to another group. There are many examples where this has occurred between sports people and business people, the military and business, and so on.

Sometimes modelling can take the form of studying whole groups of people in order to establish which skills are the most effective. Back in the 1970s, the Huthwaite Corporation set out to research effective sales performance by studying the behaviours of almost 10,000 sales people making 35,000 sales calls over a period of 12 years (Rackham, 1988). This is a very impressive example of behavioural modelling on a very large scale. Clearly this research paid off as the Huthwaite Corporation went on to pass on the outcomes of their research to over 200 of the world's leading sales organisations and many more smaller businesses. For anyone wishing to gain an understanding of how such a study is undertaken or wishing to go up a gear in their selling technique I thoroughly recommend this book.

It is interesting to note that there has never been just one brand of behavioural psychology in use in business. Towards the end of the 1970s there were around 100 different schools of psychotherapy recognised in the USA, most of which happily stayed within the domain of therapy. However, some were drawn towards the business world as the rewards there were so much greater than working with individuals or small groups of people in therapy. Consequently, a whole range of weird and wonderful psychological techniques were released upon the business community with varying degrees of success. Many turned out to be rather like Hans Christian Anderson's emperor's new clothes whilst others have made significant beneficial contributions to management science and business in general. However, never forget that there is a long-standing psychological conundrum here which goes something like this: "To attempt to understand the functioning of the brain without the use of models would be just about impossible. However, the truth of the matter is that the brain is far too complex to be turned into a model or even a collection of models". Having now confused at least some of my readers, let me now turn my attention specifically to NLP.

* * *

Modelling has had a central role within NLP since its very inception. In Chapter Three, I explained how the two originators of NLP used modelling techniques largely derived from general semantics to uncover the unique therapeutic communication patterns of Virginia Satir, Milton Erickson and Fritz Perls. This study gave rise to the first model of NLP, the Meta Model, also described in Chapter Three. In Chapter Five, I introduced models, the purpose being to provide an understanding of the inner maps of the mind that drive both our individual behaviour and collectively that of the businesses in which we work. Further models have been presented in nearly every other chapter of this book. Many of these have been borrowed or adapted from domains other than psychology, principally cybernetics and mathematics. With regard to NLP not all the models contained within this domain have direct relevance to the business world, and even fewer are applicable to the management of change.

When attempts were first made to apply NLP techniques to the business world it was very much a case of trial and error. All too often techniques that worked brilliantly when applied in a therapeutic setting failed miserably when attempts were made to use them in the business field. Often, it was not the techniques that were at fault but how they were being applied. This was because many of the practitioners applying the techniques came from a therapeutic background and lacked a sufficient understanding of how the business world worked. Similarly there was a tendency to oversell and make exaggerated claims for what could be achieved with NLP. By the mid 1980s, NLP in general had acquired such a dubious reputation within the business communities in the USA and Europe that the wise consultant stopped using the term NLP completely. Some trainers and consultants even went into denial when challenged about whether or not they were using NLP techniques. I must admit that I was reticent about using the term whilst lecturing at Cranfield University and even more so in my consultancy business until memories grew considerably dimmer.

Fortunately, over time, a number of NLP models have become more generally accepted. Many are now seen as providing very useful tools for application to a variety of human activities including business, education and training. Indeed acceptance has now reached the point where many techniques derived from NLP have become embedded in the mainstream of business and their origins in NLP are now lost. However, I still encounter situations where the misapplication of an NLP technique by an incompetent consultant or trainer has resulted in a seriously unhappy client.

It is at this point that it is appropriate to draw a distinction between NLP models which I see as providing us with some useful tools and NLP modelling which I have some problems with.

Towards the end of the last decade I became so concerned about the misuse of the NLP version of modelling in a business setting and the wildly exaggerated claims for its capabilities that I wrote a series of articles for the main organ of the NLP community, *Rapport* (Volumes 42–45). The articles were entitled "Modelling—Magic, Myth or Mirage?". The first aim of my articles was to attempt to discover if there were any demonstrable examples of the successful application of NLP modelling in a business setting. My second aim was to lay down a challenge to those modellers/trainers who claimed to have carried out a successful NLP modelling exercise in business. The challenge was to learn to fly an aeroplane by modelling alone. I would supply the aeroplane free and also my time as flying instructor. No one came forward to offer successful examples of modelling, nor did anyone take up my challenge to use their modelling skills to learn to fly!

The four articles in *Rapport* created a huge amount of comment, correspondence and yet further articles, none of which demonstrated that NLP modelling could be made to work consistently and successfully outside a therapeutic setting. Does this mean that NLP modelling has no place in business? I believe my answer will become obvious later, but at this stage let me just say it appears to have a number of severe limitations.

Before I progress to discussing these limitations it is pertinent to look at what I perceive to be the most common modelling process used by NLP modellers in business. Typically this type of modelling is a three-step process aimed at transferring the desired skill of an "exemplar" to the "modeller" and thence onwards to "others". Often this technique has been claimed to be used successfully in selling scenarios, so I will use this activity to demonstrate what I mean. For example, let us assume a situation where there is one outstanding sales person and a number of mediocre salespeople forming a sales team. The objective is to transfer the skills of the excellent salesperson (exemplar) to the rest (others). In order to do this, the modeller has first to define the desired skill(s) of the exemplar. Then the modeller has to identify the significant patterns of behaviour and experience that collectively make up these skills. The modeller then applies these acquired patterns to himself and tests them for efficacy. When the modeller is satisfied that he has acquired all the necessary behavioural skills he teaches the mediocre salespeople (others) the same patterns. The salespeople then practise these patterns under the tutelage of the modeller until he deems them to be proficient at their use, at which point these salespeople are launched upon the customers.

Now all this sounds reasonably simple until you take into account the variables that contribute to making each individual different. Just contemplating differences such as family background, education, work experience and what life itself has thrown at each person is enough to make one realise how complex this task will certainly become! It should, therefore, not be surprising to find that to learn how to carry out this process you will need to invest a considerable amount of time and brain power to acquire the necessary skills.

However, even if you do acquire the necessary NLP modeller skill set, you will still be faced with the most limiting factor of all, the individual intellect of the exemplar, the modeller and the recipient of the model. Intellect is the constituent that marks out most of the difference between one individual and another, other than obvious physical characteristics. It is also the most difficult element to model effectively using any of the current methodologies not only of NLP but of psychology in general.

I once asked Dr Ernest Rossi about how predictable Milton Erickson was in his choice of techniques when working with clients in therapy. His response was that Dr Erickson had remained almost completely unpredictable even after he had worked closely with him for seven years. Dr Rossi, apart from being a world authority on the subject of psychobiology and a renowned author in the domain of psychotherapy, is one of the most observant people I have ever had the good fortune to come into contact with.

On pondering Dr Rossi's comments some time later, I realised that no consultant, even if he happens to be a genius, has much hope of accurately and consistently understanding another's intellectual processes as a result of a few short interviews. So whilst NLP has many useful tools that allow us as change agents to be truly excellent at our task, it cannot build proficient models of human intellect. Furthermore, some of the tools utilised by others in the NLP community to carry out modelling exercises are in my opinion of dubious pedigree and severely lacking in scientific validity. The question I posed for my series of articles on modelling, "Modelling—Magic, Myth or Mirage?", and the extensive feedback that I received have led me to become firmly convinced that myth or mirage are near the truth. Of magic, I found no evidence at all.

If for a moment I suspend my belief that NLP modelling is effectively composed of nothing other than smoke and mirrors, and even if there is indeed some hidden magic in NLP modelling that

I have missed, there still remains the issue of efficiency. The task of acquiring a working understanding of the technology and more importantly the processes involved in applying it, is without doubt considerable. Therefore, having surveyed alternative approaches, I have come to the conclusion that with most applications there are much more effective ways to achieve the same end. Earlier in this chapter, I used as an example the training of a sales team. I also mentioned the Huthwaite Corporation and their SPIN Selling technique. This technique can be taught in 3 days, with the sales force achieving real results in the field just one day later, all at a cost of less than one average consultancy day. Nothing like this could possibly be achieved with the NLP approach to training a sales force. Huthwaite is not unique. There are many other organisations now offering similar sales courses and also a growing number of computer-aided modelling approaches to assist in modelling behaviours. Always keep in the forefront of your mind that well-worn but incredibly incisive phrase "keep it simple, stupid" (KISS). So would this NLP technique, even if it worked well, which it doesn't, pass the KISS test? I don't think so.

So what, if anything, can NLP offer to change managers in terms of modelling? To start with, there are the many models already covered in this book which have been proven to work well. These range from the Meta Model which can dramatically improve our own ability to communicate and just as importantly our ability to understand others' attempts at communicating with us, through to the use of time lines to construct meaningful models of other peoples' reality encompassing their past, present and future.

However, although I have firmly cast aside the more complex NLP modelling technique involving a three-step process, "exemplar", "modeller" and "others", there is validity in using just the first two steps. This is very similar to the process used in therapy where the exemplar is the patient and the therapist is the modeller. Typically, the therapist, or in our case the consultant or change agent, builds up a picture of some part of the client's behaviour that would be useful. This is achieved by applying the processes described in Chapters Two and Three, first establishing rapport with the client, then asking the Meta Model questions. In this way, we can build a reasonably accurate understanding of a particular element of a client's thinking processes or of their behaviour or even a skill. We can then add more precision, if required, by applying the techniques described in Chapters Four and Five.

To provide an example of this type of modelling, I will return to the function of sales. I had a client who some years ago had agreed in principle to commission my company to design, build and install a software product. A fully developed proposal had been made supported by a huge amount of technical detail which had been agreed by both sides. The total cost to the client at today's prices was about £2.5m ($4.25m), and the client and his superiors had agreed they were happy with this figure. However, the client would not sign the purchase contract and appeared to be prevaricating over minor details. I was completely baffled by his behaviour and was at a total loss to understand what was stopping him from signing the contract.

Initially I had carried out all the processes mentioned in the above paragraph and felt that I had built up a very good picture of the client's behaviours. During the negotiation of all the stages of the contract I had continued to use the Meta Model to assist me and felt certain that I had not missed anything of importance. Eventually I asked him out to lunch. Having enjoyed a very nice meal, I covertly and very gently went over much of what had gone on before and could find nothing new. Then I asked him about some of the items that he had bought personally and, again using the Meta Model, I discovered that he nearly always had difficulty making major buying decisions. With further gentle probing, I discovered that many years before, whilst he was at university, he had bought a second-hand car with money borrowed from his parents. His parents had wanted him to buy a small car of a particular make which they felt would be economical to run and be very reliable. Because he liked rock climbing he wanted a larger car to put all his ropes and other climbing gear in, with room to transport his friends, whom he thought would contribute towards the running of the car. He went against his parents' wishes and bought the larger car which proved to be unreliable and cost a lot of money to maintain. Moreover, his friends declined to contribute towards the cost. Eventually he was forced to borrow more money from his parents in order to keep the car going. Seemingly, both his parents from that point on took every opportunity to remind him what a poor buying decision he had made, and this had clearly left him with a bad imprint about buying anything. Once I knew all this I was able to provide him with the reassurances that he needed to buy my software. This is known as developing a model of a person's strategy, in this case, a buying strategy.

We are creatures of habit and nearly always follow a set behavioural pattern in making decisions about most things in life. Therefore, it is sometimes important to discover what these patterns of behaviour are. In the above example, I could have saved myself considerable time and inconvenience if I had been aware at an early stage in the negotiations of the problems my client had about making buying decisions.

This process works well even with small groups, always provided that you are not seeking high levels of precision. Precision is an issue here, whether it is with groups or individuals. Ask yourself the question: "How much information do I really need from this interaction and when will I know I have sufficient?" Only you will be able to decide this, and it will almost certainly vary with each interaction. However, it is vital to decide precisely what you want before you start the interaction because, if you don't, once you become involved at a detailed level, you will find it harder to assess what is useful and what isn't and you could well end up searching for things you do not need.

It is possible, using NLP, to take these processes to a very much deeper and certainly far more precise level than is laid out here. But always keep firmly in mind KISS and COST. Time really is money, and burning up the client's money for your own self gratification is not likely to ingratiate yourself with whoever is employing you.

The levels of precision used in this book have served my colleagues and myself well over the years. However, if you wish to investigate the subject further, keep firmly in mind the limitations that I have mentioned because they are demonstrably real. An excellent source of further information can be found in the highly readable book, *Expanding Your World: Modeling the Structure of*

Experience (2005) by David Gordon and Graham Dawes, PhD. This book is accompanied by an equally excellent DVD which brings the text to life.

Part Six

A
Short Consideration
Of
Popular
Packaged Solutions

Overview

Much of the main part of this book has been concerned with methods for avoiding failure in Change Management projects. One could therefore possibly come to the conclusion that perhaps the best way of avoiding failure would be to avoid making any changes. This, of course, is just plain nonsense. All businesses must continually evolve and change if they want to stay alive and prosper. However, there is a great deal of common sense in the phrase, "If it ain't broke, don't fix it". Unfortunately a considerable number of Change Management failures have resulted from tinkering with some part of a business that has not previously shown any signs of being broken. Often the tinkering has arisen as a result of attempting to apply the latest Management Science fad in the form of a pre-packaged solution.

It should also be borne in mind that managing and controlling evolutionary change is much easier than managing revolutionary change. The risks – and consequently the failure rates – are consistently lower with evolutionary approaches. However, in today's world all too often there is not enough time available to allow new working practices to evolve or for a business to change direction. Then revolution becomes the only sensible option if a business is to prosper, and revolution is best achieved through the application of packaged solutions.

Some readers may have come to the conclusion that my attitude towards modern packaged solutions is almost totally negative, but this is not the case. My chief criticism is not about the content of the techniques or the concepts behind them but the methods used in their application and their all-too-frequent misapplication. It was these concerns that were the driving force behind the formation of the Ecotech Group and the subsequent short-course programme run by them on various aspects of Change Management.

Whilst we were carrying out our research we were largely treated by the wider academic and business consultancy communities as though we were heretics. It gives me comfort now to know that we were not alone in our views; others all around the world were also having serious doubts about the efficacy of many of these modern techniques. In recent times it has become more politically acceptable to ask awkward questions about these new management theories. Perhaps this is because at last most businesses are fed up with being caught wearing yet another set of the proverbial "Emperor's new clothes". On this note I will quote briefly from an excellent book that I read shortly before completing this book, *The Witch Doctors: What the Management Gurus are Saying, Why it Matters and How to Make Sense of It:*

> *Management theory, according to the case against it, has four defects: it is constitutionally incapable of self-criticism; its terminology usually confuses more than educates; it rarely rises above basic common sense: and it is faddish and bedevilled by contradictions that would not be allowed in more rigorous disciplines. The implication of all four charges is that management gurus are conmen, the witch doctors of our age, playing on business people's anxieties in order to sell snake oil. The gurus, many of whom have sprung suspiciously from the 'great university of life' rather than any orthodox academic discipline, exist largely because we let them get away with it. Modern management theory is no more reliable than tribal medicine. Witch doctors, after all, often got it right – by luck, by instinct or trial and error.*

> *John Micklethwait and Adrian Wooldridge (1997)*

I find myself having great difficulty in disagreeing with the sentiments conveyed in the above extract. But I believe it is perhaps an overstatement of the true situation, as some businesses claim to have grown very significantly as a result of adopting these modern management theories. Many other businesses have improved in some areas of their business simply by being stimulated into reviewing their own practices in the light of new thinking created by these new management theories. However, many of our newer and vibrantly successful enterprises owe nothing to these techniques and much to the entrepreneurial spirit that is the main motivating factor contributing to their achievements.

Chapter Twelve

Packaged Solutions

Total Quality Management (TQM)

There can be no doubt that the advent of this technology has had a beneficial effect upon attitudes concerning all aspects of quality throughout the western world. However, there are two main areas of quality, best dealt with separately, and these are "products" and "services".

Possibly the raison d'être for the development of TQM was the emergence of the Japanese car industry and the competition it presented to American carmakers. Japan could produce cars not only more cheaply and efficiently but it was able to produce them to a much higher standard of quality. This came as an incredible shock to the American car makers, as before the Second World War Japan had been notorious for making poor quality replicas of products emanating from the West. What was even more ironic was that the person who invented TQM was an American who went to Japan shortly after the end of the Second World War to assist Japanese industry to re-equip, having previously had his ideas rejected by the big American carmakers. His name was W. Edwards Deming. Even today Japanese business managers speak of Deming in the same hushed tones that people normally reserve for a deity. Japan also awards an annual Deming Prize which is regarded as the highest accolade for achieving excellence in manufacturing.

After American carmakers and other manufacturers realised what was happening to them there was a rush to adopt Deming's techniques in the USA, although much of the actual "missionary work" was, I believe, carried out by Joseph Juran, also an expert in the subject. The central concept was simple: "Get rid of waste and improve quality". To the Americans at this time these were totally alien concepts. Cars were built and assembled with about ten per cent wastage of components along the way, and only when a car came off the production line was it "tested" by the quality department. Deming's concept involved continuous testing at all stages of assembly and production, mainly by the employees who were doing the assembly work rather than specialist "quality control" workers. Indeed all Toyota workers were encouraged to stop the production line as soon as errors started to appear.

Once Deming's ideas had become respectable in the USA it was not long before various management consultants were knocking on the doors of the boardrooms of American big business offering to provide them with a huge competitive advantage over their competitors by installing TQM in their companies. Consequently, there are very few American companies that did not consider adopting TQM at some time during the 1980s.

As I have said earlier, some of these were spectacularly successful, but they were only a small minority. Motorola has perhaps been the most successful at adopting TQM. It claimed that it had added $3.2 billion to its profits during the period 1987–92 by adopting this technology. However, Joseph Juran, the original missionary, estimated in 1993 that of the top 500 American businesses only ten per cent had actually achieved "world class quality" status. And, in any case, as "quality" had by this time become something that everyone was concerned with, it could no longer be seen as a factor in providing competitive advantage.

All that I have mentioned up to now relates to the quality of product and has little to do with services. No company exists without its service operation. Everyone has a switchboard, many have a receptionist, sales people, accounts people and other subsidiary functions without which a business simply cannot exist. In America it is these functions that seem to have been ignored by the TQM gurus, but it is these operations which are the most prone to errors and poor service. It is also these functions that can lose a company masses of business through not being courteous to customers and not replying punctually to letters, faxes and e-mails – all common problems with American businesses even today but rare now in Europe.

When TQM came to the UK the service functions were not ignored. Considerable effort was put into improving the quality of service to customers at all levels, and this has become the norm rather than the exception. However, many businesses achieved very significant improvements in the quality of products and services without becoming involved with TQM simply by reviewing and updating their methods and procedures.

As I have said already the downside of TQM stems not from the concepts of quality but from the misapplication of TQM techniques. In the past ten years my colleagues and I have earned a good living by undoing the damage caused to businesses by the incompetent installation of TQM. In the main, many of the problems have stemmed from failing to recognise two critical factors, the existing corporate culture and the people within the business who have to change their ideas, beliefs and behaviours.

I have often described corporate culture as the essence or the spirit of a business. Tinkering with the culture can destroy a business just as effectively as sacking all the key staff. Cultures evolve over time, and the older the business the deeper the culture. Changing culture also takes time, and even when everyone involved agrees that a change would be beneficial it still takes time for it to happen. TQM almost invariably brings with it a requirement to change part of the culture of a business, and this is not necessarily a bad thing. However, often the consultants involved in the Change Management process are not sensitive to the culture that exists and are unable to recognise the value that this adds to the business as a whole. Similarly they often do not allow sufficient time for the culture to change. When these failings occur together this is a certain recipe for disaster.

People-issues in all changes such as TQM can be huge. Many unfortunate scenarios can occur if the people involved are not consulted thoroughly at every stage of such a project. People often become confused during any change programme and constantly need reassurance as to their value and purpose in the organisation. I can remember several occasions when key personnel left a business because the consultants employed to "put in TQM" were insensitive to people-needs. In one instance a company lost nearly all its sales and marketing staff in the space of one month – the consequence of which was that it was not able to sell its products and suffered a massive cash-flow problem. At the end of the year the turnover was down by 20% and the very respectable profits of the two previous years were turned into a significant loss. The key message here is that people matter far more than some new management fad.

The good points about TQM are to be found in some of the ideas the discipline contains. Overall quality matters almost as much as the people employed in the business, but quality at all levels and in both areas – products and services. Providing quality improvement in any part of a business will eventually find its way through to the bottom line of the P & L. TQM also teaches us that quality is an on-going commitment and the quest to improve quality should never cease – not a bad sentiment to end my look at TQM.

Business Process Re-engineering

Whereas TQM was largely a Management Science fad of the 1980s, in a few years' time Re-engineering is likely to be seen as its equivalent of the 1990s. The two "inventors" of the technique are James Champy and Michael Hammer, both with consultancy and computer science backgrounds. Much of the hype surrounding Re-engineering arose from the publication of two books: Champy's book entitled *Re-engineering Management: The Mandate for New Leadership* (1995) and Champy and Hammer's *Re-engineering the Corporation* (1993), the latter being by far and away the better seller, selling nearly two million copies in 17 languages in three years. However, interest in this subject first stemmed from an article by Michael Hammer in the July/August 1990 edition of the *Harvard Business Review*, entitled "Re-engineering Work: Don't Automate, Obliterate".

For the roots of Re-engineering I believe we need to look to the background of the two inventors of this particular discipline: computer science. In the mid 1980s a new approach was being pioneered by James Martin Associates, a British computer consultancy, to analyse business functions and to assist in the automation of the process of creating software products. This was given the name Information Engineering (IE). The techniques involved in IE were to break the business down into "processes" and "entities" and to map these onto a theoretical functional map of the business. Often in the course of constructing these maps surplus or unnecessary functions would be identified which could be deleted in the new structure, thus, in theory, saving resources.

I have little doubt that the authors used the concepts in IE to arrive at their definition of Re-engineering. Many of the functions involved in Re-engineering have close parallels with IE and many of the techniques share common names. However, the methodology involved does have major differences.

IE is concerned with the design and construction of computer systems with only a passing interest in efficiency, whilst Re-engineering is concerned with only efficiency. This technology places its main focus upon team-working assisted by computers and quality. It likes to group people from different disciplines into teams dedicated to carrying out processes that span several functional areas. Thus people from marketing, design and research can be brought together in a team devoted to "new product development" or whatever is required. When this technique is applied it also has the knock-on effect of making many middle managers redundant. There is no longer a need for them, as most of the information flow and organisational needs now occur horizontally across the organisation rather than vertically as in the past.

The term "downsizing" has become largely synonymous with Re-engineering. There can be no doubt that many Re-engineering projects have been associated with considerable reductions in the workforce. However, Re-engineering appeared at a time when the world was in recession and layoffs were inevitable as businesses strived to remain competitive. Whatever the truth, a major restructuring in order to improve efficiency in any large business is always likely to produce a reduction in the workforce, whatever name is given to it.

One of the big questions that remains unanswered about Re-engineering is whether or not it is likely to prove beneficial to business in the long term. There is much evidence to suggest that in the short term and in a recession the process is likely to seem beneficial. However, currently many management thinkers and senior executives are airing doubts about the longer term effects. Professor Charles Handy of the London Business School saw problems with Re-engineering at an early stage and, in an article in *Fortune* dated 31 October 1994, declared that "blowing organisations apart is not conducive to a state of commitment and euphoria ... The trouble with Re-engineering when it is done badly – which it mostly is – is that it leaves people shattered, even the people left behind." Professor Handy's sentiments have been echoed elsewhere and with growing frequency ever since.

Many businesses that chose to re-engineer in the recession of the early 1990s have come to regret their decision. Many have found that once the recession was over there was no "fat" left in their business to take advantage of the growth that was on offer. This has led to Re-engineering's being termed by some observers "the corporate anorexia of the 1990s". Similarly, the problems mentioned by Professor Handy have led to managements finding it extremely difficult to motivate staff to provide yet further increases in productivity when they have already reached the limits of their capacity. Often these same businesses have found themselves re-hiring staff dispensed with at the time of "downsizing". Many of these have been middle managers whose skills were not appreciated by the consultant brought in to re-engineer the business.

An even more damning charge was made against the process in late 1995 by the *Californian Management Review* who, having carried out an extensive survey of re-engineered American companies, concluded that Re-engineering was having a major adverse effect upon innovation within businesses.

The book that had perhaps even more influence on management in the mid 1990s is *Competing for the Future* by Gary Hamel and C. K. Prahalad (1994). The authors had this to say about Re-engineering: "Re-engineering has more to do with shoring up today's businesses than creating tomorrow's industries. Any company that succeeds at restructuring and Re-engineering, but fails to create the markets of the future will find itself on a treadmill, trying to keep one step ahead of the steadily declining margins and profits of yesterday's business." Four years later there is no clear indication of this occurring on a widespread basis. Perhaps the timely warning given by the authors caused managements to reconsider their position and they then took effective action to avoid this pitfall.

All the major consultancies have jumped on the Re-engineering band wagon and some have a whole division dedicated to this discipline. Many have chosen to repackage the product into a slightly more benign form by knocking off some of the rough edges, taking more notice of the human factors, and finally renaming and relaunched it as the "practical approach to high performance business" or some other high-sounding term, all of which, I submit, tends to suggest that the consultants are at least attempting to learn from their mistakes.

Whatever the critics of Re-engineering have had to say about it, there is no doubt that many businesses, large and small, have benefited from applying this technology. In fact many stayed alive through the recession of the late 1980s and early 1990s only by reconstructing their businesses with the aid of Re-engineering and large doses of downsizing. However, doing it once a decade is probably as much as any one business can take. The shock effect alone of Re-engineering can take many years to dissipate, and if repeated a second time can prove fatal. It is vital therefore to get it right first time, and the techniques outlined in this book can be a valuable asset in ensuring that this happens.

There are a significant number of businesses that rue the day that they became involved in Re-engineering. Not surprisingly some of these featured as statistics in the Ecotech survey. As far as we were able to detect, these failed for similar reasons to all the other Change Management failures. Statistics arising from other sources suggest that failures are high but not as high as those for TQM. The same statistics suggest that failure rates were highest in the period 1994 to 1996 and have declined since. There could be several reasons for this. As this was the period when the UK recession was ending, Re-engineering could have been a last desperate effort by some businesses to survive. The sudden rush by the major consultancies to market this technology could also be a factor. It is doubtful whether they would have had enough time to provide adequate training for their staff and give them the necessary field experience to make them fully competent.

Re-engineering in whatever guise forces companies to consider the methods by which they conduct their business and to assess what improvements they can make. Many of the world's largest corporations have lumbered on through several decades without really reconsidering what business they are in or whether or not they can improve overall efficiency. All will have made changes on a more or less continuous basis throughout this period but mainly at a component level rather than across the total business. Re-engineering offers a practical approach to addressing this issue. However, it should be undertaken in a circumspect manner and with a fair degree of caution.

Whilst I would never claim to be a disciple of Business Process Re-engineering in toto, I have used various parts of the technology for at least the last five years. The XYZ Company quoted as an example throughout this book is in fact made up in the main of three different sets of experiences with different business, and all involved application of some elements of Re-engineering.

Information Technology

Often Management Science has followed in the footsteps of the innovation provided by the IT industry. There is a strong case for placing IT, rather than Management Science, at the top of the list when considering the drivers for change over the last thirty years. I believe that Re-engineering is a case in point, as close examination suggests that it is largely an attempt to keep pace with the technology provided by the IT industry. However, there are also many counter-examples where IT has attempted to introduce technology which was either under-developed or inappropriate to the business needs of the time.

I believe that many of today's problems have their roots in the early days of the computer, and that a quick recap of this history is worthwhile.

Since the early 1960s IT, Data Processing or Computing, call it what you will, has enabled massive changes to take place in the way we manage, control and operate our businesses. However, the mechanisation of office processes had begun several decades before with the advent of the punch card, comptometers, etc. It was, however, the arrival of the electronic, stored-program computer that facilitated and accelerated change in a way previously only dreamed of by the likes of George Orwell and H. G. Wells.

The development of the electronic computer was the cause of much new Management Science thinking from the mid 1960s onward. Initially the main thrust was to mechanise processes which required large amounts of human effort but which followed well-established processes and rules. Typical of this was computerisation of payroll functions, rapidly followed by many of the other clerical operations in business and industry. Their introduction gave rise to considerable "downsizing" of the clerical workforce, thus creating the first fear of the computer age: losing your job to a computer.

Back in the 1950s when managements became more focused on achieving increased productivity in their businesses they were inspired by one particular Management Science guru, Peter Drucker. In 1946 he had written a highly incisive book about the American car giant General Motors entitled *The Concept of the Corporation* (1946). The book proved so popular with managers that it rapidly became a bestseller around the world. In the early 1950s he followed this book up with another entitled *The Practice of Management* (1954) which proved even more popular. This book is seen by many – including Tom Peters, Michael Porter and Charles Handy – as the original catalyst for all modern management thinking, and I would not argue with them on this matter.

The publication of Drucker's second book caused managements to recognise that to create increased efficiency it was necessary to have clear objectives for the business. Managers should also have their incentives based upon subsets of the business objectives. It also focused on the need to translate long-term strategy into short-term goals which were closely coupled to the managers' objectives. However, perhaps the most revolutionary element was the concept of setting up an elite group of managers who would be responsible for determining strategies and setting the objectives to achieve them. Drucker's concepts were largely responsible for the creation and development of the Organisation and Methods (O & M) departments which then reshaped UK businesses over the next two decades.

It was the O & M departments that originally started to apply computers to the work of clerical functions, and not the programmers and analysts who ran the computers. Similarly it was the O

& M people in the late 1960s and early 1970s who began to apply computers to more advanced applications aided by other professions such as accountants, engineers, architects, etc. During this period the computing part of the business was usually referred to as the Data Processing Department (DP). Most of the people found in the DP department had been chosen for their ability to write computer programmes or to operate the computers. Few had any practical experience in line functions or as managers in other parts of the business.

In the early 1970s the growing complexity of the computer systems being developed prompted a growing need for a bridge between the O & M and DP functions. In most companies the two departments were merged, with the DP department becoming dominant. The merger of the functions resulted in a need to cross-train staff in the skills of the other department. Predominantly this meant training the O & M staff to be systems analysts. By the mid 1970s virtually no DP departments were still actively training their staff in O & M skills.

I have heard many different reasons given for this shift of emphasis but I have never been really sure of the true one. Pressure over increasing costs and the growing backlog of undelivered systems probably contributed, as did the gradual growth of mechanisation of the development of computer systems (Information Engineering). However, I am absolutely certain that the absence of the skills associated with the O & M specialists caused a significant increase in the number of IT camels being delivered instead of the thoroughbred race-horses that the end-users had been expecting.

Regrettably, not much seems to have changed over the intervening years in respect to the delivery of unsatisfactory or unacceptable IT systems. Hardly a year goes by without another survey pointing out the current high level of failures of new IT developments. It was attempting to solve these problems that first led to my involvement with the International Ecotechnology Research Centre at Cranfield University.

One of the short courses I became involved in running at the Ecotech was entitled "From Technology Push to Organisational

Pull". These courses were dedicated to providing help and guidance to senior management and senior IT professionals in the development of more effective IT systems. The courses proved so successful that they ran for a number of years and in turn gave rise to other courses concerned with different aspects of Change Management.

As many of the ideas in this book arose from these courses and the associated consultancy work that they generated, all I can do is recommend that you apply them wisely to your IT problems.

Other Management Science Theories

As I have been writing this book I have become aware of yet other, newer Management Science theories which are about to burst upon unsuspecting managements across the world. At the same time some of the older more established technologies seem to be about to be re-launched, smartened up in new clothes, while still basically being the same product as before.

Knowledge Management, or KM as it is becoming more widely known, appears to be the newest Management Science methodology. As with its predecessors, it has been acclaimed by the early users as nothing short of the panacea for all ills. Some people, however, with perhaps fingers still burning from encounters with previous such products, see it as nothing short of good old-fashioned snake oil. No doubt the efficacy of this methodology will remain a source of much debate well into the future.

For the uninitiated, KM is mainly concerned with obtaining the maximum value from the knowledge existing within an enterprise. This is something I and many others have been preaching for over thirty years with varying degrees of success. For over two decades vast untapped resources have existed in the databases of just about every business in the western world. The reason why this vast repository of data was not turned into knowledge baffled me in the early 1970s when I was charged with designing and building what would now be classified as an Executive Information System (EIS) for my then employer, International Computers Ltd (ICL).

At that time I was employed within their Group Strategy and Development Division, not the IT department. I spent the best part of two years battling against the IT function over gaining access to the corporate databases that they so jealously guarded. My main problem was to persuade the heads of the IT function that the knowledge which I could derive from the stored data was in many respects more valuable to senior management than the limited information provided by the financial accounts. Eventually I obtained what I needed by escalating the issue to Group Director level with a covert threat from my immediate boss to take the matter up with the CEO. The system was given the name "COMBAT" which was a acronym for COntrol and Monitoring of Business Objectives And Targets.

The system, when completed, was not perfect. If it had been, it would not have needed to be replaced by later, better and more powerful systems. However, it was a significant move away from the then current practice of accumulating data and presenting it in simplistic reports, towards a full-blown, modern, knowledge-based system. It was also one of the first systems to have the capability to use the concept of "feed forward" as well as "feed back", and this was some years ahead of the first commercially available spreadsheet. Having this capability presented senior management for the first the time with the opportunity to ask complex "what if...?" type questions about the overall business plan. It also facilitated the complex simulation and evaluation of future marketing and manufacturing strategies. This was seen as a giant step forward by senior directors and most particularly the Group Marketing Director. Some years later the system became the main inspiration behind the introduction of the highly effective Just-In-Time (JIT) system in the mid 1980s.

My success in developing this corporate management tool can largely be attributed to the vision and plain, down-to-earth ideas of Peter Drucker. My main source of inspiration was Chapter Seven of *Managing for Results* (1964) entitled, Knowledge Is the Business. The chapter ends with this statement:

> *Marketing analysis and knowledge-analysis, when superimposed on the analysis of results, revenues, resources and on the analysis of cost structure and cost centres, should not*

only yield new facts. They should give management the knowledge to say: "This is what our business could be"; and the sense of direction needed to say: "And this is how we might get from where we are now to where we could be.

I find it mind-numbing that thirty-five years after these words were written, Management Science has been forced to reinvent Dr Drucker's "wheel" and call it Knowledge Management. But as so many businesses have still not reached a sufficiently good understanding of the value of the knowledge locked up in the vast accumulations of raw data stored in computer systems, and the even larger pool of untapped knowledge extant within their employees, obviously something urgently needed to be done.

My problems in obtaining raw data to drive the COMBAT system were not unique but all too common in the 1970s when managers felt that data should not be made freely available even if it could be put to good use by the person seeking it. This situation still pervades many companies today, where it is felt that information equates to power. As the basis of KM is this belief that everyone in an organisation should be able to access any required information, a massive change in attitudes will be required for it to be successful.

Managements will undoubtedly remain as confused by these technologies as they have been by all the previous ones. Some will rush to put them into practice, others, and perhaps the wiser ones, will sit on the sidelines awaiting the outcome of their more adventurous colleagues' endeavours.

Whatever happens, Management Science will continue to evolve and will espouse other, newer packaged solutions in the future. Similarly, the problems involved in business will also evolve and change, requiring newer and more sophisticated techniques to control and manage them. Overall, the future is likely to generate far more opportunities for Change Management failures than previously. A straightforward and common-sense approach is always more likely to resolve the problems than a complex one. The tried – and now thoroughly tested – technologies presented in this book are intended to equip modern managers and consultants with Change Management tools suited to the challenging environment presented by the advent of the 21st century.

Appendices

Appendix One

The New And Updated Meta-model

Patterns/ Distinctions	Responses/ Challenges	Predictions/ Results
1. Simple Deletions		
"They don't listen to me."	Who specifically doesn't listen to you?	Recover the Deletion.
"People push me around."	Who specifically pushes you around?	Recover the Ref. Index.
2. Comparative and Superlative Deletions (Unspecified Relations)		
"She's a better person."	Better than whom? Better at what? Compared to whom, what? Given what criteria?	Recover the deleted standard, criteria, or belief.
3. Unspecified Referential Indices **(Unspecified Nouns and Verbs)**		
"I am uncomfortable."	Uncomfortable in what way? Uncomfortable when?	Recover specific qualities of the verb.
"They don't listen to me."	Who specifically doesn't listen to you?	Recover the nouns of
"He said that she was mean."	Who specifically said that? Whom did he say that you call mean? What did he mean by "mean"?	the persons involved. Recover the individual meaning of the term.
"People push me around."	Who specifically pushes you around?	Add details to the map.
"I felt really manipulated."	Manipulated in what way and how?	
4. Unspecified Processes—Adverbs Modifying Verbs		
"Surprisingly, my father lied about his drinking."	How did you feel surprised about that? What surprised you about that?	Recovers the process of the person's emotional state.
"She slowly started to cry."	What indicated to you that her starting to cry occurred in a slow manner?	Enriches with details the person's referent.
5. Unspecified Processes—Adjectives Modifying Nouns		
"I don't like unclear people."	Unclear about what and in what way?	Recovers the speaker's
"The unhappy letter surprised me."	How, and in what way, did you feel unhappy about the letter?	projected sense of feeling "unclear" or "unhappy."
6. Universal Quantifiers		
"She never listens to me."	Never? She has never so much as listened to you even a little bit?	Recovers details about the extent of a process and counter-examples.
7. Modal Operators (Operational Modes of Being)		
"I have to take care of her."	What would happen if you did?	Recovers details of the
"I can't tell him the truth."	What wouldn't happen if you didn't? You have to or else what?	process, also causes, effects, and outcomes.

8. Lost Performatives
(Evaluative statement(s) with the speaker deleted or unowned)

"It's bad to be inconsistent."	Who evaluates it as bad? According to what standard? How do you determine this label used, of "badness" etc.?	Recovers the source of idea or belief—the map-maker, standards.

9. Nominalizations
(Pseudo-Nouns that hide processes and actions)

"Let's improve our communication."	Whose communicating do you mean? How would you like to communicate?	Recovers the process and the characteristics left out.
"What state did you wake up in this morning?"	How specifically did you feel, think, etc.? What behaviors, physiology, and internal representations make up this "state"?	Specifies the verb and actions.

10. Mind-Reading
(Attributing knowledge of another's internal thoughts, feelings, motives)

"You don't like me ..."	How do you know I don't like you? What evidence leads you to that conclusion?	Recovers the source of the information—specifies how a person knows

11. Cause-Effect
(Causational statements of relations between events, stimulus-response beliefs)

"You make me sad."	How does my behavior cause you to respond with sad feelings? Counter-example: Do you always feel sad when I do this? How specifically does this work?	Recovers understanding of how a person views causation, sources, and origins—specifies beliefs about how world works.

12. Complex Equivalences
(Phenomena that differ which someone equates as the same)

"She's always yelling at me, she doesn't like me."	How do you equate her yelling as meaning she doesn't like you? Can you recall a time when you yelled at someone that you liked?	Recovers how the person equates or associates one thing with another. Ask for counter-examples to the meaning equation.
"He's a loser when it comes to business; he just lacks business sense."	How do you know to equate his lack of success in business with his lack of sense about it? Could other factors play a role in this?	

13. Presuppositions
(Silent Assumptions, Unspoken Paradigms).

"If my husband knew how much I suffered, he would not do that."	How do you suffer? In what way? About what? How do you know that your husband doesn't know this? How is it that you assume that his intentions would shift if he knew? Does your husband always use your emotional state to determine his responses?	Recovers the person's assumptions, beliefs, and values that he or she just doesn't question. Specifies processes, nouns, verbs, etc. left out.

14. Over/Under Defined Terms (O/U)

"I married him because I thought he would make a good husband."	What behaviors and responses would make a "good" husband for you? What references do you use for the word "husband"?	Recover the extensional facts about the terms used.

15. Delusional Verbal Splits (DVS)

"My mind has nothing to do with this depression."	How can you have "mind" apart from "body" or "body" apart from "mind"?	Recovers the split that someone has created verbally in language.

16. Either-or Phrases(E-O)

"If I don't make this relationship work, it proves my incompetence."	So you have no other alternative except total success or failure? You can't imagine any intermediate steps or stages?	Recovers the continuum deleted by the Either-Or structure

17. Multiordinality (M)

"What do you think of yourself?"	On what level of abstraction do you refer to "self"? "Self" can have many different meanings, depending on context and usage—how do you mean it?	Recovers the level of abstraction that the speaker operates from. Specifies the context and order.

18. Static Words (SW)

"Science says that ..."	What science specifically? Science according to whose model or theory? Science at what time?	Recovers the deleted details.

19. Pseudo-words (PW)

"And that makes him a failure."	What do you mean by "failure" as a word that modifies a person?	Challenges a map that uses words that have no real referent.

20. Identification (Id.)

"He is a democrat." "She is a jerk."	How specifically does he identify with the term "democrat"? In what way? Upon what basis do you evaluate her using the term "jerk"?	Recovers the process of Identification or prediction. Invites one to create new generalizations.

21. Personalizing (Per.)

"He does that just to irritate me."	How do you know his intentions? How do you know to take these actions in a personal way?	Challenges the process of personalizing.

22. Metaphors (Mp)

"That reminds me of the time when Uncle John ..."	How does this story relate to the point you want to make?	Recovers the isomorphic relationship between the story and the person's concepts.

The above text used by permission of the author and extracted from *The Secrets of Magic* (Hall, 1998).

Appendix Two
Dr Mayon-White's Change Management Strategy

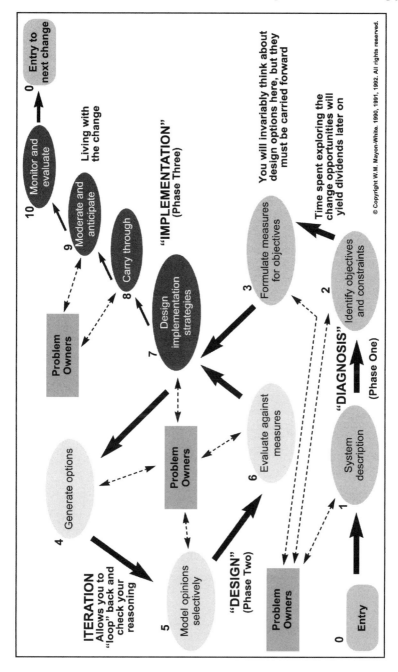

The Key Features Of Dr Mayon-White's Change Management Strategy

The phases of the strategy	The steps of the strategy	What kinds of actions are appropriate?
		Remember that iteration is useful when using this strategy
DESCRIPTION **AND** **DIAGNOSIS**	0 Entry. 1 Description. 2 Identify objectives and constraints. 3 Formulate measures for your objectives.	Start by recognising that change is a complex process. Structure and understand the change in systems terms. Get other points of view on the change problem or opportunity. Set up some objectives for the systems you are examining. Think of the objectives of the change. Decide on ways of measuring if an objective is achieved.
DESIGN **AND** **DEVELOPMENT**	4 Generate a range of options. 5 Model options selectively. 6 Evaluate options against measures.	Develop any ideas for change as full options. Look at a wide range of possibilities. Your objectives may suggest new options. Describe the most promising options in detail. Ask of each option: What is involved? Who is involved? How will it work? Test the performance of your options against an agreed set of criteria.
IMPLEMENTATION **AND** **INNOVATION**	7 Design implementation strategies. 8 Carry through the planned changes *Reviewing* 9 Monitor and evaluate 10 Moderate and anticipate	Select your preferred options and plan a way of putting the changes into place. Bring together people and resources. Manage the process. Monitor progress. *and Re-learning* Bring in new person, sympathetic to project to conduct review. "Re-union" Reviews. Encourage team to "stand down" and recover. Scan environment for new opportunities.

The Key Features Of Dr Mayon-White's Change Management Strategy

What techniques are available?	People issues to consider?	Computer mediated Decision Support software to consider?
Make use of the concepts of "mess" and "difficulty". Use Diagrams: Rich pictures, Systems maps, Multiple cause, Fish Bone etc. Set up special meetings (NGT, DELPHI, etc). Create a model of things as they are. Set up an "objective tree". Prioritise your objectives for change. Use "£s" or quantities where possible. Scaling or ranking methods elsewhere.	Identify: "Change champion" or patron. Appoint project leader. Identify all "problem owners" and "users". Allocate resources. Review and reconsider.	COPE/SODA STRAD I.S.M. Freelance Drawgal CorelDRAW Hexagons Lotus Notes
Brainstorming. Idea writing. Interviews and surveys. Comparisons with best practice in other orgs. Diagrams are simple models: Input/Output. Activity sequence, Control models, Cost-benefit analysis, Cash-flow models. Computer simulations. Set up a simple matrix to compare the performance of your options. Score each option against the measures. Look for reliable options.	Bring in ideas from outside the project team. Involve change champion in evaluation process.	ESI Case STRAD I.S.M. Dynamo Comet Stella I Think System Architect Lotus Excel HIVIEW/EQUITY "00" Work Bench Products CASE - Foundation - I.E.F. MAUD
Check back to the "problem owners". Plan time and allocate tasks. Sort out who is involved. Allocate responsibility. Review and modify plans if necessary. (Critical path analysis etc.) User questionnaires and surveys. Metrics in place. Review workshop with project team. Reward system for team. Social and emotional recovery.	Consider change in leadership for implementation. Consider long term position of project team members. New management input needed to help evaluate change. Audit the impact of change on people and performance.	Harvard Total Project Manager PERTMASTER etc.

Adapted from "Problem solving in small groups: Team Mentors as agents of change" by Bill Mayon-White in *Tackling Strategic Problems,* edited by Colin Eden and Jim Radford, Sage 1990.

Appendix Three
NLP Resources And Contact Points

NLP is taught in over sixty countries throughout the world. Many of these countries also have umbrella organisations operating at a national level. These are marked with # to aid identification. The following is a list of organisations providing training at various levels within the UK, USA and Canada.

UK NLP Centres

The Association of NLP (ANLP)#
PO Box 3357
Unit 14
Barnet
EN5 9AJ
0870 787 1978

Calabor
Calabor House
48 St James Road
Carlisle
Cumbria
CA2 5PD
01228 599899

Centre NLP
PO Box 178
Leicester
LE3 8ZU
0845 456 9297

Dr Susi Strang & Associates
31 High Street
Skelton
Saltburn-By-sea
North Yorkshire
TS12 2EF
01287 654175

Frank Daniels Associates
Tall Trees
Coashill
Critch
Matlock
Derbyshire
DE4 5DS
0845 226 9088

Hidden Resources
2 Tyersal House
Tyersal Lane
Bradford
BD4 0RE
0845 123 5890

Integration Training Centre
12 Prince of Wales Mansions
Prince of Wales Drive
London
SW11 4BG
020 7622 4670

International Teaching Seminars
ITS House
Webster Court
Websters Way
Rayleigh
Essex
SS6 8JQ
01268 777125

John Seymour Associates
Park House
10 Park Street
Bristol
BS1 5HX
0845 658 0654

Mental Combat
71 Falinge Road
Rochdale
Lancashire
Ol12 6LB
01706 663245

NLP Academy
The Pavillions
35 Brighton Road
Croydon
Surrey
CR2 6EB
020 8686 9952

NLP Northeast
Bongate Mill Farmhouse
Appleby
Cumbria
CA16 6UR
01768 351934

NLP World (Terry Elston)
24a Westbourne Gardens
Hove
East Sussex
SN3 5PP
07974 565585

Organisational Healing
Unit 7, Asher Court
Lyncastle Way
Barley Castle Trading Estate
Appleton, Warrington
Cheshire, WA4 4ST
01925 861600

Paul McKenna Training
33 Drayson Mews
London
W8 4LY
0845 230 2022

Performance Partnership
Rosedale House
Rosedale Road
Richmond
Surrey
TW9 2SZ
020 8992 9523

Post Graduate Professional Education
PO Box 506
Halifax
HX1 5UF
01422 343165

PPD Learning
17 Cavendish Square
London
W1G 0PH
0870 7744321

PPD Personal Development
30A The Loning
London
NW9 6DR
0208 201 3333

Realisation at Stenhouse
36 Plasturton Gardens
Pontcanna
Cardiff
CF11 9HF
02920 377723

Salad Ltd
38 Mount Road
Hinckley
Leicestershire
LE10 1AF
01455 445607

Sensory Systems Training
162 Queens Drive
Queens Park
Glasgow
G42 8QN
0141 424 4177

Training Changes
7 Spenser Avenue
Cheltenham
Gloucester
GL51 7DX
01242 580640

USA and CANADA

This list was compiled by Dr Michael Hall and Barbara Belnap
and is reprinted here with their permission.

"P" stands for Practitioner Training, **"MP"** stands for Master
Practitioner Training, **"T"** stands for Trainer Training. As the field
of NLP grows, more and more specialised trainings have been
developed and will continue to be developed. Centres that offer
courses in Photoreading, Core Transformation, Hypnosis, etc., are
annotated accordingly.

Canadian Association of NLP (CANLP) #
338 First Avenue
Ottawa
Ontario
K18 2G9
Canada

Success Strategies
220 Townsend Avenue
Burlington
Ontario
L7T 1Z4
Canada

The Northeast Institute for NLP
Zero Kinsley Street
Nashua, NH 03060

NLP Center of Connecticut
Jack H. Bloom
23 Sherman Street
Fairfield, CN 06430

Institute for Education and Cognitive Psychology
c/o FEA,
12 Centre Drive
Jamesburg, NJ 08831
(690) 860-1200
Fax: (609) 860-6677
NJPSA@aol.com   www.njpsa.org
Specialises in training in redirectional thinking and accelerated learning. Most of the Institute's work centres on improving education and the lives of children. Also conferences on peak performance, personal and professional development.

New York Training Institute for NLP
155 Prince Street
New York, NY 10012
(212) 674-3194
www.nlpcenter.com
P and MP trainings, hypnosis, teaching in USA, Europe, and Israel.

The NLP Center of New York
24 East 12th Street, 4th Fl., Ste 402
New York, NY 10003
(212) 647-0860
1-800-422-8657
Fax: (973) 509-9599

nlp@earthlink.net   www.nlptraining.com
P, MP, and T; Ericksonian Hypnosis, Core Transformation, Workshops for Educators, Corporations, Businesses.

NLP of Gastonia / Institute Of Neuro-Semantics
1516 Cecilia Dr.
Gastonia, NC 28054
(704) 864-1545
Fax: (704) 864-1545
Bob@neurosemantics.com
www.neurosemantics.com
P and MP trainings with an emphasis on personal integrity and training both the conscious and the unconscious mind.

Rivijon Training Institute
1093 A1A Blvd., #390
St. Augustine, FL 32084
(904) 471-7161
rivijon@aug.com
P and MP trainings, with a special interest in health, wellness, personal and professional development, PhotoReading. Located in Jacksonville, FL.

Southern Institute of NLP/ International NLP
PO Box 529
Indian Rocks Beach, FL 33785
(813) 596-4891
Fax: (813) 595-0040
Sunnlp@intl-nlp.com
P, MP and T trainings. Focuses on international trainings in Europe.

NLP Institute of Chicago
1532 W. Victoria St.
Chicago, IL 60660-4223

The South Central Institute of NLP

PO Box 1213
Mandeville, LA 70470
1-800 347-3615
Fax: (504) 626-7424
sidjacob@pipeline.com
Offering P and MP training, emphasis on NLP in business and education, international training
Also:
Singapore: Integrative Learning Corp.,
197 Jalan Pelikat,
Singapore,
537650. (65) 784-7905.

The NLP Center of Texas

4600 Post Oak Place, Suite 204
Houston TX 77027
(713) 439-0011
1-800 625-1925
Fax: (713) 439-0030
rodas@blkbox.com
www.nlpcenteroftexas.com
NLP Centre since 1981. Emphasis: NLP as applied in business and corporate settings, P and MP trainings, Meta-States training.

NLP Comprehensive

PO Box 927
Evergreen, CO 80437
(303) 987 2224

Institute Of Neuro-Semantics

PO Box 9231
Grand Junction, CO 81501
(970) 523-7877
Michael@Neurosemantics.com
www.neurosemantics.com

Anchor Point Associates

505 East 200 South Suite 250
Salt Lake City, UT 84102

Success Design International
11934 Oceannaire Lane
Malibu, CA 90265
800-807-5666
(310) 457-7062
NLPIDEA@worldnet.att.net
P and MP Trainings, Core Transformation, Personal Productivity, IDEA, ENVoY. Emphasis on making a positive difference for individuals and businesses.

NLP University/ Dynamic Learning Center
PO Box 1112
Ben Lomond, CA 95005
Offering training in P, MP, and Trainers levels along with most of the other trainings associated with NLP.

Quantum Leap
PO Box 67359
Scotts Valley, CA 95067

The NLP Connection
PO Box 7818
Santa Cruz, CA 95061

Advanced Neuro Dynamics
615 Piikoi Street, Suite 501
Honolulu, HI 96814
1-800-800-MIND (6463)
Fax: 1-808-596-7764
email: info@nlp.com

* These details are all correct at time of going to press.

Appendix Four
About The Author

On leaving school at sixteen years of age in 1955 the author joined a firm of chartered accountants as an articled clerk. Within a month he regretted taking the decision to become an accountant and rapidly sought a means of escape.

This was the period when all fit young men were required to spend two years' National Service in the military and were normally called up at the age of eighteen. The author approached the Royal Air Force hoping that they would let him join up a little younger. This was not possible, but he was persuaded to join as a regular. He left the RAF some six years later having enjoyed the experience but not sufficiently to encourage him to make it a permanent career.

Back as a civilian it became apparent that to succeed he needed a formal qualification. For the next five years he successfully mixed working with studying for a degree-level qualification in mechanical engineering. Shortly after qualifying he joined International Computers and Tabulators, a predecessor company to International Computers Ltd (ICL). After a short period working in a production control function he was selected to become a programmer/analyst.

For several years his work involved computerising all aspects of the production control processes on the manufacturing side of the business and the provisioning of spares in the field. During this period he became an avid reader of the writings of Peter Drucker and was strongly influenced by two books in particular, *The Practice of Management* (1955) and *Managing for Results* (1964). The information he gained from these books proved immensely useful when he was assigned to develop a system to control and monitor a Management By Objectives project intended to manage an incentives scheme for middle management.

The system was successfully implemented and it was adopted in various forms by other parts of the company. This brought him into contact with other senior managers in different parts of the organisation. On the completion of this project he was invited to take up an appointment as Senior Systems Planner within the Group Strategy and Development Division at the head office in London. His main assignment in this role was to develop what would now be known as an Executive Information System (EIS) for use by the company's most senior directors and their immediate staff. He had total responsibility for the design and development of the system, although no one had previously attempted such a task. This he felt was a great opportunity to learn more about management, as his task brought him into almost daily contact with Board-level directors whilst he was establishing their precise requirements.

The project took three years to complete and was fully implemented by the mid 1970s. It was whilst working on this project that he started to become fascinated with the subject of Change Management. His next assignment was concerned with unbundling the software business from that of hardware. This in many ways was far more challenging than developing the EIS system. It involved not only the separation of products but also convincing people that this was in the long-term interest of the company. This represented a paradigm shift in the manner in which the company marketed its products. It required, therefore, a major change in the attitudes and beliefs of the whole sales force. Now looking back over two decades, this process in which the author was involved can be seen as the first steps by ICL in becoming what it is today.

Several years later, when this "conversion task" was finally completed in 1981, he left ICL to form his own systems consultancy. In 1985, the systems consultancy was sold, and the author spent the next two years studying, but this time the subject was psychology. He had been fascinated with the subject for many years and had learned how to hypnotise people during his period of service with the RAF. In the late 1960s he had developed an interest in applying psychological and quasi-psychological techniques to business problems and by the early 1970s he had also become interested in Behavioural Modification and Transactional Analysis. He felt at the time that he needed to do this in order to gain a better understanding of the needs of senior managers for whom he was designing systems.

In 1987 he joined part of the European Division of the American-owned Raytheon Corporation as a Principal Business Consultant. In this role he was able to practise much of what he had learned in the previous two years coupled to his now extensive knowledge of good Change Management practice. His assignments included many with large British and EC corporations as well as internal assignments within the Raytheon Group. It was during this period that one of his colleagues introduced him to Cranfield Institute of Technology (later to become Cranfield University), and he became involved in the short-course programme. Later he was appointed as a visiting research fellow of the University.

In 1992 he formed, with his wife Glenys, the Anglo-American Book Company and shortly afterwards left Raytheon to set up his own consultancy. In the intervening years the book company has grown very significantly but his interest in working with business to assist in solving their problems continues unabated.

Quite when the author became interested in NLP he is not sure but thinks that it was in the early 1980s when he read a book entitled *Frogs Into Princes* (1979). On first reading he was not too impressed, as it presented a number of ideas that challenged some of his beliefs about the process of change in individuals. But on further consideration he realised that the concepts presented in the book were valid. This aroused his curiosity and he then read everything that had been written on the subject.

During the 1980s many new applications were developed in the field of NLP, and some of these were directly focused on business and commercial applications. It did not take him long to start to use these techniques in his consultancy assignments. Also, during the same period, much new thinking occurred in the business community concerning the nature of Change Management. This was also a period when managements were more open to new ideas to improve their businesses, much of this openness possibly fuelled by the recognition that, to survive, let alone grow, they had to become more competitive. For the first time in his working life management in the western world suddenly became open to experimentation and ready to accept new ideas and concepts. He feels that this was a marvellous time to be a Change Management consultant and he has had a great time learning and developing new ideas and then having the challenge of making them work in the real world.

In his spare time, the author enjoys fishing for salmon and, for thrills, harking back to his youth by flying a light aircraft with the occasional dash of aerobatics thrown in.

Bibliography

Ackoff, R.L., (1974) *Redesigning the Future*, New York: John Wiley.

Ackoff, R.L., (1981) *Creating the Corporate Future*, New York: John Wiley.

Andreas, C., and Andreas, S., (1987) *Change Your Mind and Keep the Change*, Moab, Utah: Real People Press.

Andreas, C., and Andreas, S., (1989) *Heart of the Mind*, Moab, Utah: Real People Press.

Andreas, C., and Andreas, S., (1994) *Core Transformation: Reaching The Wellspring Within*, Moab, Utah: Real People Press.

Andreas, S., and Faulkner, C., (1994) *NLP The New Technology of Achievement*, London: Brealey Publishing.

Ashford, Martin., (1998) *Con Tricks*, New York: Simon & Schuster.

Bandler, R., and Grinder, J., (1975) *The Structure of Magic Vol. I*, Palo Alto: Science and Behavior Books Inc.

Bandler, R., and Grinder, J., (1976) *The Structure of Magic Vol. II*, Palo Alto: Science and Behavior Books Inc.

Bandler, R., and Grinder, J., (1975) *Patterns of the Hypnotic Techniques of Milton H. Erickson, M.D., Vol I*. Cupertino, California: Meta Publications.

Bandler, R., and Grinder, J., (1977) *Patterns of the Hypnotic Techniques of Milton H. Erickson, M.D., Vol II*. Cupertino, California: Meta Publications.

Bandler, R., and Grinder, J., (1979) *Frogs into Princes*, Moab, Utah: Real People Press.

Bandler, R., and Grinder, J., (1982) *Reframing: Neuro-Linguistic Programming and the Transformation of Meaning*, Moab, Utah: Real People Press.

Bandler, R., Grinder, J., and Satir, V., (1976) *Changing With Families*, Palo Alto: Science and Behavior Books Inc.

Bandler, R., (1985) *Using Your Brain for a Change*, Moab, Utah: Real People Press.

Bagley, D.S., and Reese, E.J., (1987) *Beyond Selling: How to Maximize Your Personal Influence*, Cupertino, California: Meta Publications.

Beer, S., (1972) *Brain of the Firm*, London: Allen Lane.

Berne, E., (1964), *Games People Play*, New York, USA: Grove Press.

Bateson, G., (1972) *Steps to an Ecology of Mind*, New York: Ballantine Books.

Benson, I., and Lloyd, J., (1983) *New Technology and Industrial Change*, London: Kogan Page.

Bodenhamer, R.G., and Hall, L.M., (1998) *The User's Manual For The Brain*, Carmarthen, Wales: Crown House Publishing Ltd.

Cameron-Bandler, L., (1985) *Solutions: Enhancing Love, Sex and Relationships*, Moab, Utah: Real People Press.

Cameron-Bandler, L., Gordon, D., and Lebeau, M., (1985) *The Emprint Method: A Guide to Reproducing Competence*, Moab, Utah: Real People Press.

Cameron-Bandler, L., Gordon, D., and Lebeau, M., (1985) *Know How: Guided Programs for Inventing Your Own Best Future*, Moab, Utah: Real People Press.

Cameron-Bandler, L., and Lebeau, M., (1986) *The Emotional Hostage: Rescuing Your Emotional Life*, Moab, Utah: Real People Press.

Champy, J., (1995) *Re-engineering Management: The Mandate for New Leadership*, London: HarperCollins.

Champy, J. and Hammer, M., (1993) *Re-engineering the Corporation*, London: Nicholas Brealey.

Checkland, P.B., (1982) *Systems Thinking, Systems Practice*, London: John Wiley.

Chestnut, H., (1967) *Systems Engineering Methods*, New York: John Wiley.

Chomsky, N., (1957) *Syntactic Structures*, The Hague: Mouton.

Chomsky, N., (1965) *Aspects of the Theory of Syntax*, Cambridge, Massachusetts: MIT Press.

Clegg, C., et al, *(1985) Case Studies in Organisational Behaviour*, London: Harper and Row.

Clutterbuck, D., and Crainer, S., (1988) *The Decline and Rise of British Industry*, London: Macmillan.

Clutterbuck, D., and Crainer, S., (1990) *Makers of Management*, London: Macmillan.

Dilts, R., Grinder, J., Bandler, R., and DeLozier, J., (1978) *Neuro-Linguistic Programming: The Study of the Structure of Subjective Experience, Vol 1*, Cupertino, California: Meta Publications.

Dilts, R., (1990) *Changing Belief Systems with NLP*, Capitola, California: Meta Publications.

Dilts, R., (1994) *Strategies of Genius, Vol 1.*, Capitola, California: Meta Publications.

Dilts, R., (1996) *Visionary Leadership Skills*, Capitola, California: Meta Publications.

Drucker, P., (1946) *The Concept of the Corporation*, New York: Mentor.

Drucker, P., (1954) *The Practice of Management*, London: William Heinemann Ltd.

Drucker, P., (1964) *Managing For Results*, London: William Heinemann Ltd.

Drucker, P., (1967) *The Effective Executive*, London: William Heinemann Ltd.

Drucker, P., (1977) *Management*, New York: Harper's College Press.

Drucker, P., (1985) *Innovation and Entrepreneurship*, London: William Heinemann Ltd.

Fodor, J.A., (1987) *Psychosemantics*, Cambridge, Massachusetts: MIT Press.

Gordon, D., and Dawes, G., (2005) *Expanding Your World: Modeling the Structure of Experience*, Tucson, USA: David Gordon and Graham Dawes.

Grinder, J., and Bandler, R., (1981) *Trance-formations: Neuro-Linguistic Programming and the Structure of Hypnosis*, Moab, Utah: Real People Press.

Hadamard, J., (1945) *The Psychology of Invention in the Mathematical Field*, New York: Dover Publications.

Hall, A.D., and Fagin, R.E., (1956) "Definition of System." *General Systems Yearbook*, 1:18-28.

Hall, E.T., (1959) *The Silent Language*, Garden City, New York: Doubleday and Co Ltd.

Hall, E.T., (1975) *Beyond Culture*, Garden City, New York: Doubleday and Co Ltd.

Hall, L.M., (1996) *The Spirit of NLP: The Process, Meaning and Criteria for Mastering NLP*, Carmarthen, Wales: Crown House Publishing Ltd.

Hall, L.M., (1997) *The Secrets of Magic: Communications Excellence For The 21ˢᵗ Century*, Carmarthen, Wales: Crown House Publishing Ltd.

Hamel, G., and Prahalad, C.K., (1994) *Competing for the Future*, Boston: Harvard Business School Press.

Hammer, M., and Stanton, S., (1995) *The Re-engineering Revolution: The Handbook*, New York: Harper Collins.

Handy, C.B., (1981) *Understanding Organisations*, London: Penguin.

Handy, C.B., (1989) *The Age of Unreason*, London: Arrow Books.

Handy, C.B., (1995) *Beyond Uncertainty*, London: Hutchinson.

Harris, C., (1998) *The Elements of NLP*, Shaftesbury: Element Books Limited.

Harvey-Jones, Sir J., (1993) *Managing to Survive*, London: Heinemann.

Jacobson, S., (1983) *Meta-cation*, Cupertino, California: Meta Publications.

Jacobson, S., (1986) *Meta-cation Vol II*, Cupertino, California: Meta Publications.

Jacobson, S., (1996) *Solution States*, Carmarthen, Wales: Crown House Publishing Ltd.

James, T., and Woodsmall, W., (1988) *Time-line Therapy and The Basis Of Personality*, Capitola, California: Meta Publications.

Jung, C.G., (1969) *Jung Extracts: The Psychology of the Transference*, Princeton, New Jersey: Princeton University Press.

Jung, C.G., (1971) *Psychological Types*, Princeton, New Jersey: Princeton University Press.

Korzybski, A., (1933) *Science and Sanity, 4th Edition*, Lakeville, Connecticut: The International Non-Aristotelian Library Publishing Co.

Kanter, R.M., (1985) *The Change Masters: Corporate Entrepreneurs at Work*, London: Allen and Unwin.

Koestler, A., (1964) *The Act of Creation*, New York: The Macmillan Company.

Kotter, J.P., (1978) *Organisational Dynamics*, New York: Free Press.

Kotter, J.P., (1995) *The New Rules: How to Succeed in Today's Post-Corporate World*, New York: Free Press.

Laborde, G.Z., (1984) *Influencing With Integrity: Management Skills For Communication And Negotiation*, Carmarthen, Wales: Crown House Publishing Ltd.

Laborde, G.Z., (1987) *Fine Tune Your Brain: How to Sell Your Idea to Someone Else*, Redwood City California: Syntony Publishing Inc.

Lankton, S., (1980) *Practical Magic: A Translation of Basic Neuro-Linguistic Programming into Clinical Psychotherapy*, Cupertino, California: Meta Publications.

Lazarus, A., (1976) *Multimodal Behaviour Therapy*, New York: Springer Publishing Co.

Lewis, B., and Pucelik, F., (1982) *Magic of NLP Demystified: A Pragmatic Guide To Communication and Change*, Portland Oregon: Metamorphous Press.

Lewis, B.A., (1996) *Sobriety Demystified: Getting Clean and Sober with NLP and CBT*, Santa Cruz, California: Kelsey and Co.

McDermott, I., and O'Connor, J., (1996) *NLP and Health*, London: Thorsons.

McLuhan, M., and Flore, Q., (1967) *The Medium is the Message*, New York: Random House.

McMaster M., and Grinder, J., (1980) *Precision: A New Approach to Communication*, Beverly Hills, California: Precision Models.

McNeill D., and Freiberger, P., (1993) *Fuzzy Logic*, New York: Simon & Schuster.

Mehrabian, A., (1971) *Silent Messages*, Belmont California: Wadsworth Publishing Co. Inc.

Micklethwait, J., and Wooldridge A., (1997) *The Witch Doctors: What the Management Gurus are Saying, Why it Matters and How to Make Sense of It*, London: William Heinemann.

Miller, G.A., Galanter, E., and Pribram, K.H., (1960) *Plans and the Structure of Behavior*, New York: Holt, Rinehart and Winston, Inc.

Nadler, G., and Hibino, S., (1997) *Breakthrough Thinking: The Seven Principles of Creative Problem Solving*, Rocklin California, USA: Prima Publishing.

O'Connor, J., and Seymour, J., (1990) *Introducing NLP: Psychological Skills for Influencing People*, London: Thorsons

Overdurf, J., and Silverthorn, J., (1994) *Training Trances: Multi-Level Communication in Therapy and Training*, Portland Oregon: Metamorphous Press.

Peters, T.J., and Waterman, R., (1982) *In Search of Excellence: Lessons From America's Best Run Companies*, New York: Harper & Row.

Peters, T.J., (1987) *Thriving on Chaos: Handbook for a Management Revolution*, New York: Knopf.

Peters, T.J., (1994) *The Tom Peters Seminar: Crazy Times Calls for Crazy Organisations*, London: Macmillan.

Perls, F., (1969) *In and Out of the Garbage Pail*, Moab, Utah: Real People Press.

Perls, F., (1973) *Gestalt Approach: Eyewitness to Therapy*, Palo Alto: Science and Behavior Books Inc.

Porter, M.E., (1980) *Competitive Strategy: Techniques for Analyzing Industries and Competitors*, New York: The Free Press.

Porter, M.E., (1985) *Competitive Advantage: Creating and Sustaining Superior Performance*, New York: The Free Press.

Rackham, Neil, Huthwaite Inc., (1988) *SPIN Selling*, New York: McGraw-Hill Book Company.

Richardson J., (1987) *The Magic of Rapport: How You can Gain Personal Power in any Situation*, Cupertino, California: Meta Publications.

Robbins, A., (1986) *Unlimited Power*, New York: Simon & Schuster.

Roberts, Martin, (1998/9) *Rapport: The Magazine of the Association of Neuro-Linguistic Programming*, Volumes 42–45, London: ANLP.

Satir, V., (1986) *New Peoplemaking*, Palo Alto: Science and Behavior Books Inc.

Shaw, G.B., (1903) *Man and Superman*, London: Macmillan.

Shore, E.J., (1994) *Psychotherapy Through Imagery*, Santa Barbara, California: Fithian Press.

Taylor, J.C., (1988) *Your Balancing Act: Discovering New Life Through Five Dimensions of Wellness*, Portland Oregon: Metamorphous Press.

Watzlawick, P., Beavin, J., and Jackson, D., (1967) *Pragmatics of Human Communications*, New York: W.W. Norton.

Watzlawick, P., Weakland, J., and Fisch, R., (1974) *Change*, New York: W.W. Norton.

Zedeh L.A., "'Fuzzy Sets' Information Control," *Radio Engineer*, 8(3), June 1965, pp. 338–53.

Glossary Of Terms

Abstract noun: See **Nominalisations.**

Accessing cues: Unconscious behaviours, including breathing, gestures, head movements and eye movements, that indicate specific sensory modalities such as thoughts or other experiences stored in the brain.

Analog: Any form of output (behaviour) exclusive of word-symbols.

Anchor: : A specific stimulus: sight, sound, word or touch that automatically brings up a particular memory or state of body or mind. An example may be a favourite song or perfume.

Associated: Seeing the world through our own eyes, immanently.

Auditory: The hearing/speaking sensory modality, including sounds and words.

Behaviour: Any activity we engage in, from major muscles movements to the act of thinking.

Behavioural flexibility: The ability to vary one's actions in order to elicit a desired response in another person.

Beliefs: Generalisations about yourself and/or the world about you. In other words, our beliefs are what we take as being "true" at a particular moment. Beliefs guide us in perceiving and interpreting reality. Note that beliefs relate closely to values.

Cause and effect: A Meta-model violation in which the speaker indicates a belief that one person can directly cause another person to have a particular emotion.

Chunk size: The amount of information or level of specificity considered at one time. People who are detail-orientated are "small chunkers" whereas "large chunkers" tend to see the "big picture". Chunking Down is the act of setting out to break problems down into their component parts in order to solve them. (How do you eat an elephant? Answer: One chunk at a time.) Chunking Up is the act of accumulating all the components in order to be able see the "Big Picture".

Complex equivalents: The relationship between a word or action and the *meaning* attached to it by the observer. It is called "complex", because the equivalent verbal description is much more detailed than the word or action being defined ("a picture is worth a thousand words"). A person's complex equivalent is a more accurate representation of his deep structure associations to the particular word or action.

Congruence: When goals, thoughts and behaviours are all in agreement. A state of unity, internal harmony, absence of conflict.

Consensus reality: Due to similarities in the neurological mechanisms within each of us and shared social and cultural experiences we are able to create similar representations of the world called consensus reality.

Constraints: Filters on the map-building processes. Neurological, social and individual constraints affect our maps of the world by providing experiences to be generalised, deleted and distorted.

Content: The specifics and details of an event. Contrast with process or structure. Answers obtained from "What", "Where", "When" and "How" Meta-model challenges.

Context: The setting, frame or process in which events occur and provide meaning for content.

Criteria (Value): The standard by which something is evaluated. Obtained by asking, "What's important to you?"

Cues: Information that provides clues as to another's structures, i.e. verbal predicates, breathing, body posture, gestures, voice tone, etc.

Deep structure: The most complete linguistic representation of an experience. A person's deep structure is a linguistic map of his or her map of the world.

Deletion: The universal human process which screens out or prevents the awareness of experiences. A primary function of the brain and central nervous system is to filter out most sensory input so that we can attend to our various activities uninterrupted. In language, deletion is the process of simplifying deep structure representations by leaving things out in the surface structure.

Derived feelings: See **Emotions.**

Dissociated: Viewing or experiencing an event from outside one's body. Such as, for instance, seeing yourself on a movie screen or seeing yourself floating above an event.

Distortion: The universal human process by which we manipulate our perceptions and remembered experiences. This process often alters experiences in a way which will better fit our own maps and models of the world, and it is also important in the creative processes of visualising, planning ahead, and enjoying works of art and literature.

Ecology: Concern for the whole person/organisation as a balanced, interacting system. When a change is ecological, the whole person or organisation benefits.

Elicitation: Evoking a state by word, behaviour, gesture or any stimuli. Gathering information by direct observation of non-verbal signals or by asking Meta-model questions.

Emotions: A complex set of physical sensations combined with other thought processes such as internal images and thoughts. Emotions are also commonly called "feelings", possibly because of the important role the physical sensations play in our ability to attach meaning to these complex "derived feelings".

Empowerment: Process of adding vitality, energy and new powerful resources to a person or a group of people.

Feedback: The visual, auditory and kinaesthetic information as what you get as a response to your behaviour.

Filters: See **Constraints**.

First Position: Viewing/experiencing the world through one's own eyes and with one's own body. See **Associated.**

Flexibility: Having behavioural choice in a situation. Requires minimally three possible options. If you have only one choice, you are a robot. If you have only two choices, you are in a dilemma.

Future Pace: The process of mentally rehearsing an event before it happens.

Generalisation: The universal human process of drawing from a set of experiences to understand and make predictions about similar new experiences.

Incongruence: When goals, thoughts and behaviours are experienced as being in conflict, e.g. a person may say one thing and do another.

Individual constraints: The collection of our past personal history: our complete set of stored and remembered experiences through which we filter our ongoing experiences.

Intention: The underlying desire or goal of a behaviour, assumed to be positive.

In Time: Having a time line that passes through the body: where the past is behind and the future in front, and "now" is inside the body.

Kinaesthetic: Sensations, feelings, tactile sensations and emotions.

Leading: Changing your own behaviours after obtaining rapport so another follows. Being able to lead is a test for having good rapport.

Logical typing errors: Mistaking the "map" for the "territory" it represents. Assuming that what you perceive (which is based on your own model of the world) is *reality*, and that it is the same as what other people perceive.

Lost performative: A Meta-model violation in which a person makes **a value** judgment or expresses a belief in a way that deletes the judge or the originator of the belief.

Map of reality: Model of the world, a unique representation of the world built into each person's brain by abstracting from experiences, comprised of a neurological and a linguistic map.

Meta-model: A linguistic tool for using portions of a person's spoken or written behaviour to determine where he has generalised, deleted or distorted experiences in his model of the world. It includes specific "Meta-model responses" to these "Meta-model violations" which aid in obtaining a more complete representation from the person's deep structure. Certain responses also help to reconnect the speaker with his deep structure in ways which can expand his perceptions and give him more choices about how to feel and behave.

Meta perspective: An awareness of the *patterns* involved in the processes of communication as well as the content.

Meta-program: A mental program that operates across many different aspects of a person's life.

Mind reading: A Meta-Model violation in which a person expresses the idea that it is possible to know what someone else is thinking or feeling with little or no direct feedback.

Mirroring: See **Rapport.**

Modal operators: Meta- model violations which identify limits to a person's model of the world. Modal operators of necessity are exemplified by imperatives such as "should" while modal operators of possibility are exemplified by words such as "can't".

Model: A representation of a thing or process which is useful as a tool for better understanding of what it represents and for predicting how it will operate in various situations. A model is a generalised, deleted and distorted copy of that which it represents.

Model of the world: See **Map of Reality**.

Motivation Direction: A mental programme that determines whether a person moves *towards* or *away from* experiences.

Neurological constraints: The filters of our brain and sensory organs. Differences in people's "sensitivity" to various stimuli accounts in part for differences between people's models of the world.

Nominalisation: A Meta-model violation in which an"abstract noun" is formed by taking a verb (such as "relate") and changing it by the process of linguistic distortion into a noun (such as "relationship"). A nominalisation differs from a "concrete noun" which names a person, place or thing.

Pacing: See **Rapport.**

Parts: A metaphor for describing responsibility for our behaviour to various parts of our psyche. These may be seen as sub-personalities that have functions that take on a "life of their own". When they have different intentions we may experience intra-personal conflict and a sense of incongruity, e.g. "A part of me wants security, whilst another part wants to just go for it".

Perceptual enhancer: The effects of language on our perception. See also **Social constraints.**

Perceptual filters: Unique ideas, experiences, beliefs, values, meta-programs, decisions, memories and language that shape and influence our maps of the world.

Perceptual position: Our point of view; one of three mental positions: first position – associated to self; second position – from another person's point of view; third position – as an observer, from a position outside the people involved.

Predicate preference: The habitual use of certain predicates – verbs, adverbs, and adjectives – which indicate systematic use of one of the representational systems in preference to others to express our thoughts. Predicate preference is often a good indication of a person's preferred representational system.

Preferred representation system: The system in which a person makes the most number of distinctions about himself and his environment. The habitual use of one system more often than the others to sort out and make sense of experiences.

Presuppositions: Ideas or assumptions that we make about the world about us that may or may not be true.

Rapport: During effective communication, rapport is established through communicative behaviours called "pacing". These subtle forms of feedback elicit in the observer a sense of *being like* and of *trusting* the communicator. Two methods of pacing that result in rapport are matching a person's predicate preference and "mirroring" (matching) a person's posture, gestures, rate of breathing, etc.

Referential index: A Meta-model violation in which the person or thing doing or receiving the action of the verb in a sentence has been deleted, unspecified, generalised or reversed.

Reframing: Changing the frame or reference of an experience so that it has a different meaning.

Representational systems: The Sensory Modalities: Visual, Auditory, Kinaesthetic, Olfactory and Gustatory. Called representational because it is the way memories and ideas are represented by human beings.

Requisite Variety: Flexibility in thinking, emotion, speaking, behaving; the person with the most flexibility of behaviour controls the action; the law of Requisite Variety derived from systems-theory.

Resource State: Whilst any experience can be a resource state, typically a positive, action-orientated, potential-fulfilled experience in a person's life. A desirable state for all those involved in the act or process of Change Management.

Second Position: Viewing/experiencing an event from the perspective and experience of the person you are interacting with.

Sensory Acuity: Awareness of the outside world, of the senses, making finer distinctions about sensory information we get from the world.

Sensory Modalities: The five senses through which we take in experience of the world: sight, hearing, touch, smell and taste.

Social constraints: Cultural filters on our ability to perceive. Language, for example, can either enhance our perception of something by naming it ("perceptual enhancer"), or it can limit perception by not providing labels for certain aspects of experience.

State: Holistic phenomenon of mind-body-emotions, mood, emotional condition; the sum total of all neurological and physical processes within an individual at any moment at time.

Strategy: A sequencing of thinking-behaving to obtain an outcome or create an experience. Referred to sometimes as "running your own programme/s".

Stress: An important factor in determining how a person will respond in certain situations. Stress will often cause a person to "retreat" into the representational system in which he makes the most number of distinctions (his preferred system), thereby limiting both his awareness of the world and his choices about how to respond.

Sub-modality: The components that make up a sensory modality, e.g. in the visual modality the sub-modalities will include colour, brightness, focus, distance, etc.

Surface structure: The spoken or written portion of communication which is derived from the Deep Structure using the processes of generalisation, deletion and distortion.

Third Position: Perceiving the world from the position of an observer: From this position you see both yourself and other people.

Time-line: The unconscious arrangement of a person's past memories and future expectations. Typically seen as a "line" of images.

Trust: Within the context of effective communication, trust is the sense a person gets when he believes he is being understood. Trust is a necessary ingredient in the "magic" of effective communication and especially in Change Management.

Unconscious: Everything that is not in conscious awareness in the present moment.

Universal human modeling processes: Three mechanisms common to all model-building activities; the processes of generalisation, deletion and distortion.

Universal quantifier: A Meta-model violation in which a generalisation has been made in a way that indicates that the speaker is not aware of any exceptions to his statement as with such words as "every" and "never."

Unspecified verbs: A Meta-model violation in which a person uses a verb which deletes such qualities as how, when or where the activity took place or the duration or intensity of the act.

Values: What is important to you in a particular context. Your values are what motivate you in life. All motivation strategies have a kinaesthetic component.

Visualisation: The process of seeing visual images in your mind.

Well-formed Condition: The criteria that enable us to specify an outcome in ways that make it achievable and verifiable. A well-formed outcome is a powerful tool for negotiating win/win solutions.

Index

Accelerated Learning, 8, 268
Andreas, Steve, v, 3–4, 159, 277
Association, x, 70–71, 91, 97–98,
    106, 128, 151, 207, 263, 267

Badly-formed problems, iii, 82,
    98
Bandler, Richard, v, 3–7, 19,
    30–32, 71, 98–99, 160, 164,
    277–280
Bateson, Gregory, 5–6, 167, 169,
    278
Behavioural flexibility, 25, 285
Behavioural Modification, xi, 7,
    115, 274
Berne, Eric, 6, 167, 278
Breaking state, 208
Business Forces Diagram, iii,
    133–135
Business Process Re-engineering
    (BPR), xiii, 12, 76, 113, 224,
    242–246

Cameron-Bandler, Leslie, v, 6,
    164, 278
Cause and Effect, 46–47, 75, 285
Champy, James, 242, 278
Chomsky, Noam, 5, 279
Chunking, 162, 167, 285–286
Cognitive Behavioural School,
    The 7
COMBAT, 250–251
Competitive advantage, 11, 78,
    124, 133, 136, 144, 240, 284
Corporate maps, 71, 73
Covey, Stephen, 8
Crane, Roger, vi, 81

Critical Success Factors (CSFs),
    iii, 80, 89, 108, 113–120, 122,
    129–130, 146, 148–150, 153,
    162–163
Culture, 6, 44, 71, 106–107,
    110–111, 115, 120–121,
    128–132, 146, 172–173, 177,
    241, 280
Cybernetics, 6–7

Deming, W. Edwards, 239–240
Deletions, 34–35, 37, 49, 255
DeLozier, Judith, v, 6, 279
Developmental Behavioural
    Modelling, 109
Dilts, Robert, v, 6, 29, 115, 121,
    167, 170, 178, 180, 279
Dissociation, 70
Distortions, 34–35, 39
Drucker, Peter, 247, 250–251,
    273, 279–280

Einstein, Albert, 201–202
Ellis, Albert, 6
Erickson, Milton H., 5, 30, 277
Executive Information System
    (EIS), 249, 274

Family Therapy, 7
Fawlty Towers, 27–28
Feldenkrais, Moshe, 6
Ford, Henry, 9
Fuzzy Logic, 86–87, 283

General Semantics, 31
Generalisations, 34–35, 37–39,
    82–83, 85, 107, 118, 143, 164,
    285
Gordon, David, 6, 280

Grinder, John,   v, 3, 5–6, 19, 30–32, 98–99, 160, 277–280, 282

Hall, L. Michael,   v, 33–34, 167, 257, 267, 278, 280
Hamel, Gary,   244, 281
Hammer, Michael,   160, 242, 278, 281
Handy, Charles,   243–244, 247, 281
Hollerith, James,   9

IBM,   10, 166
Identity conflict,   iii, 176
Information Technology,   vi, xiii, 7, 9, 11, 23, 122, 143, 246
International Ecotechnology Research Centre,   vi, xiii, 55, 75, 78, 81, 84–85, 88–90, 94, 97–98, 113, 116, 122–124, 128, 140, 142, 156, 158, 237, 245

James Martin Associates,   242
Janov, Arthur,   7
Juran, Joseph,   239–240

Knowledge Management (KM),   249, 251
Korzybski, Alfred,   5, 31–32, 281

Lewis, Byron,   6, 282
Logical Levels,   iii, 167, 169–173, 175–178
Long-term Planning,   203

Management By Objectives (MBO),   10, 273
Map/territory,   32
Maps of reality,   34–35, 45, 57, 59, 156, 193
Mayon-White, W.,   ii–iii, vi, 55, 81, 88, 259–261
McLujan and Flore,   20

McWhirter, John,   v, 109
Mehrabian, Albert,   283
Meta-model,   ii, iii, 6, 29–38, 41–42, 45, 47, 49, 51, 57, 59, 65, 70–71, 73, 75, 86, 98–99, 118, 129, 146, 164, 205, 255, 285–287, 289–291, 293
metaphors,   73, 131, 257
Mind Reading,   45–46, 289
Modal Operators,   42–43, 255, 289
Modalities,   61, 73, 195, 285, 291–292
modelling,   viii, 7, 8, 104, 221–233
Motorola,   240
Moving towards,   129–130, 132, 149, 213–214
Moving away from,   129–130, 132, 149, 213–214
Multiple cause diagram,   iii, 92

Nadler and Hibino,   140–141, 145

Organisation and Methods (O & M),   10, 247–248
Organisational Identity,   iii, 175
Orr, Leonard,   7
Orwell, George,   246

Pascale, Richard,   12
Perceptual Positions,   iii, 179–182, 184, 188
Perls,   4–6, 30, 283
Peters, Tom,   79, 247, 283
Porter, Michael,   133, 247, 284
Prahalad, C.K.,   244, 281
Problem Definition,   81–83, 99, 140, 161
Pucelik, Frank,   6, 282

Rapport,   i, 8, 19–26, 28, 32, 73, 164, 284, 288–291
Reagan, Ronald,   202

Rich Picture,   iii, 95–97, 183, 203
Rogers, Carl,   6

Sabotage,   158
Satir, Virginia,   6, 30, 278, 284
Senge, Peter,   8
Sensory acuity,   21, 28, 292
Short-term Planning,   202
Strategic Planning,   201–202, 212
Stuart, Jim,   vi, 81
Stuck state,   58–60, 65, 205
Sub-modalities,   61–63, 65, 67,
     69–71, 73, 197, 209, 292

Taylor, Frederick,   9–10, 284
Thatcher, Margaret,   202
Time-Line,   iii, 197–211,
     214–217, 281, 293
Time-lining,   203
Total Quality Management
     (TQM),   xiii, 12–13, 76,
     93–94, 105–107, 113. 116, 120,
     126, 133–134, 161, 176,
     185–188, 239–242, 245

Transactional Analysis,   xi, 6–7,
     167, 274
Universal Quantifiers,   42–45,
     255

Verbal Predicates,   73, 286

Watzlawick, Paul,   31, 284
Well-formed Outcome,   99,
     145–146, 293
Well-formed Problem,   iii, 48,
     98–100, 118–119, 128, 140,
     145–147, 159, 183, 214
Well-formed Solution,   iii, 139,
     146–147, 150–151, 153, 159,
     163, 183–184, 205, 214
Wells, H.G.,   246

Zedeh, Lotfi,   87, 284